HOUSE OF STICKS

A Memoir

Ly Tran

SCRIBNER

New York   London   Toronto   Sydney   New Delhi

Công cha như núi Thái Sơn
Nghĩa mẹ như nước trong nguồn chảy ra
Một lòng thờ mẹ kính cha
Cho tròn chữ hiếu mới là đạo con

The good of your deeds, Father,
as great as the highest peak
of the Thai Son mountains

The purity of your soul, Mother,
like spring water from the source
gushing forth,

Revering Mother, Respecting Father,
to fulfill the duties of filial piety,
that is my religion.

—Vietnamese proverb

*This book was written for my mother and for my father.
Not out of a sense of duty, but because I love them.*

Summer 1993. Ly in front of 1725 Bleecker Street with her first bag of potato chips.

Awake

A DIN OF NERVOUS *voices, a shuffle of restless bodies, a dome of bright blue tarp.*

It was nighttime. I was hungry, fretful, struggling out of my mother's arms. My father had gone to trade a ceramic bowl for eggs with soy sauce. We sat on narrow, overcrowded benches waiting for him. My senses were just beginning to activate, some more than others. Vision dominated. And smell. I remember the strong odor of eggs drenched in soy sauce as my father entered the tent and carried the food back to us. And the vague presence of blurry faceless people all around.

I don't remember my three brothers being there. I knew only that we were not in a familiar place. And that shock of unfamiliarity is perhaps what has preserved this earliest memory of mine, sitting on a bench in a tarpaulin tent in a refugee camp in Thailand. I was three years old, only vaguely conscious of the world around me. But in that singular moment, it was as though a light had flickered on in the uncharted rooms of my mind. I have no recollection of the moments before, of how I got there, or of what came after.

But the blue remains. I can almost touch it, a country of blue as big as Antarctica, frozen in the geography of my consciousness.

And the eggs. I can still taste those eggs. Rubbery whites infused with soy sauce and a creamy yolk at the center.

I know from what my parents have told me in the years since, that we stayed in that camp for three weeks. Then we boarded planes that took us from Thailand to Denmark, from Denmark to France, from France to America. From that time, I remember only hazy glimpses of airports and an isolated sensation of burning coldness, but nothing lasting, nothing of shape. My father tells me that on the plane ride from France to America, he'd awakened to find that I was gone. Panicked, he and my mother searched the plane, approaching the stewards and stewardesses in their broken English. "Ah, esi kew me, where ees bay bee?" They cradled an invisible baby in their arms.

Turns out, I had waddled down the aisle to an empty seat and curled up at its base to sleep.

I, of course, have no recollection of this. I was asleep.

But sometimes, I think I remember it. I see myself as a toddler, walking down the aisle beneath the unseeing gaze of strangers. I remember dim lighting and a sudden sensation of dizziness. Of crawling into a quiet, empty space. Then I feel strong arms encircle me and carry me back to my family. I feel the weight of sleep descend upon me once again. . . .

Part I

Spring 1993. Thinh, Phu, Long, and Ly with Ba.

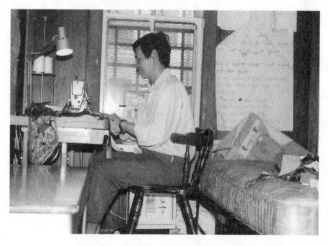

Winter 1994. Ba at the sewing machine, making silk paisley ties.

Nước Mỹ

WE ARRIVE IN THE blizzard of 1993, coming from rice paddies, mango trees, and the sun to February in the Empire State. We feel sick from turbulence and three weeks of travel, with that nauseating airplane smell, a combination of pleather and cleaning product, clinging to our hair and skin. Thinh, Phu, Long, and I step off the plane, ahead of our parents, holding clammy hands. We're here.

My mother is flushed with excitement. She rushes up to a confection stand and gives the man behind the register five thousand dong. *Gandy*, she says to the man brightly, *for my childs*. Before the man can reply, my father slaps her hand away and calls her an idiot. The five thousand dong falls like a feather to the ground. I don't understand what's happening. I wait for the candy, but it never comes. Thinh, the oldest of my brothers, grabs my hand and leads me away. He knows something I don't.

Our sponsor, an old family friend who fought in the war with my father, was supposed to meet us, but we don't see him anywhere and have no means of contacting him. It's up to my father to figure out how to get to the address he'd given us. Outside the airport, a blizzard rages. *The map is in your mouth*, my father tells himself, reciting a Vietnamese mantra, as he stops strangers to ask for directions in his broken English. He produces a small piece of paper, upon which he writes the instructions they give him: "Tek A tren tu Brotway Junksun." My mother stands by, smiling and bowing to the people who try to help us. We come back into the airport to figure out next steps and to escape the cold when a man runs up to us holding a sign.

"We've been looking for you all over the place," he says in Vietnamese, breathless. "We checked the arrival time, but your plane must have been delayed because of this weather. My goodness, how long it's been. You two have not changed. How was the trip?" Then, looking at me, "I didn't know you had a fourth child! How old are your children now?"

"Kỳ Thịnh is nine, Kỳ Phú is eight, Kỳ Long is five, and Kỳ Lý just turned three," my mother says.

My parents call him Ông Sáu. Mr. Six. Tall and wearing a thick coat, he stands with perfect posture and an air of refinement. He looks to be a little older than my father, with gray peppering his hair. They embrace him, clutching his forearms, grateful to find a familiar face fourteen thousand kilometers away from home. He leads us to the bus we need to take, and his son, who is also tall, materializes shortly after, to help carry our luggage.

My mother holds on to me tightly. My brothers and I flinch every time the bus makes a turn, thinking it's about to crash into a nearby pole or car. We have never been on a bus. It screeches to a stop: Howard Beach. We scramble off and Mr. Six takes us to a set of stairs leading under the ground. Staring at the sign, a white *A* in the middle of a blue circle, my father checks his handwritten directions and realizes that this is what the strangers at the airport had meant by "A tren." He looks wildly around for another way, wary of going into a confined space after spending nearly a decade in prison. In a loud, panicked voice he asks Mr. Six if there are any trains aboveground.

Meanwhile, my brothers and I trudge around in the snow, our feet freezing and numb. We don't mind the cold or the grown-ups' hesitation. We dart through the soft flurries falling all around us. *White!* we shrill to each other. We have never seen snow and don't know what else to call it. Down the block, we see a group of children having a snowball fight. We imitate them and use our hands to pack the snow into small clumps. They're wearing thick coats, gloves, boots, and woolen hats. We have only the blue hoodies handed out to us in the refugee camps. Slushy water breaks through the thin fabric of our shoes and slides around between the cracks of our toes. We watch the children play, and we throw the clumps of snow when they throw. Their snowballs land on targets. But because we are not yet adept in the art of packing hard snowballs, ours fall apart midair, glittering in the winter light like fairy dust. This is magic, I think to myself: cold and powdery light.

After Mr. Six manages to convince my father that he will not be held captive for another decade, we all descend into the subway. The roaring sounds scare us. On the train, my mother sits near us, shutting her eyes tight while we cover our ears. My father stands and stares outside the windows at the graffitied tunnel walls, a crazed look in his eyes. A slim, nervous man, he walks from one window to the next. I gaze at him in silent wonder, perhaps because this man is my father, and perhaps because on an unconscious level I also sense his fear. But exhaustion eventually sets in. My hands drift from my ears, and I fall asleep on my mother's lap, the rumbling of the train carrying me off to a faraway land.

My mother wakes me up as we leave the train. She holds my hand and walks swiftly, following Mr. Six. I stumble along beside her. That sensation of being pulled is something I can feel to this day: that hand, my stumbling, my fright and bewilderment, and most of all a sense of never being able to catch up.

We've arrived at our new neighborhood, a place called Ridgewood, a name we can't pronounce. Cars line both sides of the black asphalt, trampled snow in the short spaces between them. We can barely make out big white letters painted in the middle of the street right before a section of raised asphalt: B-U-M-P. We walk through the snow on wide concrete pathways, under trees that tower over us, one tree in front of every large three-story apartment building, each building identical to the next.

Sai-wok, Mr. Six, who lives a few blocks away, says in English. He points downward to the tree-lined pathways. I had never seen sidewalks, never seen buildings this tall, never seen this kind of uniformity. In Vietnam, huts are scattered haphazardly throughout the village where we lived. Made of dried coconut leaves and twigs that came crashing down every July during monsoon season, the huts are different sizes, different shapes, different colors. Trees and plants grow wildly there, not in rows. Everything is so neat here in New York City.

We stop in the middle of the block. We have arrived. Gazing up at the brick building where Mr. Six, with the help of the International Rescue Committee, has secured an apartment for us, we stand with our mouths open, awestruck. Stretching half the length of the block and impervious to the snow, our new building is not the *nhà lá* we knew from Vietnam, the house made of sticks and dried leaves that we lived in. No typhoons will be able to hurt us here, to rip holes into our home.

My parents climb the seven gray steps leading up to the first floor, the landlord's apartment, and ring the doorbell. Standing in the concrete front yard of our new home, my brothers and I notice the little white clouds that form outside our mouths as we breathe. While we wait for our parents we distract ourselves, four little heads, each holding a mouthful of breath and taking turns at releasing the puff of white. Because I am the youngest, my brothers pause to let me release the cloud twice in a row. Look, I say, magic.

———

We are on the third floor, in what is known as a railroad apartment. My father beams, happy because the front of it faces east. It is a good omen. We will see the sun when it rises.

Phu, the most energetic and adventurous of us, runs through the length of the apartment while the rest of us move slowly from room to room. From east to west, there is one bedroom, the room that looks out to the rising sun, then a small living room, which leads into a small kitchen with crooked cabinets and a light that doesn't turn on unless you jiggle the switch seven or eight times. Behind the kitchen there is a black-and-white-tiled bathroom, behind which there is another room. What a long house! my parents exclaim.

We have no furniture, only thin sheets, some pillows we'll have to share, and a straw mat Mr. Six has supplied us with. He leaves us with a few pots and pans to cook with and a bag of rice. Soon my mother has made congee with soy sauce, which we eat huddled together on the mat to keep warm. Because there's a problem with the boiler, we have no heat, except for the heat of our bodies and the breath we blow into our hands, which we press against the body parts that are coldest. As winter seeps through the windows and into my bones, my mother can hear my teeth chattering and gathers me up in her arms, rocking me to sleep.

That night, my father thrashes about and wakes my mother up.

"Hía, take the children and run!" he yells into the darkness with large, panicked eyes. "They're coming for us!"

My mother, well-seasoned in handling his night terrors, grabs his wrists. "What are you doing?" she asks calmly as he struggles in her grasp. "No one is coming for us. Go back to sleep." I am awake. I see what is happening. Perhaps half out of fear and half out of curiosity to watch the scene unfold, I know not to make a sound.

My father takes a few seconds to adjust his reality, as his eyes search for meaning in the darkness of our new apartment. He looks down at his four children. He remembers where he is now and slowly lowers himself back onto the straw mat. Silence is replaced with snores. The show ends, and I, too, fall asleep.

Now it is March. My father has not yet found a job. The price of our airplane tickets weighs on his mind. He must pay back the Humanitarian Operation for six tickets: a cost of $1,800. Where will we find that kind of money? Having just arrived, we are already in debt. We feel immeasurable gratitude mixed in with crushing desperation. Or rather, my parents do. Their worn-out bodies feel the cold more than ours do, and they alone know that food is scarce, that they have to ration portions of rice for us to eat, that if my father doesn't find work soon we'll have to eat even less. Thinh and Phu are caught between two worlds, but quickly adjusting, while Long and I are too young to be afraid, too young to be desperate. My memories and consciousness are only just forming, earlier memories falling out of my head as new ones enter it. Soon there is nothing else to compare this to. I am happy. I play with my brothers. I am with my family.

Food and sleep are essential. My father repeats this mantra day in and day out. He says it in the mornings when one of us sneezes from a cold, at the dinner table as we eat our hot porridge with ginger and soy sauce, at night as he and my mother get us all ready for bed, layering thin sheets on straw mats.

We eat dinner every night at exactly six o'clock. My mother cooks and my brothers and I help set the table, a rickety construction consisting of a tabletop screwed onto a cabinet, which my brothers and I like to tip back and forth, testing our parents' patience. Though the table is round, there is a designated "head of the table," where my father sits. My mother sits next to him, and the rest of us sit wherever we please.

My father spends the days building an altar high up on our living room wall to honor the Buddha and bodhisattvas. In the center of the altar is a framed picture of Bổn Sư Thích Ca Mâu Ni Phật, the great Shakyamuni Buddha, the Awakened One. He sits atop a lotus blossom with a swastika on his chest, his legs crossed and his right thumb and index finger touching, palm facing outward, his left hand resting upon his lap. This is the Abhaya mudra, the fearlessness hand gesture.

"It means don't be afraid," my father tells me. "He will protect us."

Really? I think. A picture can protect us?

To the Buddha's right is another picture, this one depicting Quan Âm Bồ Tát, Bodhisattva of Compassion, She Who Perceives the Sounds of the World. She is a radiant figure dressed in white against a backdrop of black swirling waves. She has a serene expression on her face as she rides atop a dragon flying above a stormy sea.

"Call out her name three times when you need help," my father tells me. "Her arms will reach you."

"Her arms?" I ask.

"She has a thousand arms," my father says. "Buddha gave her a thousand arms to save humanity from suffering."

I don't know what suffering is, but I look up at her, at her illuminated body. I whisper her name three times. I shut my eyes and stay still, imagining a hand on my shoulder. To the Buddha's left is a third deity, Đại Thế Chí Bồ Tát, the Great Strength Bodhisattva, dressed in bright blue robes and cradling a lotus in his arms. Also known as the Bodhisattva with a Body of Blinding Infinite Light, he endows us with wisdom and strength and generosity.

Together, they are the three sages of the Western Pure Land. Each morning, my father makes us all kneel before the altar and recite their names three times each.

"We will be okay as long as they are here to watch over us," he says. "We will find a way."

One morning in mid-March, Mr. Six takes us to the offices of the International Rescue Committee (IRC) in Midtown Manhattan. "You kids must give Mr. Six all of your respect," my mother tells us before he arrives. "He is our sponsor. He is the reason we are able to come to nước Mỹ—America."

"What's a sponsor?" Thinh, the eldest, asks.

"Someone to help us get settled into our new country," my mother says. "He came a few years before us and knows how to navigate the system now. He will help us figure it out."

At the IRC, a Vietnamese representative helps my father with immigration papers and takes photos of each of us. They help him enroll in a few free courses to learn English and basic data entry and ultimately to study for his GED. He is given instructions on how to apply for a green card, how to apply for Medicaid and food stamps, and how to enroll his children in school.

When we return home, he reviews the paperwork with a broad smile on his face. "Free health care." He chuckles in disbelief. "They're giving us free health care. And free school. And free food." He turns on the lights to the altar he's been constructing, brings his hands together, and bows to each deity. Then he makes us all bow. The gods have saved us once again.

The next day my father enrolls my three brothers in school. Thinh and Phu are placed in the third and second grade, respectively, a year behind where they should be for their ages. Long is in kindergarten, where he should be. "Why can't I go?" I wrap my arms tight around my mother's leg, crying and begging her to take me with them as they leave. I feel cheated and lonely. I know they're off having fun without me.

But the following week, I get to go to the Wyckoff Heights hospital in Bushwick, a few blocks from where we live, when my father takes us there to get us vaccinated. "No more sickness," he says. He gives a nurse the paperwork the IRC provided and communicates through a combination of broken English and a finger imitating a needle going into each of our arms.

The food stamps haven't kicked in yet, so my mother sells her last white-gold bracelet to a jeweler in Chinatown for one hundred dollars. She has learned to calculate dong to dollars and knows the bracelet is worth more but does not have the verbal capacity to fight for it. This is enough to last through another month, she says with waning hope, knowing that even with the help of food stamps, this means she'll have to choose between feeding six hungry people and buying winter clothing for us. She is prepared to give up the idea of warm clothing for a few packs of noodles and some soy sauce.

My brothers warm up some during the day, at school, but I am my mother's shadow, following her around the unheated apartment as she cleans it and prepares the day's meals. I develop hypothermia. My speech slurs and my brothers make fun of me. I laugh too, until the day I pass out and fall down the stairs of our building. I stay at the Wyckoff Heights hospital for some days, snuggling beneath warm blankets. Strange people in blue and occasionally white uniforms come in and out of my room. My parents and brothers stay with me after visiting hours end and sneak into bed with me. Long and I sleep on my mother's stomach, and Thinh and Phu sleep across the foot of the bed. My father sleeps in a chair. For the first time in what seems like forever, because two months are an eternity to a three-year-old, I am warm and I dream of sunlight in Vietnam. We hope that no one will kick us out in the middle of the night. And no one does.

Can we all fall down the stairs? one of my brothers asks the morning I am released. Yeah! the other two chime in. This is the best! Let's throw her down the stairs again. They chase me around the room and we tickle each other. Someone falls down and is crying, quite possibly me. Meanwhile, my parents sneak hospital food into their pockets to take home with them.

Some days later, Long develops Raynaud's disease from frostbite, making the blood vessels in his fingers and toes constrict in spasms. His fingertips turn blue. *You blue? You blue?* we ask, managing to rhyme in our new language and collapsing in shrieks at the sound of our own brilliance. We think we are poets and color our fingers blue with Crayola markers to be like Long. Back at the Wyckoff Heights hospital, doctors gently admonish my parents and advise them to bundle their child up more. As if they had the bundles to do so.

A month later, we have almost run out of food again. We eat rice with soy sauce and my brothers ask around in school for any food that is going uneaten. *You don like foo, you gib to me*, they say, practicing their English. They hang around garbage cans in the cafeteria to snatch up any leftovers and stick them in their backpacks. When they come home, they compare the spoils.

One day, my father shows up with a bag of used clothing and sneakers with holes in them: *Look what I found.* We don't know where he found them, but we do not ask questions. We are ecstatic as we try on the clothes, which hang limply around our shoulders. We think we look American now. We start to call each other American names. I am Lisa. My brothers, Thinh, Phu, and Long, are Tony, Peter, and David. These will be the names we choose when we earn our citizenship.

We are American! We are American! We troop around the house in our brand-new old clothes. My parents look on, wondering what to call themselves.

Twenty Thousand Cummerbunds

THERE'S A STRANGE MAN in our living room. I have not seen him before. But my father has invited him in and my mother is making him tea. My brothers are in school. And I sit on the floor at home, playing with a cockroach that has unwittingly crossed my path, making walls with my hands.

"It's really easy," the man says. "Someone delivers the materials to you every weekend. You put them together, sew them into whatever the boss wants, and you exchange your finished products for the next set of materials the following weekend. Easy." He is young and has an accent when he speaks Vietnamese, the kind my brothers and I will develop when our tongues cool like iron into western phonemic casts. He looks around at our apartment. It makes me anxious. They are seated in the living room at a table my father has just found on the street. The chairs they sit on are splintered school chairs salvaged from the schoolyard across the street.

"And we get paid enough?" my father asks nervously. Thin lines have appeared on his honey-brown face in just a few months. His eyes are wide and watery. It has been two months since any one of us has had a full meal, but thanks to my mother's shopping with Mrs. Six, we have discovered the wonder of canned sardines. I love canned sardines— a break from the rice with soy sauce.

"Oh yeah, definitely. There's so much money in this business. All the Vietnamese are doing it in this area."

I am not allowed to make eye contact with adults. It is rude. So I watch their interaction out of the corner of my eye. The man is tall, is dressed in a fancy suit and tie with shiny shoes, and has a crew cut. My mother's hands shake as she pours tea for him. He has a loud voice. He tells my parents that they will be given a Mitsubishi sewing machine to assist them in the work. Brand-name stuff, high-end. His eyes dart quickly around the apartment. He rarely looks at my parents as he speaks. But he promises that he will bring them success and provide them with a solid livelihood.

My father stands up and shakes the young man's hand, vigorously, bowing to him at the same time. There are holes in my father's worn T-shirt. His trousers do not reach his ankles, and he is barefoot. They look different, my father and this man.

"No problem," the young man says. "Glad to help." He glances over at me and furrows his brow a little before catching himself and waving goodbye.

I look down at my pet cockroach and realize that I have accidentally killed it.

Outside, the snow has turned black, gray, and yellow. The magic is over.

"Mom?" I ask as I wipe the snot running down my nose with the back of my hand. "Will it always be winter?"

My mother has begun to take daily walks around the neighborhood with Mrs. Six. In Vietnam, it is not uncommon to have more than ten children, and the children are often referred to not by their names but by their birth order, starting with the number two. The firstborn is referred to as Sister Two or Brother Two. The second born becomes Sister Three or Brother Three. Mr. Six is fifth in line, and his wife is Mrs. Six by association. In our family, I am simply *con gái út*. The Littlest Girl.

Mrs. Six shows my mother the nearby shops and streets and cautions her to walk only in the daytime. "You can't trust anyone around here," she tells my mother in a hushed whisper, as though there might be a mugger eavesdropping nearby. With my brothers in school and my father taking data-entry and English courses, I tag along with them on their missions because I am too young to be left alone at home.

Slowly, my mother and I explore the neighborhood. She learns the differences between the bodegas that dot Seneca Avenue—which ones carry the cheapest milk, which ones carry the best eggs, and which ones are not prejudiced against us. She surveys the discount department stores and nearby supermarkets. There is even a live poultry market on the corner of Bleecker Street and Knickerbocker. "Oh, I thought everything was packaged here! This is much better! A bit like home. When we make enough money, we will come back here." Mrs. Six smiles at her optimism. Her husband is still looking for a job, but cannot find one, so they must rely on government assistance.

A brown cardboard box has arrived and the Sweatshop Era begins. On the floor of the back room, which my parents have designated our workroom, my brothers and I sit cross-legged and separate the brightly colored satin and silk fabrics. They are held together at one edge with a kind of rubbery glue, like a notepad. I like tearing them off. I like the sound it makes. Then there is another bundle of a white scratchy cotton material that is harder to separate. As I tear the fabrics off the glue, small pieces of thread and dust fall all around me. I sneeze a lot.

After we are finished separating the fabrics, my mother and my brothers go to the bedroom to start assembling the neckties, and I stay behind with my father, to work on a big roll of black elastic band an inch wide, which I must cut into foot-long lengths and leave in piles for my father. Although the metal scissors are too big for my little hands, bruising my knuckles, I get used to holding them and the work soon becomes easy—so easy that the rhythmic sounds of tearing and the repetitive actions make me fall asleep. My father throws a shoe at my head. *Làm biếng*, he says. He is teaching me: don't be lazy.

He sits at our new Mitsubishi sewing machine, trying to figure out how to make a cummerbund. We see from the cover of the instruction manual that it is a pleated sash a man wears at the waist with a shiny black suit called a tuxedo, which Thinh has told us, translating from the little English he has learned at school, is something worn at "black-tie events"—though none of us has any idea what a black-tie event is. My father flips through the pages of the instruction manual over and over, but since it is in English he must rely on the pictures. He makes a few of the sashes, but they don't come out right. They are lopsided and look like colorful, crumpled bitter melons with the pleats sticking out. The sight makes me giggle. Everything makes me giggle at this age. I enjoy laughing. But my father does not. He has mouths to feed in a land that is not his own and only limited means of communication. He yells and tells me I am not preparing the materials correctly, tells me we're already behind and need to hurry up. His anxiety makes him agitated and impatient. He hurls spools of thread to the floor.

Hearing the commotion, my mother and my brothers come to my rescue. My mother scoops me up. Thinh attempts to translate the manual into Vietnamese. My father sits back down at the sewing machine, and this time, after several tries, he finally makes one that looks the way they do in the manual.

We all move into the living room, where we can spread out and each concentrate on a task. My brothers turn all the cummerbunds outside in. My mother irons the pleats flat. I attach silver buckles and a clasp. It's an assembly line. The process for the ties is similar but a little less complicated, so they are faster to make. By the end of the night, there are 150 cummerbunds and 250 ties.

We are so proud of ourselves. My brothers high-five each other, and I copy them. We raise our hands to our parents, and they stare at us blankly. We hesitate, then, laughing, take their hands and raise them up to meet ours.

The next morning at breakfast, my father, who has stayed up all night counting the pieces, unable to believe how productive we've been, confirms the total we already knew: four hundred. We made four hundred items, he announces every few minutes. Sounding newly hopeful, he tells us, *We will make it after all.*

He calls the young man, eager to know how much we will earn for our night's work.

"Hey, ah, Ken? Yeah, this is Mr. Tran. How are you? Listen, we made a hundred and fifty cummerbunds and two hundred and fifty ties in one night," he says in Vietnamese, straightening his back as though a great weight has lifted.

My brothers and I sit at the table and wait, my father's excitement spreading through us. My mother sits down on the straw mat, eyes wide. But something is wrong. We hear him repeat the number three times. The math doesn't add up, he mutters. He grabs a calculator to figure out our total, even though it's simple math and he served as a lieutenant in the South Vietnamese artillery unit at the age of sixteen, plotting coordinates for bombs.

"So you're telling me we only made eleven dollars and twenty-five cents?"

My brothers and I look at each other, not knowing how to feel. Eleven dollars and twenty-five cents could supply us with plenty of candy, ice cream, and even *McDonald's.* It sounds like a lot of money.

Isn't it?

"Faster? My family and I are not machines. You guaranteed that we would make hundreds in a week. How are we supposed to live like this? We'll have the electricity bill to deal with now that we have a sewing machine, iron, and lights running all night long. We're already behind on two months' rent. At this rate, we'll need to make five thousand cummerbunds a week. That's twenty thousand cummerbunds a month. The ties are worth even less!"

His voice cracks.

"You lied to us!" he cries into the phone, and we hear a dial tone on the other end.

My brothers and I give him our breakfast. Today, it is rice porridge with soy sauce. Food and sleep, we recite proudly. All else is unnecessary. He looks at us with red eyes, looks through us, and retires to the bedroom.

"Don't forget to set your clocks forward an hour," Mr. Six tells my parents. It is April. Mr. and Mrs. Six are over for tea.

"Set my clock forward? What do you mean?" my father asks.

"It's something we do here in America. You get more daylight that way. You set it an hour forward around springtime and an hour back in the fall. Interesting idea, isn't it?"

"Wow," my father says, trying out a new word he has learned in English class.

It is still cold. But the days are getting brighter and the birds are chirping more loudly. One day, on a trip in search of discarded furniture or appliances left out on sidewalks, my father finds a broken blue and pink bicycle. He takes it home and examines it. The brakes no longer function, and the pedals have broken off, but it still works for the most part. On the weekends, he brings us to the schoolyard across the street whenever we have a small break from work, and we take turns getting bruised, scraping our knees, learning how to ride our new bike. My mother stays home to cook and occasionally calls to us from the window.

Throughout the week, when my brothers are at school and my father does not have classes to attend, my parents and I work. I separate the materials, my father sews, I turn the item inside out, my mother irons, counting twelve of each after she is done and arranging them in neat little dozens in the cardboard box the materials came in. Then my brothers come home from school and we start up again.

Lately we have been getting gold buckles instead of silver ones. So Long and I play trading games. Hey, I'll trade you a gold buckle for two silvers and this cool piece of fabric. How about that funny-looking one? Whoa, no way, check out this piece. Finders keepers! No, that's not how it works! You touched it first, but I saw it first, so that means I found it!

Shut up! my father yells from the back room. We stare at him, momentarily quieted. Within a few minutes, though, we've started back up again.

After a few months of nonstop working, we manage to perfect the process. My father sews multiple items at the same time, all connected by a thread. We take them out from underneath the sewing machine, a long daisy chain of ties and cummerbunds. Using sharp blades, we cut the threads and divvy them up. We take the piles into the living room. We slip a chopstick through an opening in the fabric to turn the item outside in. Our small fingers are perfect for the job. We try to see who can do it fastest. It's a game.

My mother uses friendly competition to egg us on even faster. See how much Phu has done? He's so quick! Let's see how much you can do, Thinh. None of us can compete with Phu. He always wins. But I develop my own system. When I have a particularly large pile, I separate it into six smaller piles, each pile representing a family member. I pretend there is a fire. I pretend that the fire is spreading and that the only way to save my family is by completing my task. I go down the line. I save my father first, then my mother, then my brothers, in order of age, and only then do I save myself. Each time I finish a pile I imagine one of us escaping the burning building.

One day, a few months into this work, we notice black soot coming out of our noses. Thinh, a precocious child at nine, sets out to investigate the cause of it and notices a strange high-pitched sound coming from the sewing machine in the back room that we hadn't heard before. He alerts my father. After releasing the upper part of the sewing machine from its bedplate, they discover that the noise is coming from the rotors grinding against each other, sending a black cloud of metal dust into the apartment, where it ended up on our bodies and in our clothes.

My father had noticed but hadn't said a word for months, afraid of the cost of replacing the rotors, afraid of slowing down and not making enough money for rent, for clothing, for food. Only when our noses start to bleed does he cave in and buy new rotors. The air clears. We can breathe again.

Water and Angels

IN VIETNAM, THE MEKONG Delta was our backyard, its canals and tributaries spread throughout the southwestern tip of the country like capillaries. We called it the Nine Dragons, one of which wrapped its meandering yellow tail around our village and behind our hut. It thrashed and raged in the tempests of the wet season, and lay still beneath a cloudless sky during the dry season.

It was where my brothers learned to swim. I was too young, though my mother would occasionally dip me into the river water while sitting in a canoe as my brothers swam around naked nearby.

On days when the river came down from the sky, my father put out large terra-cotta vases to catch the streams of rainwater coming in through the gaps in our roof. When he ran out of vases, he used bowls and cups that inevitably overflowed.

"We slipped around the dirt floor of our hut a lot," my mother said, during one of the stories she told us about our life in Vietnam, which she liked to recount as we cut fabrics and attached buckles to cummerbunds. She dipped and slid her hands through the air. There never seemed to be enough containers for all the drips, she recalled, but it was how things were. "Water was always everywhere. And we accepted it. We exalted it. We prayed to it."

But no matter how much they prayed, the river couldn't cure everything. Once, when he was four years old, Long became very sick, she told us, as we all listened with rapt attention. He had a distended belly and large liquid-filled boils spreading across his body. After the village doctors and the shamans had shaken their heads in surrender, my father waded into the river with Long in his arms, tears running down his face. "Please," he had pleaded with the river. "Anything, anything. Please." Long was unresponsive, breathing weakly.

It was my mother who forced her husband out of his despair. "You give up too soon," she told him. "We have to go into the city. Now. Snap out of it." So they carried Long into Cần Thơ, the largest city in the Mekong Delta, but still little more than a village. They had already spent most of their life savings on local doctors and medicines that didn't work. But my mother was counting on compassion. Somewhere, she thought, someone would take pity on them.

In the emergency room of the general hospital of Cần Thơ, doctors poked and examined the little round mass that Long had become. By then the boils had reached his face, and his cheeks were swollen and shiny like glass bowls, my mother said, her hands cupping the air as though to hold Long's ballooning face. But kind as they were, the doctors shook their heads and lowered their eyes.

"We have seen this before," they said. "There is nothing we can do for him."

The state of medicine in Vietnam in the late eighties was far behind the rest of the modern world, especially in the countryside. Village doctors reused gloves and needles for lack of equipment, and treatments for certain curable diseases had not yet arrived. Antibiotics were only just reaching the big cities, and one needed money to afford them.

"I don't remember much of what I thought when we walked out of that hospital," my mother said. "I knew only that a wind was slowly and softly blowing out the flame of his life."

A nurse walking past noticed my father's grief-stricken face as he held Long in his arms, and inquired about the situation. "He's dying," my father said. My mother described her son's symptoms—the speed with which the boils had appeared, his lack of appetite, his inability to pee—to the nurse.

The nurse looked down at Long and frowned. "What, this? This is nothing. Wait here."

She disappeared into a room, leaving my parents to reconcile this "nothingness" with the imminent death of their son. When she emerged, the nurse had in her hands a slip of paper. "A new shipment of medicine just arrived from the West. Take this to the pharmacy and follow the entire course as indicated on the package. He should be fine." My parents stared in disbelief. Was this a hoax? "Don't waste time," she warned them. "Listen, if this doesn't work, I'll tear up my nursing license." They scrambled out of the hospital, prepared to be the punch line of a cruel joke.

Later, on the ferry going back home, after the first dose of medicine had been administered, Long woke up on my father's lap. Two sleepy eyes looked up at my father's haggard face. "I have to pee," Long said. My father carried his son to the side of the ferry and held him up in triumph as Long shot out a long and steady stream of urine into the river.

Days later, after Long had regained his strength and was looking healthy again, my parents returned to that hospital in Cần Thơ to thank the nurse who saved their son. But they couldn't find her.

"We asked all around for her," my mother told us. "She had written her name on the prescription she gave us, but no one in the hospital knew who she was. The receptionist even took out a directory of all the staff members. Her name wasn't listed."

"An angel," my father said as he listened to the end of my mother's story with tears filling his eyes. "An incarnation of Quan Âm Bồ Tát."

25

———

When we came to New York City, my parents were struck by the dryness and gray of all the concrete. They pined for the Mekong, the artery of Vietnam, where they washed dishes and clothing and bathed their children, where townsfolk grew their vegetables by the riverbank, where fishermen slept in boats on the murky waters with their lines, awaiting the tug of sustenance, where the river god would answer their prayers.

Eventually, my parents found a way to return to the water.

In June 1994, they discovered Coney Island. I was four years old then, and my parents decided it was time for me to learn how to swim. We were going to have a family adventure. It would be the first time we had done anything like it since coming to America, the first time we took a break from making ties and cummerbunds to explore New York City.

"We can't stay cooped up in here like this. We can't work like dogs," my father said in a moment of fearlessness and clarity. "We have to go outside. Go here and there. That's the only way we'll know the world!"

He brought out a large subway map and put on the pair of reading glasses he'd bought from Rite Aid. He circled the 14th Street–Union Square stop, where we would need to get off the L train and switch over to the Q. Then he circled the last stop on the Q, a bunch of yellow and orange lines converging at the bottom of the map, punctuated by black and white dots.

"This is where we're going tomorrow," he told us. "We're going to swim."

The next morning my father woke us all up earlier than usual. My brothers play fought with each other. My mother got us ready. It didn't matter that none of us had swimsuits; we all wore cotton shorts and my mother put on a pink tank top over her bra. My father pored over his map again and again to memorize the directions. Something was about to happen; I could feel it: a new adventure was waiting for us.

The ride to the last stop on the Q train was a long one. Before this, we had only ever ventured as far as Chinatown on the M train, back when the M train still stopped at Bowery. This time, it felt like we would be underground forever. But as we neared the end of the line, the crowd started to change. I looked around us and saw flocks of families and friends who had had the same idea we had—folks with beach bags and straw hats, flip-flops and sunglasses. A few people already had their bathing suits on, some skimpier than others. "Don't look," my mother commanded us. Anything that would remind us of our own bodies was taboo, an idea instilled in us early on. We obeyed and did not look, not because we understood why, but because we weren't interested anyway. Not yet. Not at this age.

Now there was a palpable excitement in the air. People started talking loudly and laughing a lot, and a few kids danced around the subway poles with lollipops in their mouths. I was content to sit on my mother's lap, enjoying the moment. Thinh, Phu, and Long were kneeling on the bench across from me, their backs turned, noses pressed to the dirty polycarbonate glass, watching as the world beyond moved past them like a roll of film unraveling.

Coney Island was a dream. Up until this point, we had only heard about it from Mr. and Mrs. Six, so we didn't know what to expect. But seeing the Ferris wheel loom large on the horizon as we approached was the first time I remember ever experiencing a sense of sheer amazement. My brothers and I craned our necks to admire its size, tugging on our parents and pointing up to make sure they saw what we saw. "Look!" we said. "Yes, yes, we see it!" they said.

Though we couldn't afford anything in Astroland, we walked through the park, where all the colors of a summer childhood existed, and we drank it in like some effervescent soft drink. The painted rides, the pink and blue cotton candy, its edges dark and crystalline where it had been licked, the buoyant balloons bumping against one another, the red-white-and-blue Firecracker Popsicles slow-dripping in the sultry heat, and the happy music blaring out from each of the different rides. But we had to move on. We were headed toward something even better than Astroland.

We followed the throng of beachgoers across the wooden boardwalk to the edge of the sand, where all of us except my mother took off our shirts. It was the first time I had ever seen the ocean, its limitlessness at once awe-inspiring and frightening. Barefoot and wearing nothing but a pair of red cotton shorts, I skittered across the sand with my brothers. My feet burned, pain giving way to exhilaration and the promise of cool water. Hundreds of people crowded the section of sand right at the water's edge. We zigzagged around them until we found an opening where we could claim our own little plot of sand. As soon as we marked our territory with our towels, my brothers and I ran straight to the water, our parents trailing after us.

I watched as my brothers tentatively walked into the white froth of the waves, their faces lighting up as though seeing an old friend after a long period of absence. "So cold!" they shouted gleefully, splashing each other. After a few minutes of shivering discovery, Thinh was the first to dunk his body beneath the water, emerging seconds later, hair dripping and a big grin on his face, to let us know that it was safe.

"Don't go far!" my father called out to them. "Stay between the lady right there on the right with the blue umbrella and that man over there with the green-and-yellow towel." He was like a referee, blowing an imaginary whistle each time one of them ventured too deep into the water or stepped outside the boundaries he set. Every now and then he would stand waist deep in the water and stick his head under, then straighten back up and rub the water all over his body, as though showering in the sunlight with seawater as soap.

I stood by the ocean's edge, digging my feet into the sand, instinctively aware of the dangers of the cold, murky water, which even a few feet from shore was so deep that I wouldn't be able to stand with my head above it. I bent down and grabbed a handful of gray wet sand, kneading the strange stuff onto my body. My mother appeared at my side. *"Đi đi con,"* she said, coaxing me farther into the water. "Don't be scared." She crouched down, and when I climbed onto her back, she paddled out to my brothers, with me clinging desperately to her neck.

The water was calm and peaceful, with only small waves, and I soon relaxed into feeling safe and secure on my mother's back. Looking around I saw other children playing nearby, and I wondered what their lives were like. Wondered if they were also done with their quota of ties and cummerbunds for the week and were taking a break at the beach like we were.

The air was cool, the sun suddenly hidden behind clouds. When a breeze blew by, I felt the hairs on my arm rise, goose bumps spreading across my body. Somehow, it was warmer to be in the water than outside of it, and my mother walked in deeper, taking me with her until I was fully immersed except for my head. We all stayed in the water until our lips turned blue. "Five more minutes," Phu begged when my mother and father began reeling us in. But we were cold and we knew the journey home was long, so none of us protested further when our five minutes were up. We made the trek home in a blissful state of sun- and water-induced languor, having experienced for the first time in our lives an *ocean*, not knowing, as our parents did, the oceans we had already crossed to get there.

That night I went to bed feeling the ebb and flow of the waves around my body. I closed my eyes and imagined it all over again. My day at the beach.

School Days

THE YEAR-ROUND FREE-BREAKFAST PROGRAM across the street at P.S. 81 was a godsend for my parents, who never failed to thank the Buddhas for such profound generosity. My brothers and I loved it too and looked forward to it every morning. There were six or seven different cereal options to choose from, milk to pair it with, orange, apple, or cranberry juice, and muffins and bagels. I was not a picky child and liked it all. These were foods and beverages I never got to have at home. Our own breakfasts were savory, not sweet like the American breakfast, and there was no dairy. On hot days, I especially liked to take home a small carton of chocolate milk and put it in the freezer. After a few hours, I'd take it out and open both sides of the carton to reveal a block of frozen chocolate milk. Then I'd dig my spoon into the sweet, icy shards.

In the beginning, before I was enrolled in school myself, my brothers would take me to breakfast across the street with them. Phu would sometimes carry me on his back, and it'd be the four of us at a cafeteria table. But when school let out for the summer, they headed to the park instead and my father would take me.

I watched with fascination as the kids and parents at the tables around me spoke to each other in many different languages. Even as a small child, watching other people was more interesting to me than anything else.

"*Mày ăn đi. Ngó người ta hoài, đồ ngu quá.* Eat your food. Don't be foolish," my father would always say, occasionally smacking me across the head to snap me out of it. "Stop looking at the other kids. Something could happen right now, and you could end up without a meal. Then what will you do?"

I never questioned my father's frequent violent outbursts then. I understood only that I needed to obey. There was always an urgency in his voice and in his actions, as though he were running from imminent danger. And I ran with him.

One August morning, when I was almost five years old, my father took me to the kindergarten annex on the corner of Bleecker Street and Seneca Avenue half a block from where we lived. Finally, it was my turn to go to school. A tall, pale-faced lady brought us to a room with a round blue table and motioned for us to sit down.

"What is your name?" she asked me.

"Trần Kỳ Lý," my father responded for me. She looked at my father, shook her head, and pointed to me.

"Raise your hand," she commanded. I smiled at her but did not understand. My father told me in Vietnamese to raise my hand. I shot my hand up with enthusiasm, relieved to know the answer. It was like a game and my father and I were a team. But my sense of achievement didn't last long.

"No help," the lady gently admonished my father.

"What kind of fruit do you like to eat?" she continued. Again I remained silent. Strange sounds in my ears. Having spent most of my time at home with my family working on our little home assembly line, I hadn't had a chance to play with any English-speaking kids and I didn't know the language at all. Though my brothers were learning it in school, they spoke Vietnamese at home.

" *Trái cây*," my father whispered. *Fruit.* He couldn't help himself. He squirmed in his seat. He wanted to show that *he* had been studying the language, that *he* was capable.

But the woman wagged a finger at him. "Ah-ah!" I felt him shrink, defeated, as he slid into the back of his chair. She turned toward me. "I like your earrings. Can you show me where they are?"

Silence. I began to feel nervous. I began to feel that I'd let my father down.

"Earrings," she repeated, and tugged on her own earrings to show me, but I stared at her blankly, then at my father, hoping that he could somehow tell me the answer.

"All right," she said, and marked something down on the clipboard she'd carried in with her. "We'll put her in ESL." She slid a piece of paper from the clipboard and handed it over to my father. It was a list of supplies to buy for the upcoming school year. My father beamed.

"Tankyu very motch!" he said to the lady. He took the list of supplies and walked out with my hand tightly in his.

"Xong rồi hả Ba?" I asked him. All done?

"Xong rồi," he said, looking down at me with a big smile on his face. "You're going to be a student starting next month. Study hard like your brothers. Be a good student."

So, I thought, *we didn't lose the game after all.* And just like that, my journey as a student in America had begun.

A few weeks later, my brothers reminded my parents that it was time to go shopping for school supplies, and soon the four of us were racing down Cypress Avenue toward Myrtle to the ninety-nine-cent store, followed by our mother. I was ecstatic. This time, I would be included. A world I hadn't yet glimpsed, a world my brothers already had access to, was waiting for me.

My brothers, who already understood the value of money and knew enough about our financial situation to help my parents save, looked over their supply list and mine to make sure that they didn't buy anything they didn't really need.

"We could just share a pack of pencils and erasers and crayons and glue," Thinh said.

"Yeah," Phu said. "And she doesn't need *that* many folders. Marble-covered notebooks, though, she's gotta have her own."

"And a book bag!" Long said. "She needs a book bag."

"Which one would you like?" my mother asked me as we considered all the available options. I looked up at the rows of multicolored book bags with cartoon illustrations, all hanging from a rack on the ceiling. The owner, a kind Korean man, stood by with a long metal pole to retrieve the book bag of my choice. My eyes scanned the possibilities—ponies with rainbow hair, a princess in front of a castle, a girl with red hair and a fish tail for legs—but I couldn't decide. It had to be the right one. And they were all so beautiful. I could feel the panic rising within me. I looked up at my mother. "I-I don't know," I said. It was the first time that making a decision was difficult for me. But it wouldn't be the last.

"Ugh, hurry up! Just pick one already!" Long yelled at me. He was the least patient of my brothers, a trait he'd no doubt inherited from my father.

Sensing my anxiety, my mother placed her hand on my head. "How about this one?" she asked. She pointed to a pink-and-white bag with an image of a princess and a unicorn in front of a castle. The man hooked it off the rack.

"Oh, this a good one. Very nice," he said, handing it to me with a wink.

I reached my hand out and touched it gingerly. The man nodded at me and nudged the bag toward me. "Take, take," he said.

"Go on, take it," my mother repeated.

So I took it and cradled it in my arms, breathing in that new-plastic smell. It was so perfect. And it was mine. Even my brothers seemed pleased.

"Yeah, Ly! You're gonna go to school!" Thinh said.

I ran and skipped all the way home, catching glimpses of myself in store windows, a girl with a pretty pink book bag on her back. I felt like I had suddenly become a new person, like my identity had changed somehow. I thought I was now getting closer to my brothers, in both age and experience, and might one day even surpass them. *It's about time*, I thought, not yet realizing that that wasn't quite how it works.

Kindergarten proved even more enjoyable than I imagined. We had no toys at home, and here there were wooden block letters to play with, and white cotton black-eyed dolls with blue and red yarn for hair, and a red telephone with a rotary dial. I liked hearing the click each time I landed on a number, and the soothing sounds the dial made as it returned to its resting position. I would sit and pretend to make long-distance phone calls to Vietnam the way my parents did when they had the chance. I talked half in Vietnamese and half in the English I was learning in my ESL class. I liked playing with the other kids too. Since none of them spoke English much better than I did, I didn't feel inferior.

Nap time, by contrast, was my least favorite part of the day. I'd become fidgety and mischievous, disturbing the rest of the class. Our teacher was not amused.

"Sometimes has trouble focusing," read the handwritten note on my first report card.

Not that it mattered, of course. My parents saved the card but they couldn't read English, nor did they ever ask me or my brothers to translate it for them.

Cheater

MY PARENTS ARE AMONG the millions of people of Chinese ancestry who had settled in Vietnam, and that sets them apart from many of the Vietnamese people they meet after we move to New York. It confuses me when my father calls my mother by her Chinese name, Hía. I see Diệp Hứa on her documents and wonder about this second identity, only finding out later that it's a translation of the same name, a remnant of their Chinese identity.

So when another Chinese/Vietnamese family with a young son moves into a building down the street and they invite us over one weekend, my parents are delighted. Being with them will remind us of our identity, of how we are different from the Vietnamese at the Buddhist temple we have started going to. Thinh and Phu are in middle school and have too much homework, so it is just me and Long who go.

I am six, Long is eight, and the boy is ten. We have never been invited to play at anyone else's home. It is like entering some unknown land, and we walk in nervously, the darkness of the hallway adding an air of mystery to what lies beyond. We are led into his bedroom and our eyes widen when we see how many games the boy has in his room, boxes and boxes with the label "Toys" written across the top, and a vast collection of tiny toy cars underneath his bed. Action figures litter the floor. How could one child have so many games? I think to myself.

We decide to play Monopoly, not knowing how fraught that game can be. "I want to buy it," the kid proclaims after landing on Park Place, which we've quickly learned is a highly desirable piece of real estate.

"With what money?" Long asks. "You already spent it."

"No I didn't. I still have five hundred. See?" The kid opens his hand to reveal his crumpled bills.

"Cheater. You stole that money. I just saw you take an extra five hundred when you were changing your two fifties for a hundred!"

"I didn't cheat!" He crosses his arms over his chest. "I'm telling my mom!"

His mother walks in and demands to know what is going on.

Long explains that her son has taken money from the bank when he wasn't supposed to. He isn't playing by the rules. Even at eight, Long already cares deeply about what is fair and what isn't.

"Look, if you can't play nice, then this game is over," she says. "Put everything back. You can go on home now." She turns around and walks away, the sound of her heels echoing across the wooden floorboards. I want to cry. The kid sticks his tongue out at us. Long throws a hotel at him. We are kicked out.

Later that night, my mother notices Long adjusting his pillow, rearranging something inside the pillowcase.

"What is that?" she asks him. When he refuses to answer, she picks up his pillow and points the opening toward the floor. Five toy cars fall out.

It doesn't take long for my mother to register what Long has done. My brother begins to cry even before she scolds him. "Can't I keep them? He has a million of them. He doesn't even take good care of them. And he cheated today."

With one swift motion, my mother smacks him across the face. "I don't care what he did. We didn't teach you to steal. You will go over there first thing tomorrow and return these to him."

I am indignant on Long's behalf—he's right; that kid is spoiled—and also in awe of his sneakiness. When had he stolen those cars? I wonder.

My mother turns on all the lights of the altar. My father has added more pictures for us to worship, this time of gods and saints. There is one of three heavily armored men, wielding large swords and scepters, with fierce expressions. One of them has a face painted red. They frighten me.

"That's Ông Quan Công, Ông Châu Xương, and Ông Quan Bình," my father later tells me. They are the legendary generals of the Three Kingdoms era of China who later became deified for their loyalty and acts of heroism. "These generals will help us fight our demons," he says.

The altar has expanded so much that it now runs continuously from one end of the wall to the other. Whenever we do something wrong, my mother makes us stand in front of it and chant a meditation prayer 108 times.

"State your name and your age," she says to both of us now. "Ask the Buddha to grant you kindness and virtue. While you chant, think about what you did wrong."

Long and I do as we are told. When we are done, my mother makes us cross our arms over our chests and bow.

"Say, 'From this day forward, I will never steal again,'" she commands us.

"From this day forward, I will never steal again," we say in unison.

I hadn't stolen anything, but I guess my mother thought I needed to learn that lesson too.

In the Swim

DESPITE ALL THE DELIGHTS the beach had to offer, my father did not trust the ocean. He felt the waves were too dangerous for a child to learn to swim, the forces of nature too unpredictable, and so after a few trips to Coney Island, my father decided it was much too risky and we stopped going.

His fear was not without basis. Our family had almost drowned once in the Mekong River, he told us. Back then, he and my mother were merchants in the clothing trade. He ran a shop from our home selling fabric and women's and children's clothing, while she traveled from city to city on her Honda motorcycle, sometimes for weeks at a time, supplying vendors with the newest styles at wholesale prices. She was very popular, always giving discounts to clients she knew were struggling and never taking more than what an item was worth even if she could. Her sense of fairness, which I think Long inherited, earned her everyone's love and admiration.

One day they took me and my brothers to deliver a shipment of fabrics in the Sa Đéc region across the river. We made our return trip in the late afternoon by canoe. The sun had already set when the canoe suddenly began to spin and sink. When my parents realized what was happening, it was too late. We had gotten sucked into the vortex of a whirlpool and there seemed to be no way out. My brothers weren't strong enough swimmers yet, and I was only a few months old. So my parents clutched their four children, calling out Quan Âm Bồ Tát's name to deliver us from danger.

Somehow, nearby villagers heard their cries, and beams of light from flashlights waved back and forth in the distance.

"Over here!" my parents shouted. "Over here!" They heard voices shouting and getting nearer, and finally a voice telling them to grab hold of the ropes being thrown to us. My parents tied the ropes around our waists and the villagers pulled us all to safety.

But my parents did not emerge unscathed. The incident shocked my father, made him fearful of large bodies of water. So when he discovered that here in America, children could learn to swim in free public pools, he was relieved. It meant that he could keep us safe. He asked around at the Buddhist temple my parents attended and someone told him about Astoria Pool in Queens.

And so, in 1996, two years after our first outing to Coney Island, my father once again took out his map and charted a course to a new destination. It wasn't the ocean, but it seemed massive to us. Built in 1936 for the aquatic recreation campaign launched by legendary Park Commissioner Robert Moses, it is the largest public pool in New York City, 330 feet long, and one of the largest pools in the nation. We didn't know that, of course, but when we got there we were amazed to see a long, glimmering rectangle of blue water the size of a city block. It was divided into sections by lane markers and had a shallow wading pool for children at one end. I felt safer here than at the beach. There were no jagged rocks beneath my feet, no Styrofoam cups or plastic bags bobbing around me in the waves. There were only the clean geometric surfaces of a man-made body of water. Though I had loved the beach the few times I'd gotten to go, I viewed the pool's tidiness then as a sign of luxury, a distinct improvement over the ocean.

Every Saturday morning that summer I looked forward to going to the pool, to being in the water. It was a reward that awaited us at the end of a long week. One day in late August, as we were getting ready to go home after a day at the pool, I gathered my towel and belongings and headed back to the locker room. I walked along the edge of the concrete pool, placing one foot in front of the other as I balanced myself on an imaginary line. It had been a good day. My father had given me swimming lessons, and I was proud of all that I'd learned. I could float on my back and on my stomach and hold my breath underwater for more than thirty seconds. I could dog-paddle and swim the width of the pool, from one side all the way to the other. *"Gần tới rồi! Gần tới rồi!"* I'd hear my father yell. "You're almost there! Almost to the other side!" He was so proud of my progress.

I felt the soft burn of the sun on my shoulders, beads of water sliding down my back from my dripping hair, and the joy that comes from the feeling of learning a new skill. I was filled with fresh, budding confidence until, suddenly, my legs gave way. A charley horse had formed in the small of one of my calves, causing me to stumble. Next thing I knew, I was in the blue water at the deep end of the pool, frantically trying to stand but unable to find the ground beneath my feet.

After I'd gulped down several mouthfuls of water and thrashed around in a wild panic, my mother fished me out of the water and set me down on a nearby lounge chair.

"What were you doing playing around like that?" she asked me irritably as she dried me off with the towel. "We have to go. The sun's already setting."

"Stupid!" My brothers laughed at me. "You got snot all over you!"

I was mortified, but laughed along with them to cover up my embarrassment. As we left I turned around and took one last look at the rippling blue rectangle. It was the last time we ever went to the pool.

As the months rolled by, my father found a part-time job in a nearby sewing factory, our sweatshop shipments grew larger, our schoolwork increased, and suddenly, it was summer again. But the era of water had come to an end. We no longer had the time. And I never completely learned how to swim.

How the Other Half Lived

WE HAD A GUEST in our apartment. With round cheeks and silky skin that smelled of his mother's milk, little baby Cuong arrived like a prince in a light blue stroller filled with toys. "What a gem!" my mother exclaimed when she saw him.

"You say that now, but he's got quite a temper. If you give him back after a few days, I won't blame you," the father replied in Vietnamese.

"Oh, don't listen to him. He doesn't know what he's talking about. Baby Cuong is no trouble at all," the mother said, playfully slapping her husband on the arm.

My parents, needing our birth certificates translated into English, had originally met this couple at the translation agency they owned on Baxter Street in Chinatown. A few years later, we bumped into them again while shopping for groceries in Tan Tin Hung, a Vietnamese supermarket we had discovered on Bowery. The couple had a one-year-old baby boy and needed a full-time nanny to take care of him on weekdays while they went to work. My mother offered. They accepted.

They sat in our living room one Sunday morning, the father wearing a light blue shirt, the mother a light blue ruffled tea dress. Baby Cuong was asleep in his light blue stroller, a round rubber ring in his mouth. I was struck by the monochromatic scene, all that light blue casting a brightness on our otherwise dull apartment. Everything seemed to glow in this family's presence.

They looked around at our apartment and remarked, curiously, on its lack of furniture. My parents had moved all our work materials to the bedroom and closed the door. Only a few straw mats lined the floor.

"We like the spaciousness," my mother said.

The couple was kind. The man had handed me a bag of M&M's upon arrival, which my brothers and I promptly devoured. He had a square face with black hair neatly gelled to one side. The lady wore a pearl necklace with pearl earrings, and had hair that flowed to her waist, blown out and beautiful. She winked at me whenever she looked my way. "I've always wanted a daughter," she told my mother.

"We can trade," my mother said, reaching out to tickle me. I dodged and stuck out my tongue.

The man assembled a crib for the baby. He wrapped the plush little mattress in sheets with a candy design and put a blanket with a solar system theme on top. Then he dropped in a stuffed bunny and a teddy bear. So it was settled. My mother was to watch the baby from nine to five every weekday for three dollars an hour, all food and diapers provided.

With bills piling up, this was a welcome addition to our income. For me, it would be an exciting change in our routine. I was endlessly curious about this new arrival in our home. He was cute. He clapped with both his hands and his feet whenever he was happy. He cooed and demanded hugs from all of us whenever he wanted attention, and we gave it to him. My brothers and I crisscrossed our arms and held hands, creating a little throne for him as we carried him around the apartment. I caressed the little soft tufts of hair on his head, gave him my finger so he could grasp on to it, and kissed and nibbled his supple cheeks. The first thing I did when I came home from school was go to his crib and make sure he was still there.

But a few weeks after my mother started babysitting, my fondness was replaced with a different feeling. I began to feel jealous. I had been the baby of the house. Now that Cuong had arrived, I no longer received as much of my mother's affection or my brothers' attention. It seemed as though their love for me had been transferred to Baby Cuong, who hadn't done a single thing to deserve it. He had his own parents to love him and take care of him. What was he doing in my house and stealing my family? With the primitive spite of a six-year-old, I plotted to eat the mushy food in pretty little jars set aside just for him, hoping that I too could achieve a level of plumpness that matched that of the baby on the label. No sooner had I eaten the contents of two of the little glass jars than my mother caught me.

"What is wrong with you?" she demanded. "You know these are not for you. Now I have to go out and buy more."

I decided to be subtler in my tactics. I hid his toys from him. I no longer smiled at him or kissed him or hugged him as I once had. One day, my mother caught me as I yanked a rubber dinosaur out of his hands and sent him into a fit of tears. She picked him up in her arms and patted and rubbed his back to soothe him, glaring at me as she walked away, her abandonment stinging more than any smack. I knew I had gone too far. It was, after all, not the baby's fault that he had sailed into a life where his every need and comfort were met.

Still, when I looked at him through the light blue bars of his crib, asleep in that soft heaven, I wanted badly to pinch him.

Cuong's mother took him back from us some months later. She couldn't bear being without her baby for such long stretches, and decided to be a stay-at-home mom. The couple thanked us for our help and gave us treats, and the three of them disappeared into the light blue world from which they came. And my own world felt much emptier without him. As jealous as I'd been, I was still sorry to see him go.

Though Cuong's time with us was short, it had its revelations. We looked at ourselves, emaciated, marked with cuts from the blades we used, tired, and we realized that we were different from other children. Cuong had a nice soft mattress to sleep on. We had only the floor. He had toys. We didn't. He was plump. We weren't.

"Remember that baby we used to take care of?" we'd say to each other years later.

"Yeah, Baby Cuong. Man, he had it good."

A Bedtime Story

MOST NIGHTS MY FATHER makes us get ready for bed promptly at nine, no matter how much work we have left to do. To him, sleep is important above all else. But one night my father is in a rare reminiscing mood. He lights incense and turns on the altar lamps, whispering prayers of gratitude to the Buddhas.

"You know, if it weren't for that turtle, we wouldn't be here today," he says to us. I can see that he is somewhere far away.

"I saved that turtle from getting eaten by a neighboring prisoner."

I've heard this story before but never understood it. But now I'm seven, and I want to know more.

"What's a prisoner?" I ask.

"A person who lives in a prison," my mother says.

I nod. "What's a prison?"

"A bad place," my mother says, taking me into her lap.

"It's where I went after the war," my father says.

What is war? I want to ask, but have learned by this age not to ask too many questions.

"We prisoners weren't fed very often," my father tells us. "So we

49

had to come up with creative ways to stay alive. I grew plants from the seeds my sisters would sneak in for me whenever they were permitted to visit." Other prisoners, like his neighbor, whose family members had all been killed in the war, would set out traps for animals and leave their carcasses out in the sweltering Vietnam sun to roast, risking death by food poisoning rather than death by famine.

"One day, a small turtle got its leg caught in a trap my neighbor had set out. 'Just my luck,' the man said as he removed the turtle from the trap. 'What the hell can I do with this?' Then he tossed it aside.

"When I saw this, I felt sorry for the little turtle. He was struggling to stand, and for some reason, I didn't want him to die." My father was a deeply pious young man and Buddhism had taught him, if not a love for living creatures, the idea that liberating them from unnecessary death would guarantee his own painless death in the arms of the great bodhisattva Quan Âm Bồ Tát.

"'Hey, you!' I called out to my neighbor. I had a few scallion bulbs that had just grown in, so I figured I could trade with him.

"'Trade what?' the guy asked me. 'This stupid thing for your scallions? Do you know how to cook it?'

"'No, I don't know how to cook a goddamn turtle,' I said. 'You crazy? I just want it.'

"'Yeah, all right. Fine. But what the hell are you gonna do with it?' he asked me.

"I didn't really know. I just felt like it deserved a better fate. Hunger won out and the man agreed to give it to me. He picked up the turtle by its foot and flung it over as far as he could into my cell. The turtle landed on its shell a few inches away. I flipped it upright, gathered some leaves to soak up the blood oozing out of its leg, and tied clean ones around the wound like a bandage.

"And I swear, when I released that turtle, it turned around to look at me. I mean, it *faced* me and nodded three times."

Here, my father stops. My brothers and I watch him. We see his large eyes looking out toward something we cannot see.

"And then what happened?" I ask him, rousing him from his reverie.

"Well, I didn't know it then, but that turtle was trying to tell me something. It had *phép lạ*. Strange magic." At this point in the story, my father gets animated. He stands up, his eyes glistening, his face red, his gesticulations becoming wilder, taking up more space.

"Later that night, one of the prisoners got hold of the keys somehow. Desperation had taken over. We had seen other prisoners slowly die over the years from famine or disease, a fate we wanted to escape. He managed to unlock three cells, his own, mine, and one other. And just like that, we were free. We walked out of our cells, not really knowing which direction to go. I was so scared. We all were. It was death either way, and we knew it. But we figured we'd rather die trying to escape than give up.

"We ran the whole night long," my father continues. "We ran until our lungs nearly gave out. But it didn't matter, because in those moments, we tasted freedom for the first time in years. After years in shackles, nothing felt better than being able to move, to walk, to not sleep in our own piss. But the feeling didn't last long. We couldn't see where we were going in the dark, and we had no plan. We were also too weak to make it very far. They hadn't fed us in weeks. We were thin as toothpicks."

"Like a real toothpick?" I ask, trying to imagine my father as thin as a toothpick. I laugh, because I think my father is making a joke.

"Don't interrupt, stupid," Long scolds me.

My father ignores us both and continues. "They found us not long after, hiding behind some bushes. We didn't even hear them coming. We pissed ourselves. A bunch of grown men unable to control their bladders because we were so fucking scared. They tied us up and dragged us back by the hair. I thought my scalp was going to rip off my head." He grabs a fistful of his hair to demonstrate, yanking his head backward. "The next morning, they transferred us to a new encampment. They took all the prisoners out to watch. The Vietcong soldiers lined us up and tied us to stakes in the middle of a field. Then they took out their rifles and shot my friend straight between the eyes. He slumped down." My father's body goes limp in the telling and he makes as though he is about to fall, knees buckling, to plant this image in our imaginations. It works. The image is seared into my mind. I want to hold on to his hand, to tell him that he is okay now.

"I couldn't see my friend, because of where I was positioned, but when I heard the shot and the thud, I knew what had happened and I went cold. I got so cold I thought my soul had already left my body. But I prayed to Quan Âm Bồ Tát. I called out her name. Boom. Another shot and my other friend was now dead. I closed my eyes." He takes a moment to catch his breath here. He is flushed with emotion. And although this is not the first time I've heard this story, it is the first time I have a rudimentary understanding of life and death, of the stakes involved, of his absolute fear and despair.

"Just as the soldier was walking up to me, I heard a voice. It was the warden's voice. 'Hey, what the fuck are you idiots doing? Did I give you permission to do this? Who the fuck do you think you are?' The soldier saluted him and he smacked the soldier across the head. 'I'll shoot you myself next time you go shooting anyone on my premises, motherfucker. Get this asshole down,' he said, referring to me. 'Look, he even shat himself, the poor idiot. Clean this fucking mess up! That's an order! Get this idiot back into his cell.'"

Three days later, the warden released him from prison, he tells us.

"Why?" we ask him.

"It was the turtle. That turtle saved me. That turtle was Quan Âm Bồ Tát. . . . She heard my prayers." As he says this, his voice quivers and he turns around to our altar. He brings his hands together and whispers the goddess's name three times.

I look up at Quan Âm Bồ Tát, glowing bright as she glides across the black sea on her dragon. I think again of her thousand arms, one of which must have reached out to save my father that day as he called her name from the wooden post he was tied to. I whisper the goddess's name three times.

Nam mô Quan Thế Âm Bồ Tát.
Nam mô Quan Thế Âm Bồ Tát.
Nam mô Quan Thế Âm Bồ Tát.

The Hunters and the Animals

SUMMERS ON BLEECKER STREET were never-ending block parties, open fire hydrants that sprayed automobiles as they drove by, and an asphyxiating heat that intensified the smell of asphalt and turned the waistbands of our underwear yellow from sweat. Car radios blasted through the Ridgewood streets with the bass turned up, setting off car alarms, and we could feel the rumbling of the bass in our chests. Everything and everyone was in motion. The fenced-in schoolyard across the street hosted daily barbecues and handball games, which people poured out of their homes to attend.

Despite the paranoid warnings of the few Vietnamese friends they had found, my parents released my brothers and me to the raucous frenzy outside, where we immediately came across a group of prepubescent delinquents. Or rather, my brothers did, since I was too young to play with the big kids. I mainly watched them from the front stoop of our building, hoping that one day—I had no idea when that would be—I'd be able to join my brothers.

"Chinos! Gooks! Flat-face! Chinky-eyes! Black-tooth!" they called us.

In a way, I preferred these epithets to what they called us after learning our actual names. "Chinos" and all the others were blanket insult terms for Asians. I understood that. But when they called me Ug-Ly or my brother Tin-man, it was personal. The kids who gave us these names probably had little clue of their devastating power, thinking only perhaps of how clever they were and enjoying their solidarity against us. We didn't have the vocabulary to retaliate.

But acceptance, not revenge, was the goal. Though my parents knew nothing of the perils of this outside world, my brothers had an intuitive sense of what they needed to do to survive the streets of Ridgewood and Bushwick. In exchange for being allowed to participate, they had to offer something these kids did not possess. It came in the form of a basketball hoop.

On the cyclone fencing surrounding the yard across the street, someone had affixed a square of cardboard with a black X Sharpied in the middle. You'd get points in a game for getting the ball to land on the X. But that was as close as the kids in the neighborhood got to an actual hoop. Occasionally, the neighborhood kids would reluctantly allow one of my brothers to join if there was an odd number of players. My brothers were always thrilled to be included, despite being chosen last.

Thinh especially loved playing basketball, and he was good at it. When there was no one around, he would spend his time practicing on the sidewalk in front of the fence, using a basketball someone once left behind and never claimed. He would wake up in the early morn and put on faux Adidas shorts (with two white stripes instead of three), and I could hear his dribbling from outside our third-floor window, the slightly metallic sound of the ball hitting the concrete. He was short, which was not ideal for basketball, but that didn't stop him. He practiced fancy dribble moves: between the legs, behind the back, around an imaginary opponent. Or he would attempt to spin the ball on the tip of his index finger. Long and Phu often joined him.

Seeing how much my brothers longed to fit in, my father carved out the bottom of a plastic milk crate he'd found on his way home from one of his evening classes. A few nights later he bought galvanized fence wire from a hardware store and attached the crate to the schoolyard fence high enough so that it could serve as a basketball hoop. Thinh was elated when he saw it the next morning. "That my hoop!" he'd say if someone tried to use it. He demanded respect.

Soon, the kids on the block were asking Thinh if they could use his hoop, if they could get a game in, and hey, man, what's your name, slapping him a high five and offering friendship in exchange for a chance at the hoop.

I seemed always to be watching my brothers, observing their actions from afar and envisioning myself joining in one day. But in the meantime, I stayed away from the boys and their games, playing mostly by myself in our front yard, or else keeping company with my mother, who at every opportunity took it upon herself to train me in the art of housewifery. As my brothers roamed the streets and played basketball, I learned to fold clothes, sweep and mop the floors, wash dishes, and cut vegetables. "How come I have to do this and my brothers don't?" I'd often ask, annoyed that they were treated differently, that they had privileges I didn't.

Her responses varied. The usual: "This is a woman's duty." Or: "Stop comparing yourself to your brothers. I'm doing this for your own good. One day you will thank me." Or: "Again you are asking this? Fine, go play. Don't learn, but you'll regret it when I die and you'll have no one to blame but yourself."

I chanted Buddhist scriptures with my mother every morning. Inhaling the thick fumes from the incense she lit and banging metronomically on a little gong set my father had purchased in Chinatown, we chanted stories of the great Shakyamuni Buddha and his journey to enlightenment, of his disciples and successors, of the cycle of suffering we must attempt to escape through the power of prayer and compassion, of the realm of ghosts and lost spirits, trapped in a hell where their own sinful acts are carried out against them, the undulating sounds of the gong rippling through the air as our synchronized voices carried us off to a trance-like state.

My mother would have me copy down passages from multiple books of scriptures, and I had to memorize the precise pronunciation and spelling of each word. I didn't appreciate it then, but it was during this chanting that I learned to read and write in Vietnamese. My brothers did not. They were off playing basketball and handball.

But learning Vietnamese from my mother didn't help me with my English. When I entered kindergarten after our first summer in New York, I knew almost none. At home, we spoke to each other only in Vietnamese. My brothers couldn't practice the English they learned in school because my parents didn't want them to lose their Vietnamese. So even in first grade, I was still having a hard time understanding the language and communicating with it.

I was also socially awkward. Most of the time I refused to speak at all to any of the boys and girls in my classes out of shyness, but when boredom occasionally got the better of me, I was prone to speaking too suddenly and to breaking into others' conversations. I also spoke too loudly, because I hadn't yet learned to control the volume of my voice. The rules and rhythms of normal conversation eluded me. I felt different from the other kids. I felt like I was missing something. It seemed they felt it too.

To make matters worse, my precocious brothers left a legacy of excellence that my teachers expected me to live up to as soon as they recognized my last name on the roster. "Oh, you must be Phu's sister" or "Oh, you're Long's little sister." Not only could I not escape being someone's little sister, but everywhere I went I was observed through the lens of my brothers' achievements.

It was Thinh who set the highest bar for academic achievement. I still remember the year he entered the Ezra Jack Keats Bookmaking Competition. He was in the fifth grade, and his school had participated in an annual citywide competition open to students from third to twelfth grade. The goal was for students to create a handmade children's book. There were no limitations on theme. Thinh labored on different ideas for days, eventually deciding that he would make an origami pop-up book about animal cruelty. He titled it *The Hunters and the Animals*. On each page, a scene would unfold in which a paper man would shoot a paper duck or a paper water buffalo. There were tabs that you could pull on to make the hunter move his gun or make the animal flee in fear. "That's what it's about," he explained, "a bunch of hunters slaughtering animals." So in the end, it wasn't the animals that were animals.

I loved seeing him fold and cut the beautifully patterned origami paper that the librarian had given him for the project. I watched him from afar as he folded the papers into a wing here, a beak there, horsemen with spears. He handled every piece of origami daintily between his thumbs and index fingers, moving in slow, careful, deliberate steps. "You guys better not touch this," he'd warn us.

Thinh won the competition that year. The award was a brass plaque with Thinh's name and the title of his book inscribed on it. I wanted to be like Thinh, to possess his dedication, his drive, his vision. He was a source of inspiration—and envy, I imagine—for all of us.

In school, Phu was the first to be compared to him, and probably the one who resented it the most. Did he have the creativity and ingenuity of his older brother? "We so adored your brother," the teachers said, their eyes full of admiration. The stage was set early then for Phu to compete with Thinh, to be compared with him, and to always follow behind in the wake of his achievements. It was no different at home. Thinh had long earlobes that my parents associated with wisdom and a wide forehead that meant he was destined for greatness. He was the eldest son. My mother would often place four fingers sideways on his forehead and beam. "Look! Four fingers. This forehead is good luck. This forehead is intelligence and a prosperous life."

I took my mother's fingers and held them up to my own forehead. But only three could fit.

Roses Are Red

EVENTUALLY MY TONGUE WARMED up to the sounds of English, the *th*'s, the *st*'s, and the *x*'s. By the second grade, I was fluent. This allowed me to blend in with my classmates more easily, to become less of an outcast. It was Nicholas, a small, mousy boy in my class, who now had the misfortune of carrying that title.

At the beginning of the year, the kids would just stare at Nicholas, as if they were trying to figure out where he belonged. He wore the same outfit to school every day, a poorly fitting light blue, long-sleeved shirt with navy-blue slacks. It was a uniform, even though our school did not enforce uniforms except during assembly days, but he didn't seem to own any other clothes. He bit at his nails and cuticles until they bled. And he always seemed to smell like he'd peed himself.

It wasn't long before the boys started mocking him and the girls began to snicker whenever they passed him. They made him do pranks just to get him into trouble, ordering him to throw paper balls at the teacher or write curse words in the bathroom stalls. Being accepted was so important to him that he could be persuaded to do just about anything. I didn't understand it then. It just seemed to me that he had no self-respect.

"Don't do what they tell you to do," I told him one day, fed up after seeing him bullied to the point of tears yet again. I was aware that my own social standing was precarious and I had empathy for his situation. So I began to defend him.

At first he was taken aback by my support, even suspicious. Then, little by little, he would look for me in the schoolyard where we lined up every morning. He would look for me during lunchtime and would sit with me. And he would look for me at the end of the day as we said our goodbyes. Not wanting my classmates to associate me with him, I began to feel uncomfortable, but I didn't know what to say.

"Remember to be kind." My mother sent me off to school every day with some version of that mantra. "You never know what people go through. You don't know their story. So choose kindness."

I thought about what my mother told me and, despite my misgivings about what it would do to my reputation to keep associating with Nicholas, I continued to spend time with him. Then, on Valentine's Day, as class was dismissed, Nicholas shoved something into my hand and quickly walked away.

It was a little booklet of four small pieces of paper stapled together. "To: Ly, From: Nicholas," it said on the first page. On the second page, there was a picture of a little girl with a ponytail holding on to a balloon. The third had the words "Love, Nicholas." And the last page had a drawing of a rose, a red rose with a green stem and green leaves.

I thought it was beautiful.

I rushed home to show my mother. "Ly. Don't think about boys," is what she told me as she examined the pleats on a freshly ironed red satin cummerbund. It was a phrase she often repeated throughout my childhood, afraid that I would end up head over heels in love with some boy and forget my duties and responsibilities. "When boys and girls come together, bad things happen. It makes you stupid. You need to focus on your schoolwork. Stay away from the girls that always hang around boys. And stay away from boys. And that goes for you too," she said to my brothers. "Forget about girls. Now, start working on those piles over there. We have to finish all of this in a few days. And we're already behind."

I put the stapled booklet back into my book bag, then settled down with my brothers to work on the mound of neckties and cummerbunds that needed to be flipped and sorted. I didn't think any further about Nicholas.

But at lunchtime in school the next day, as our tables were called to line up for our meals, Nicholas sidled up next to me, and a group of our fellow classmates broke into song: "Ly and Nicholas sitting in a tree, K-I-S-S-I-N-G . . ."

I was horrified. I didn't know what being someone's girlfriend or boyfriend meant, but I knew from my mother that it was a bad thing.

"He's not my boyfriend!" I shouted.

But it was too late.

"Ew," they said. "You smell like him," they said.

I narrowed my eyes and looked at Nicholas with disdain. "You are *not* my boyfriend," I said sternly, leaving my place in line to stand at the back where I could get away from him.

The episode ended almost as quickly as it began. The other kids soon moved on, and we settled back into the daily routine of school. I tried to vary my seating choices to avoid accusations of being too friendly with Nicholas, but there were times when I could sense his loneliness and, inevitably, I would wander over to sit next to him.

One afternoon during group work, someone yelled out, "Nicholas said a bad word, Ms. Hout!" I was sitting next to Nicholas at the time and was sure he hadn't done any such thing. But soon the other students around us were also chiming in.

"Ooh, Nicholas just said the F-word. I heard it," one kid said.

"Yeah, I heard it too!" said another.

Ms. Hout came over to assess the situation.

"What's going on over here? What's all this noise? Nicholas, do I have to put you in detention again?"

"No," Nicholas said, at once bewildered and resigned, shrinking into himself. "I didn't do anything. I swear." He looked at me. "Ly, tell them I didn't say anything."

Everyone turned to me. I didn't know what to do. I was sure my response would determine where I stood among my classmates. It would either redeem me and save me from joining Nicholas's rank, or it would forever mark me as Nicholas's "girlfriend." And suddenly, a surge of anger went through me. I was furious that I was being teased for simply trying to be someone's friend. And I was furious that Nicholas had somehow dragged me into this.

"Well, Ly?" Ms. Hout prompted.

"Come on, Ly. You *know* he did it," the others goaded me. "You *heard* him say it."

I looked at Nicholas and I looked at the teacher and I looked at my classmates' expectant faces, which seemed to me to hold out the possibility of friendship. *Choose kindness*, I heard an inner voice say, but I ignored it.

"Just tell the truth, Ly," Ms. Hout said. It seemed even she wanted him to be the culprit, because she'd had such a tough time with him. She knew that the other kids picked on him sometimes, but he also made her job difficult with all his pranks, and he wasn't a very good student, so by then he had racked up a number of bad behavior marks in her grade book. What would one more bad mark matter? I asked myself. It wouldn't change anything for him. That's what I wanted to believe, anyway.

I looked down at my notebook, careful not to make eye contact with anyone. "Y-yeah," I said quietly. "It was Nicholas. I heard him say it."

"Nicholas, Nicholas." Ms. Hout sighed. "Another phone call to your mother, I guess."

And he burst into tears.

That incident haunted me. I knew I had done wrong the moment I lied, but there was no way to take back what I had done. Years later, after not seeing him for a while because we were attending different middle schools, I ran into Nicholas as he was walking home with a group of boys. I was happy to see that he was with people, and I hoped they were his friends. I thought of saying hello and asking him what middle school he was in now.

But before I could say anything, one of the boys noticed me and said, "What are you staring at, you ugly chink?"

They jeered and gave each other fist bumps as though the boy had done something worthy of praise. I was shocked and humiliated and frightened, hoping that Nicholas might acknowledge and defend me, his old friend.

But he did no such thing. He merely glanced up at me, a faint look of recognition in his eyes, then put his head down and walked on. I watched his hoodied back for a long time as he moved farther and farther away down the block. I was disappointed and hurt, but I understood why.

I knew, deep down, that I deserved it.

Mantras and Monsters

SEVEN O'CLOCK ON A Saturday morning. Sunlight shines relentlessly through the curtainless windows. Annoyed, I turn my back to the light and close my eyes, but pots and pans bang against each other, the faucet runs, and I can't shut out the sound of my father's voice yanking my brothers from sleep, my mother rushing them into the bathroom. The television is on too, with its familiar noises of static and the loud crackle of music.

My father allows me to sleep a little longer because I'm the youngest, but now that I'm awake, I figure, why sleep when there is such a savory aroma in the air, a mix of garlic, lemongrass, star anise, paprika, and chili oil? This morning my mother is cooking *bò kho*, rice vermicelli in a beef-and-carrot stew, fish sauce and sriracha drizzled on top, one of my favorites. I roll off the straw mat and follow my nose to my mother's cooking.

We were never asked what we wanted for breakfast. Years later, my boyfriend would ask his son what he wanted for breakfast, and I would think it strange. My mother never asked and we never requested. We ate what there was to eat, and we weren't picky. We couldn't afford to be picky. Today, it is a treat: we all love *bò kho*.

"You're up, baby girl? Go wash your face and brush your teeth after Long gets out of the bathroom, and I'll make you a bowl," my mother says.

I sit down on a chair and wait my turn in the bathroom. My father is counting cummerbunds, ready to send out our most recent batch and receive a new shipment of fabrics. Flight attendant scarves are next in the queue. On the television, an electric guitar solo whines as two members of opposing gangs are tied wrist to wrist in a knifing duel. Michael Jackson appears in a red leather jacket singing the chorus to "Beat It." My father pauses his counting to watch.

He was a big fan of Michael Jackson, my father. He loved the way Michael would grab his privates during performances. I think, to him, the action represented a kind of raw freedom that he could emulate vicariously by listening to Michael's music. It was an act of sovereignty, the opposite of my father's days sitting upright, chained at the ankles to a slab of stone and at the wrists to a wall. Michael's movements, his moonwalk, his proclamation of manhood as he swept across the stage, were emblematic of a liberation my father could only dream of in his caged sleep.

Sometimes, we'd catch one of Michael's videos on MTV2, a channel dedicated to commercial-free music videos, which we'd mistakenly received for free through some defect in the cable wiring. Whenever he heard Michael's voice my father would put aside whatever he was doing and come in to watch, and when the moment came, he'd exclaim, "Look, look at him grabbing it!" Then chuckle loudly to himself. "What a guy."

It was rare to see my father happy or smiling or laughing. And because my brothers and I also loved Michael, it was something special that we could share with him, like a joke we were all in on. Of course, this was years before we knew anything about Michael's life, what he endured as a child, and what that trauma led to. We knew him only as the King of Pop, the famous man on the television who was black in one music video and white in the next. I thought it was amazing that, not only did he want to change his skin color, but he had done so. It was a feeling we could all relate to—wanting to be something other than what we were—and we understood the anguish and humiliation that accompanied that desire. "What a crazy guy," my father would say, in a tone not of condescension but of admiration.

Music was the only form of entertainment that my father allowed himself to enjoy. "Nothing is real on television except for the news and the nature channels," he'd declare. "Movies, shows, it's all fake. All people dressing up and acting out fake lives. They trick you into thinking these lives are livable." As for art—it was either for those who had too much time on their hands, which we did not, or for those destined for a life of poverty, which we were desperately trying to escape. .

But music spoke to my father. It was one of the few things that could put him in a good mood. I imagined it might have been a source of pleasure to him during all those years of sitting in his prison cell. At least he would have had the memory of music. After all, a tune can linger in the mind: it's something no one can take away. Did my father sing to himself when he was locked up? Did he hum quietly to the tune of his favorite song when he was sweeping for mines? Did he bob his head along silently to a melody only he could hear?

Among the few possessions we brought over from Vietnam, besides our clothing and important legal documents, were two cassettes: one of Vietnamese singers belting out American tunes from the 1960s and 1970s in slightly accented voices, the other a Boney M. album. Boney M. was a popular German-based disco-era group of four black singers: Bobby Farrell, Maizie Williams, Marcia Barrett, and Liz Mitchell. Our first year in America, my father had found a beat-up black radio/cassette player while walking around the streets of Ridgewood. He popped in one of the tapes after tinkering with some of the broken buttons, and to our immense surprise, it worked!

We listened to the songs again and again—songs like "500 Miles" by Peter, Paul and Mary, "Silence Is Golden" by the Tremeloes, "All I Have to Do Is Dream" by the Everly Brothers, and "Runaway" by Del Shannon. They were the background music of our childhood and adolescence and they would shape our musical taste for years to come. When my second-grade teacher, Ms. Hout, asked us what songs and singers we liked, I raised my hand and declared, " 'Summer Wine' by Suzi Jane Hokom and Lee Hazlewood!" It had been a hit in 1967.

"What the heck?" my classmates asked. "What song is *that?*" The music they loved, by current artists like the Backstreet Boys and Christina Aguilera, was as foreign to me as my life would have been to them had they known anything about it.

Before "Beat It" ends, Long emerges from the bathroom with a dripping-wet face. He wipes it down with his shirt the way my father does. Now it is my turn to wash my face. I am seven years old so this should not be difficult. Yet somehow it is.

I stand before the bathroom sink, clutching its sides and staring at myself in the cabinet mirror, slow to move. There she is again. Yesterday, she was me. Or so I thought. Today, someone else.

I am beginning to develop a habit of experimenting with different "faces" in the mirror. A few months earlier, on a trip to the supermarket, I caught a glimpse of myself in the storefront window and was surprised by my own reflection. I didn't look at all like what I'd expected. I didn't recognize myself. That day, I started making faces to see if I could find one that squared with who I thought I was, unable to shake the uneasy feeling that I was not the girl I saw in the mirror.

But who, then, did I expect to see if not her?

I pull my face into a frown. She does it too. I tug at my cheeks. She follows suit. Of course, of course. She's a reflection: nothing more, nothing less. What I see is a round face with disproportionately large eyes, a small flat nose, and full lips protruding from an overbite. Even at this age, I know that I am my father's daughter. I have inherited his face.

But the more I look at my reflection, the more frightened I feel. There's something in her eyes I can't quite place, an expression I know is not my own but that I can't figure out. I don't want to look at her eyes. *Look down*, I command myself. *Wash your hands. Brush your teeth.*

That too has become difficult. I have begun to develop a strange aversion to the transition from dryness to wetness and vice versa. Something about the change in state of being causes me real distress, and I must force myself to do these simple actions. I particularly hate taking showers, make excuses not to, but must eventually obey. Once I jump in, wetness becomes the standard, and then it is difficult for me to stop. Eventually, this kind of anxiety will expand to encompass many areas in my life. It will get to a point where even the breeze from a fan will make me unbearably uncomfortable. But it all began with water.

"Kỳ Lý!" my mother cries out. "What are you doing in there? Quickly, your noodles are going to expand." She is referring to what happens when you leave noodles in liquid for too long and they soften and thicken. The delicate balance of noodle and broth is ruined and you are left with soggy noodles, a sin in Vietnamese cuisine. Short of finding a bug in your noodles, having them expand and become waterlogged is the most undesirable thing that could happen to them.

I don't want to be waterlogged either. But I will myself to turn on the water and dunk my hands and wrists underneath the stream. I proceed to brush my teeth as quickly as possible, counting seconds in my mind to distract myself from the discomfort.

At the dining table, my mother sets the bowl before me and squeezes a lime over my noodles. One of my brothers changes the station from MTV2 to channel 11. Saturday-morning cartoons are the only time that my brothers and I get to watch television uninterrupted by my father yelling at us or turning it off. This is also the only time we can watch television during a meal. At any other time, if something distracts us while we are eating, my father will say, "Turn that off right now. Focus on the meal."

"The meal" was important to my father. He ate as though at any moment some unknown perpetrator would pop up and steal his food right out from under him. I didn't know why, because I didn't know enough to connect the dots of his past to the dots of his present. I'd heard my father's turtle story so many times that I too now thought of turtles protectors. From the story, I also knew that he had been in prison, but that man and the father I knew seemed, in my mind, to be two separate entities.

As school got harder and our workload increased, my brothers and I tried to rebel against focusing on the meal. We wanted to do our homework while we were eating dinner. To us, it made sense: kill two birds with one stone. To our parents, it was a different matter. "You're going to swallow the words," they told us and forbade us from doing any homework or reading at the dinner table. I never questioned the validity of that statement. I didn't dare disobey. The idea of swallowing words, with all their sharp edges, terrified me. And if I swallowed them, I wouldn't have any left, I thought, and then what would happen? Would I not be able to speak? Or read? Or write?

Mantras followed us everywhere we went. Strange rules abounded. I couldn't part my hair in the middle. None of us could. "If you part your hair in the middle," my parents told me, "this family will fall apart. You will split us all down the middle." So I always parted my hair on the side.

"You can't take photographs with three people."

"Why not?" we wanted to know.

"Because the soul of the person in the middle would be lost forever in that photograph, wedged between the two people flanking him." The matter was settled. No three-person photographs.

Each morning as my brothers and I walked out the door on our way to school, my mother would leave us with two nuggets of wisdom:

"Going ninety is not yet halfway." This was meant to teach us never to rest before we had attained our goal, because anything short of completion didn't count. For my mother, there could be no reward for almost making it. "You are either at the finish line or you're not. There's no such thing as almost," she'd tell us. "There is no such thing as try."

To prevent us from getting spoiled and learning bad behaviors from other students in school, she'd remind us, *Gần mực thì đen, gần đèn thì sáng*. When you are near ink, you will be stained; when you are near the light, you will shine. So don't hang out with the bad kids in school. Seek out only the good kids, the well-behaved kids, the kids with good grades."

I thought often about this one because I liked the imagery of ink and light and loved the way the Vietnamese aphorism sounded on my tongue. It was poetry, as many of them were, and it was in listening to such lessons that I developed a newfound love for language—the beauty not just of the sounds but also of the images and meanings. *Gần mực thì đen, gần đèn thì sáng*. But something about this one didn't sit right with me.

One morning, as my mother reminded us yet again to stay near the light, I asked her, "But, Mom, what if *I'm* the light?" I was pleased that I had found a loophole, but my mother would not hear of it. "Don't talk back," she said simply.

Still, I was preoccupied with my revelation. I found comfort in the idea that I was not under the sway of either ink or light, that I could *be* the light. Being the light also meant that I could somehow eradicate the dark, which was a great source of fear for me at this time. At night, it was hard for me to go to sleep because I was terrified of the monsters and ghosts lurking in the shadows. I'd feel tingling sensations that I imagined to be cold hands touching the parts of my body exposed to air, pulling me into the darkness, ripping me apart and putting me back together as one of them. I would try to cover myself up as much as possible without suffocating, eventually leaving just a small opening in the blanket for me to breathe through. Then I'd begin to feel those same cold hands creeping beneath the blanket itself, pulling me out from under it. The blanket wasn't enough to save me. I thought and thought of how I could protect myself and concluded that only an invisible crystal shield would work if I wanted to survive the night, and so I began to build one. In my mind.

The task was long and arduous. On principle, I felt that real labor needed to be put in if it were to work properly, so I envisioned a shield that fit tightly around every inch of the contours of my body. Though I was racing against time, I knew that I couldn't rush the process, that patience and precision were key. I was obsessive, accounting for every part of my body, and when I was finally satisfied, safe inside my snug crystal dome, I would lower the blanket from around my head and breathe freely. It was a success. The dome was impenetrable.

But before I drifted off to sleep, I thought of my parents. I thought of their vulnerability, and of my thoughtlessness. So I began the process again, beginning with their toes and imagining the contours of their bodies as well as I could conjure them in my mind. Midway through, I would think of my brothers, who were also exposed. I couldn't construct these domes one at a time; it needed to be done simultaneously if I wanted to save them before time ran out.

Then, of course, I'd think of my extended family, my classmates, my kind teachers, all their loved ones, pets, plants, wildlife. What about them? I panicked. Okay, I thought. The only thing to do would be to construct one for all the beings on earth. I imagined what I thought would be the biggest number in the world. A trillion. I imagined putting everything that was alive on this earth into a trillion crystal domes, simultaneously. This was hard work, but I knew I could do it. And I did. I tinkered through the night, building all these domes until I was satisfied.

But even after my task was complete, after I felt I'd done a sufficient job, I could not sleep. I couldn't shake the thought that someone, something, somewhere out there was still alone and in need of protection. I thought of the monsters. Tried to make out their faces from within the safety of my dome. *You can't hurt us now*, I thought, proud of all the work I'd done. But terror soon gave way to sympathy. Even the most monstrous of faces that I could conjure always had the same pained look in their eyes. And I imagined that they feared the dark just as much as I did.

Okay, okay, I'd sigh to myself as the first waves of sleep finally began to wash over me. *You guys get one too.*

The Snellen Chart

THE THIRD GRADERS LINE up in the gymnasium on a November afternoon after lunchtime. Winter has arrived early and the gymnasium is drafty. I pull my arms into the body of my sweater so that the sleeves dangle empty, and I hug myself beneath the tattered cotton. Our teachers usher us over to bleachers set up on the far end of the gymnasium. Friends rush to sit next to each other, saving each other seats. I sit with the people I think of as my friends, but feel somehow apart from them, as though I don't belong. There is something I can't quite put into words, something that separates me from them.

"Sit with your section," a teacher orders. "When your name is called, walk up to the white line in front of your section and follow the nurse's directions."

While I wait, I run my fingers over the bright blue fabric covering the bleachers. It reminds me of blue tarp. It reminds me of Thailand. And for a moment, I am back there, back to the smell of eggs drenched in soy sauce.

"Tran!" a teacher standing in the center of the gymnasium yells out.

She has a roster in front of her. "Tran." She hesitates. "Ly." She pronounces it "Lie," instead of "Lee." "Lie Tran, please step down."

I step off the bleachers and walk up to the white line. I am accustomed to people calling me Lie. I don't correct them because I'm afraid to tell them they are wrong. I am more concerned with their comfort than my own.

In front of me, there is a large white poster with a hefty *E* at the top center of it and a column of random letters beneath it in varying sizes. The nurse hands me a small wooden paddle.

"Put this over your right eye," she instructs me. She walks up to the poster and points to the big *E* in the middle of the poster.

"What letter is this?"

"*E.*"

"Good, read this row." She points to the row beneath it, then another row beneath that, and I read all the letters correctly. Then she skips down a couple of rows.

I squint. Was that an *F* or an *E*? Was that a *D* or an *O*? The edges blur and bleed into each other.

"*F? O? Z, T, H? R?*"

This time, there is no affirmative response from her. She hesitates, then points to another row. All I make out is a line of blurred dots against the white background. I'm suddenly aware of my heartbeat. The hand holding the wooden paddle begins to shake. I can't find my voice.

"Come on, sweetheart," she coaxes. "What do you see?"

If you don't know the answer to something on a test, take a guess, never leave it blank, my parents have told me. "*T, U, V, W, X, Y, Z,*" I burst out. She jots down a note on her pad.

We repeat the steps, this time with the wooden paddle over my left eye. The results are pretty much the same and the nurse scribbles furiously on her notepad. I look over, frustrated and nervous. I failed a test, I think. I'm in trouble.

She tears off the first page on her pad and walks over to me.

"You have to give this to your parents. They need to take you to an eye doctor. You need glasses, honey."

"Ba, I have a note for you from school," I announce to my father as he sits at our green-and-gray Mitsubishi sewing machine, sewing the last remaining cummerbunds for the weekly quota. He is at peace, the sound of needle puncturing fabric the only break in the silence of the room. A shaft of cold winter light streams through the gated window, illuminating him.

He is godlike to me, this man with all the answers, this man responsible for my safety and well-being. This man, my father.

"What is it?" he says, not looking up at me. I've been agonizing over whether I should give the note to him, not because of any specific danger I anticipate, but because I can never be certain how my father will react.

Once, when I was about seven and we were on our way home from a trip to the supermarket, my father stepped into a nearby bodega and bought me a Popsicle. My brothers were at the park that day, my mother at home ironing, and I was out with my father, who had just given me a Popsicle, which made me feel special. I held on to the Popsicle stick with one hand and my father's hand with the other, skipping happily. I looked up at him. Was he enjoying this outing as much as I was? I wondered. He looked down at me, his eyes meeting mine, and, for a moment, seemed to consider me, consider my gaze. Then he smacked me across the back of my head.

"Don't look at me like that," he said.

I was so confused I don't even think I cried or registered that my Popsicle had been knocked out of my hand. I simply walked on in silence, averting my eyes from him. Perhaps it was around then that the girl in the mirror started to become someone I no longer recognized.

It was as though she were the one responsible for doing something bad without my knowledge, something I didn't understand, but I was the one getting in trouble for it. But what I did gather, from that and other equally out-of-the-blue eruptions from my father, was that it was always best to proceed with caution—or not proceed at all—where he was concerned.

Still, I did not want to get into further trouble at school. I take a deep breath and translate: "Please take your daughter to the eye doctor to have her eyes checked. She is nearsighted with the possibility of astigmatism"—I don't translate this word because I don't know how but instead say it slowly in a Vietnamese accent, drawing out each syllable—"and may need corrective lenses."

The rhythmic sounds of the sewing machine stop. My father looks up, wide-eyed. For a moment, nothing happens. My words are suspended in the air. Then I recognize the expression on his face and I brace myself, already flinching.

He snatches the piece of paper out of my hand. His face has turned a deep shade of red. The veins in his forehead bulge.

"Don't be stupid," he says.

"What? Wh-what do you mean?" I stammer. I don't understand his anger, but I have the instincts to take a step back.

"Don't be stupid," he repeats, this time shouting. "This is a bunch of crap. Your vision is fine. Do you think it's cool to wear glasses? What is it, you want to be blind for the rest of your life?"

"I don't know what you're talking about!" I start to cry, sensing that I will be punished. For what, I do not know, but I feel I must have done something to deserve it. The shaft of light no longer seems like a heavenly manifestation of my father's godliness, but takes on the color and confusion of his rage.

"Just because all these American kids are wearing glasses doesn't mean you have to. I know what you're thinking. You think it's cool. Long 'needed' glasses last year too. That's what they said, but I know better, and he can see just fine. Listen to your father. I know you think it's the next new fashion trend. That's what they want you to think. I'm telling you, it's a government conspiracy."

"But d-don't you wear glasses?" I ask.

"That's different," he says. "I'm older and I'm only using these glasses to see the needle on the sewing machine. No young person should be wearing glasses, and especially not my children. If you can see well enough to make these ties and cummerbunds, then you can see. If you can see enough to walk down the street without bumping into anything, then you can see. If you can see enough to recognize people, then you can see. Once you put on those glasses, you'll be blind forever. Do you want that? Do you want to be blind? Listen to your father. I know what's really going on."

His energy is manic and menacing, and there is something else, something far away in those big eyes of his—so like my own—a feeling I can't yet process.

"But the note says—" I try again, against all reason, choking back my tears.

"You motherfucker! *Đụ má mày!*" he says. Words I hear often. He slaps me hard across my face. "*Đụ má mày!*" he yells again and tears the note into tiny pieces.

I dare not speak. I am suspended in time and motion. My father sits down at the sewing machine and resumes his work, breathing heavily. He replaces the bobbin in the bobbin compartment, takes pieces of the fabric I had arranged for him the night before, and aligns them on the throat plate. Then he presses the foot pedal. The sound of the needle echoes in my head like bullets raining down.

Broken Erasers

I FIGURED IF LONG had been told he "needed" glasses the previous year but could still see, then my father must be right, and the school was playing straight into the government's hands. I could still see everything I needed to see—at least if my teachers wrote in large enough letters on the blackboard, and if I sat close enough to the front of the room. Only the classes in which I sat at the very back proved challenging, but if I squinted, that took care of the problem. The year before I had done very well in school, even being selected to join the Math Olympiad team, and I was still a good student.

Besides, if all else failed, my mother told me, I could pray to Quan Thế Âm. I prayed plenty, but later I would wonder if maybe the problem was that I hadn't prayed enough. Who knew how much was enough? Who knew when her arms would reach me? She had a thousand, but there were billions of people on this planet. Perhaps there was a backlog of requests, I reasoned. She hadn't gotten to mine yet.

But my father was wrong that I wanted glasses to be cool. It gave me a measure of comfort to know that I could at least trust that not to be the case.

There were other ways to be cool.

Every year in elementary school, my teachers handed out little Scholastic catalogues. They featured items such as books, toys, colorful pencils and pens, cute erasers of all shapes and sizes, and stickers. I thought that if only I could somehow possess those items, I'd be more like the other students in my class. I'd feel as though I belonged. But at temple and at home, I was taught not to want. My mother reiterated this lesson daily. Paintings of beautifully clothed bodhisattvas floating on clouds in the sky embellished the covers of our prayer books. "This is where you want to go," my mother told me. "But first you have to renounce materiality. Don't give in to greed." I longed to please her. But I also longed for a book of my own or a fancy pencil or rubber ball.

So each year I filled out the order form, choosing carefully what I would buy if I could, and took it home to my parents, knowing they would never sign off on it, and couldn't sign off on it even if they wanted to because they didn't have the money. I read the book blurbs and looked at the covers, watching out for the gold and silver emblems that signified awards like the Newbery or the Caldecott, because I figured that if a book had won an award, it would be worth reading. Then I decided which toy in the catalogue I should get, allowing myself only one toy. Plus one pencil. One eraser. One sticker. Sometimes I did not choose a sticker. Whenever I received a good grade on a test, a sticker would appear in the top right-hand corner, for free, so I deemed it an unnecessary item. After all, I did not want to disappoint my mother; I did not want to be greedy.

Whenever the Scholastic shipments arrived, there was always a handful of kids whose names were not called to pick up an order. Though I knew I belonged to this group, I still always sat on the edge of my seat, waiting for my name to be called. I was a very optimistic child—a triumph of hope over experience.

One of the kids whose name *was* always called and who always received a package was Veronica. Everyone loved Veronica, teachers included. Not only was she a stellar student, but she could draw well and had a knack for arts and crafts. She was sweet and without pretension. At lunchtime, every girl wanted to sit next to her. I too wanted to be her friend. She was Chinese-Indonesian, and since we were the only Asian students in the class I was hoping she'd think we had to stick together. But while I stumbled awkwardly through social interactions, Veronica was popular.

How did she do it? I wondered. Her parents were immigrants too. She had three siblings just like me and was the youngest just like me. What did she have that I didn't?

One day at lunch I asked Veronica if I could see her famous collection of erasers, which I'd heard about from the other kids. She kept it in a small brown wax-paper bag with the words "Veronica's Erasers" printed beautifully with big block letters in different colors on the front. She emptied the bag's contents onto the table, and erasers of all shapes, sizes, and colors tumbled out like jewels.

I looked longingly at them: there were animal-shaped erasers, Christmas-themed erasers, cartoon-character erasers, and a rainbow-colored Lisa Frank eraser.

"This one's my favorite," she said, taking the Lisa Frank eraser in her hands. "I have another one that I use, but this one I keep clean because it's so pretty."

That night as my brothers and I sat on the living room floor preparing cummerbunds for my mother to iron, slipping buckles onto the elastic bands, I asked her if she could buy me a pack of erasers even though I knew what the answer would be.

"A pack of erasers? Don't you have erasers on the ends of your pencils already? Just use those. Don't spend money frivolously."

Still, I did not give up. I began to look for erasers everywhere I walked. I knew that kids often lost their erasers on stairs, in the bathrooms, in the hallways, or in the classrooms, and I also looked for spare change on the floor so that I could save up for a pack at the local ninety-nine-cent store. My plan worked. Little by little, I managed to amass a small collection.

"Look," I told Veronica one afternoon at lunchtime. It had taken me several months, but I had finally gathered enough erasers to fill a quarter of a brown paper bag not dissimilar to the one she had. I held the bag open for her.

"What is it?" she asked, picking out bits of the salad that had spilled over into the ravioli on her tray. I admired her neatness, her perfection.

I took the erasers out in a fistful and unloaded them onto the table. They were mostly used or broken erasers, of the generic pink parallelogram variety, with no fun shapes like the ones she had. Still, I was proud to have collected so many. And I could imagine even the broken erasers taking on amusing and lovable shapes, a little deformed bunny here, a misshapen cloud there. I had drawn little hearts and stars on some of the plainer ones to give them character.

"My eraser collection!" I beamed. "Just like the one you have. Well, not just like it. I still have a lot more to get, but look, I have the Lisa Frank one that you have. It took me a long time to get it. But aren't they all so pretty? This one is my favorite. No, wait, maybe this one." I prattled on, examining each eraser as though I were actually making a choice. In truth, I loved them all.

"Oh, I stopped collecting a while ago." She shrugged indifferently. "I decided to move on to something else."

I froze.

"Oh. Wh-what did you move on to?" I stammered after composing myself, attempting to sound interested in her new collection. Slowly, I began to gather up my little erasers, dropping them back into the brown bag one by one. I bit my lip, not understanding then why I felt my tear ducts welling up, threatening to erupt, my face hot with embarrassment and something else, something, perhaps, akin to rage. The beginning of an idea had begun to form in my mind. The idea that life wasn't fair. That there was a difference between me and other children, and that maybe, no matter how hard I tried, I might never be like the others.

"Fuzzy stickers, I think," she said. "Or maybe pencils. I can't decide."

"Oh," I said, defeated. It was so simple, and yet, why hadn't I thought of that? She was so creative, so clear about what she wanted. All I knew how to do was copy others, and not even well. I sat back and tried to eat my lunch, hiding my disappointment as best I could. How was I ever going to be cool? I thought. How would I ever be the girl that other girls wanted to be friends with?

I looked at my little bag of broken erasers and saw myself as one of them, worn and discarded, unworthy of admiration.

But the feeling was momentary. I took that bag home and put it in a small black purse a neighbor had given me. Despite their having failed to impress Veronica, I still cherished those erasers that I had worked so hard to collect. And one day, I thought to myself, I'd have the money to buy my own erasers and my own stickers and my own books with silver and gold medallions on them. And when the day came for the packages to arrive, my name would finally be called. And I would stand up, walk slowly and ceremoniously to the teacher's desk to claim my hard-earned prize, and savor every moment of it. I didn't know exactly when that day would come, but I was sure that it would. I felt like it was right around the corner.

Part II

Spring 1982. Ý and Ba on their wedding day in Vietnam.

Ý

MY MOTHER TAUGHT US how to count from one to ten in Teo-chew, the Chinese dialect she and my father used when they discussed money matters. "We don't know how to speak Teochew well enough to teach you, but you have to remember where you come from." It was in ways like that that they tried to hold on to their identity as Chinese-Vietnamese.

But this confused us. We were accustomed to hearing the grown-ups in our temple make distinctions between Chinese and Vietnamese people. "That one's a Han. She is not to be trusted," they might whisper—Han referring to the Han dynasty that in 111 BC began the millennia-long domination of Vietnamese territories. Imposing their own culture and customs, the Han were responsible for a significant loss of Vietnamese language and identity, and the Vietnamese still resented their former conquerors.

"No, we are not that kind of Chinese," my mother explained when I asked. "We are the *tiê-chiu nang* people from the Tang dynasty, not the *hang nang*." And somehow we were not just Chinese but Vietnam-ese too.

When Thinh was a teenager, he noticed something strange. "Hey," he said to us one day. "Do you ever wonder why we call our mother 'aunt'?" Phu and Long and I looked at each other, puzzled. In Sino-Vietnamese, the portion of the Vietnamese vocabulary originating from Chinese, the word for aunt is *ý*, pronounced like the letter *e*, and that's what we called her. Did that mean we were adopted? I'd never thought about it until now. When I finally worked up my nerve to ask her, she explained that calling your mother "aunt" makes room for friendship in the mother-child relationship. The practice came from the idea that we often treat our friends better than we treat our family. Since treating our parents as our friends would be disrespectful, calling them "aunt" and "uncle" was the next best thing.

So on Mother's Day in the third grade, when we made cards with big foam hearts glued onto the front that started with "Dear Mom," I wrote "Dear Aunt" instead. Word got around that I didn't have a mother.

I went home and cried to Thinh that the kids in school were making fun of me because of my mistake. "Don't worry, Ly. They'll forget in a few days," he said. "Don't even try to explain it to them. They won't understand." Thinh had just started the ninth grade at Francis Lewis High School and took an hour every morning before school to spike his hair in just the right way. He had started to care very much about his appearance, the way he looked, the way he presented himself. And it was also around this time that he immersed himself in Eastern philosophy. He read books about Huineng, the illiterate monastic who eventually became the Sixth Patriarch of Ch'an Buddhism, and books on Taoism and Confucianism. He meditated for long periods of time. He even had a mentor named Govinda, the same name as Siddhartha's best friend, who took him on as some sort of disciple. To me, Thinh was like a sage, omniscient and imperturbable. I wanted to be just like him.

Long was not so wise or so sympathetic. "Give me a break," he said, rolling his eyes. "You really couldn't figure out you were supposed to write 'Dear Mom' instead?"

My mother met my father after the war. She had been avoiding marriage for almost a decade. She wanted to work and make money for her family. "I jumped into the river once when I saw a matchmaker come to the house and I swam to the other side. To the other side! Can you believe it? I was a good swimmer. They could never catch me."

But they did. When she was thirty-one, her sister-in-law had a friend whose brother had just come home from the re-education camps, and arranged for the two of them to meet. It was an urgent matter. My mother was in danger of becoming an old maid. Her older sister had married at eighteen and her younger sisters at ages not much older than that. There was pressure from friends and family. "After this age, you will no longer be desirable. Nobody will come for you," they told her.

So when it was time for *Lễ xem mặt* (the looking-face ceremony), where the potential bride and groom meet each other for the first time, my father arrived at her home bearing small gifts. My mother offered him tea, as part of the ritual. He was so nervous that he turned bright red, which my mother found charming. And it was settled. Though they knew close to nothing about each other, my mother accepted his hand in marriage and they had a beautiful wedding in which my father showed up at her house in a flower-laden canoe to bring her across the river from her village to his, as was the custom of their time.

But her marriage to my father was not a happy one. She now had to serve him as a housewife, and that also meant serving his family, his five sisters in particular, who lived with them and never failed to remind her of her lowly station in their household. When they discovered that my mother did not know how to cook, they abused her both physically and verbally. When my father was angry, they egged him on to beat her.

And he did. He once beat her so badly that my mother jumped into the Mekong River to escape and swam all the way back to the other side, to the village she came from, and ran home to her father.

"You can't stay here," her father told her. "What will people think of a wife who has run away from home?"

My mother would remind my father of this when they fought, and I would listen, trying to piece the story together. I was always listening. The subjects of their quarrels were usually either money-related or terrible-sisters-related—for despite the distance my mother had put between herself and her sisters-in-law when she came to America, my aunts still caused her trouble. They sent letters to my father asking for money. When he didn't have enough to send back home, they called him names and blamed my mother for his poverty. This led to many vicious fights between my parents, and their relationship was so marred by animosity and bitterness that my brothers and I never witnessed a trace of tenderness between them.

They were poor in a strange country. They had four young children to raise. They missed Vietnam and missed their families. My father took it out on my mother. My mother in turn would recite the injustices she had suffered under his sisters' regime, fueling my father's rage.

Often my brothers and I would hide when they fought, but my mother would always find us and make us go back to work. Work was the priority. My mother couldn't even take a break to cry when things got to be too much for her, so she just cried right there in front of us while she was ironing cummerbunds, her tears dripping onto the silk fabric and evaporating as she passed the iron over it.

But my brother Long could always figure out what to do to entertain her. He is the funniest of all of us and he made her laugh when she wanted to cry. My parents called him *cáo sọi*, the little pup. He made faces, picked his nose, farted loudly, jumped dramatically at the noise as though he had surprised even himself. At this, my mother would laugh. She'd begin with a sigh, as if to say, "What is the little pup up to now?" Then she'd erupt, laughing for a long time, cheeks red, shoulders shaking, every exhalation accompanied by a wheeze.

I wished I could make my mother happy too, but I lacked my brother's charm. All I could do was try to make her life a little easier by doing some of the household chores and keeping her company. Sometimes when I was helping her with the dishes after dinner she would sigh and tell me that one day, she'd run away and never come back.

"Can I come with you?" I would ask.

"No. I'm leaving by myself. No one will know I'm gone until it's too late."

At night, when I lay in bed with her, I would take all my clothes and pile them along the length of the bed between us like a mountain range, my pillow used to further increase the space between us. I'd sleep with my back to her, as far away as possible, at the edge of the bed, wounded.

In the morning, I'd wake up in her arms, the pile of clothes neatly folded in a corner.

About a year after we arrived in the US, my father completed his free courses in ESL and basic data entry at the YMCA. He was granted a certificate, which he proudly framed and displayed on the wall in our living room. It was the only thing on our walls other than the holes he'd made from using screwdrivers as hooks from which to hang our clothing. Shortly after, he found a data-entry job working at the Michael C. Fina factory. The company sold fine goods like luxury tableware and engagement rings and employee-recognition items like desk clocks and fancy pens. Their store was on Fifth Avenue, but my father worked at their factory in Long Island City, overseeing the mail and inventory. He earned four dollars and twenty-five cents an hour, minimum wage in 1995. When added to the income from our sewing, this gave my parents just enough to pay all our bills, feed us regular meals, and save a little too.

We were taught from our earliest years to be thrifty. If we weren't wearing secondhand clothing, my mother bought us clothes and sneakers that were two sizes too big so we could grow into them over several years. We diluted our dishwashing liquid with water. We diluted our detergent with water. We bought two-in-one shampoos, and separated one roll of two-ply paper towels into two rolls. And virtually all the furniture in our apartment was something we had found on the street.

Every once in a while, however, something had to be bought new. Since my brothers and I were getting too big for all of us to be able to sleep on the floor, my father had determined that upward was the way to go and bought a red metal bunk bed from a Sleepy's on Myrtle Avenue. After assigning me to the top bunk, he jury-rigged a third bed above mine that ran perpendicular to it. It was a wooden board set atop part of a wire fence, which he attached to L-beams reclaimed from an industrial-steel pallet rack he found in a junkyard on his way to work. He used duct tape and masking tape, whatever tape he could find, and yards of stretchy fabric to hold everything together. That was where Long slept. He would have to climb up the ladder to my bed, then walk across my bed to get to his bed, which wobbled as he climbed atop and with every shift of his weight. But despite the way it looked and felt, it was sturdy, and we didn't complain.

At night, Long and I would sign to each other in the manual alphabet we learned from the back of a book about Helen Keller, and we created a secret handshake that we made sure to do every night before falling asleep.

Thinh and Phu slept on two mattresses on the floor, while my parents slept on the bottom of the bunk bed, next to them. Because he hated any signs of clutter, every morning my father would lift my brothers' mattresses and set them against the wall so that they'd be out of the way.

One evening, my father came home with a box of donuts from Dunkin' Donuts and a big grin on his face. My brothers and I gathered around the table and fought each other to open the box. Stores like Dunkin' Donuts and McDonald's were out of reach for us. To us, they represented all that was American. We stared at children holding Happy Meals and coveted the toys inside. With its powdered jellies, Boston creams, and chocolate éclairs, the box of donuts was one step closer to that. We were starting to eat what the others ate. And if we could eat what the others ate, then we could be like the others. We could be American.

The next night, my father brought home another box. I like to call this the Chocolate Éclair Era of our lives. We'd wait at the top of the stairs for our father to come home every night, bobbing up and down, clamoring, laughing, fighting each other. It was around this time that we had learned how to use the term "dibs." We ran around our living room calling dibs on the donuts.

"Dibs on the chocolate éclair!"

"Dibs on the pink with the rainbow sprinkles!"

"Dibs on the French cruller!"

"No fair, you had the French cruller last night!"

Someone would always end up crying. And someone would end up having to share. My mother looked at my father with surprise, wondering how he got the money to buy a whole box of donuts.

"Relax," he said. "It's a Michael C. Fina treat."

"Every night? Are you sure you're allowed to take the whole thing? Are you leaving enough for everyone? It will be hard to find another job, you know." But he assured her that it was perfectly fine.

A few nights later, my mother took me for a walk down Bleecker Street to pick up my father at the bus stop on his way home from work. She left Thinh in charge of the boys.

"Your father will appreciate seeing us there," she told me. We got dressed, my mother donning a black trench coat she'd brought over from Vietnam and I a light gray sweatshirt. We stepped out into a crisp autumn night and made our way toward Forest Avenue. When we reached Grandview Avenue, the aroma of freshly baked bread and pastries wafted from Grimaldi Bakery on Menahan Street one block over. We stopped and closed our eyes, letting the smell engulf us.

Though it was only a few streets from where we lived, the apartments were much nicer on these blocks and the porches and sidewalks better kept. Along the way, we stopped to admire the little gardens in the front yards of the houses. People kept potted plants and fishponds in their front yards, and dog owners curbed their dogs, which nobody did on our own littered street. It was easy to feel envious. Yet because of its physical proximity to us, we allowed ourselves to dream that living like this might eventually be within reach. My mother would talk about moving into a house of our own one day. A big house with a big chandelier and a big garden.

We reached the bus stop just in time and spotted my father climbing out of the Q39. I waved to him, excited, but he didn't notice or walk toward us. He turned the corner instead.

"Where is he going?" my mother wondered aloud. She grabbed my hand and we followed him around the corner to the front of a Dunkin' Donuts shop. My mother kept her distance, standing behind a dark blue minivan as I held on to her. We observed my father gesturing to the manager inside to come out through the door. Dusk had begun to fall like a blanket of periwinkle blue upon the scene.

"Do you hap lep obas to-nigh?" my father asked loudly.

"It's 'leftovers,' you idiot," the manager said, opening the door and handing over a box of donuts. He was a stocky white man with a big nose and thinning black hair.

"Yes," my father said. "Yes, lep oba. Tankyu so motch, okay?" He bowed to the manager several times, grinning broadly.

"Yeah yeah, get outta here," the manager said.

A few moments later, my mother and I were running home as fast as we could.

"And when we get home, wait with your brothers for your father. And act like you do every night. Don't tell them about the donuts."

It wasn't difficult for me. I called dibs on the French cruller.

It was only later that I understood my mother. She did not want my father's victories, however small, to be taken away from him.

"I Will Never Marry"

TAKING AFTER MY BROTHERS, I thrived academically in school and viewed it as a much-welcomed escape from home. Our school across the street was crowded, with thirty-six to sometimes forty students a class, but it never seemed that way to us and never got in the way of our education.

The year I entered fourth grade we had a teacher I adored. Ms. Weisenthal was a young woman with a mane of frizzy red hair, a sharp nose, and bright blue-gray eyes. She admitted that we were her very first class out of school and she was determined to make the fourth grade our most enjoyable year.

She succeeded. There was never a tedious moment in her class. Because we didn't have recess that year due to construction in the schoolyard, Ms. Weisenthal was always coming up with projects for us to do. Once, she separated us into groups and assigned each group a decade. We would then research the fashion trends of the time, the music, and the politics. On the day the project was due, each group put on a performance showcasing the popular dance of their decade. My group had been assigned the 1920s so we danced the Charleston. She loved to dress up. One day, she surprised us all when she arrived in a pink ball gown and tiara. She was a princess that day. She also loved to read aloud to us, taking on different voices for each character in the story. She was different from other teachers. She was an adult, but she was also one of us.

Seeing Ms. Weisenthal dress up made me want to be a princess too. But I barely had any clothes, let alone costumes. I went home and thought about what I could do to remedy this. Rummaging around, I found leftover pieces of fabric from our shipments. Then I asked my mother to sew them together and I tied the whole thing around my neck like a cape. *I can't be a princess*, I thought, *but I can be a superhero.* Long joined me too, making his own cape, and we ran around our apartment with our arms out pretending to fly. Sometimes, I'd catch myself in the mirror, a stranger with a funny-looking patchwork cape, and it somehow didn't matter that I couldn't recognize myself. For the moment, the girl in the mirror was a superhero too.

On Valentine's Day, Ms. Weisenthal set up a dance party and brought drinks and snacks and candied hearts to class. She had us write down the name of the person we'd like to pair up with on a small index card with our initials signed at the bottom. She chose our partners based on these cards. Those pairs who had written in each other's names were lucky, although there was no way to tell. I'd left mine blank, but was matched with Henry, a quiet Chinese boy with a raspy voice. There was nothing wrong with him, but I was horrified that we were put together. Romantic love was never spoken of in my home. Physical intimacy was nonexistent between my brothers and me. We never hugged each other or our parents. Not only did my parents never exhibit affection toward each other, but they forbade us from even so much as watching a scene on television of a couple hugging or kissing. If we were caught watching, my mother would slap us.

"Turn that off this instant! That's disgusting!"

On the day of the dance, Ms. Weisenthal put on a Backstreet Boys CD. The students danced shyly and awkwardly around one another but eventually loosened up and tried out some silly moves, all except for Henry and me. We remained on the sidelines.

"Come on, guys," Ms. Weisenthal said to us. "Why aren't you dancing?"

"She doesn't want to," Henry said, his arms crossed.

"But why? You don't know how to dance? Here, I'll show the both of you."

She held out her hands, but I refused her invitation. "I don't believe in Valentine's Day," I told her.

She gasped in an exaggerated way, putting her hand over her open mouth. "You mean, you don't believe in *love*?" she asked teasingly.

"No, I don't," I declared. "And I'm never getting married either!"

"Oh ho! That's a pretty bold statement. Why don't you write it down?"

"What do you mean?" I asked.

"I want you to write it down on this piece of loose-leaf." She calmly pulled a sheet from atop her desk. "Write it down, sign it, and date it."

I did as I was told and handed it back to her.

"Wonderful." She took the note and put it in her drawer. "I am going to show up to your wedding one day with this note," she said with a wink.

Fat chance, I thought. What was marriage good for anyway? If my parents were any indication, I didn't want anything to do with it. Why would I want to endure the kind of treatment my mother was subjected to?

———

A year later, I came home one day from school to find my father in the front yard of our apartment. He lit a cigarette. It was a habit he'd had for decades, since his time in the war, an expensive one that we couldn't afford and that caused my mother grief.

"What are you doing home so early, Ba?" I asked him. "You didn't go to work today?"

"I did," he said, a big grin appearing on his face. "But I left early. I'm going to surprise your mother with this." He took a little box out of his pocket and opened it, revealing a diamond ring glistening inside.

I was stunned. Who was this man grinning like a child in a toy store? Surely not my father. Surely not the man who often made my mother cry. Surely not the man who was often impatient and had fits of rage.

"What is that for?" I asked.

"A gift," he said. "Today is our fifteen-year anniversary."

I observed him cautiously, as if it were not my father who stood before me but a man disguised as him. A gift? I couldn't recall a single time my father had ever given a gift to my mother, or vice versa. In fact, gift giving was a concept completely foreign to me. It was something others did, not us. But in the golden light of the afternoon sun, this man I thought I knew was nervously admiring his choice of a diamond ring, puffing away at his cigarette, his features softened by the glow of excitement. I suddenly felt the old warmth I had felt toward him when I was a small child and he was much gentler with me. It was a rare moment. I didn't say anything. I just stood there, beneath the shade of the maple tree in our front yard, desperately trying to understand. It wasn't only that he was inaccessible to me but that he was inaccessible to himself.

In the end, the ring didn't fit my mother's finger, and my father didn't have the money to get it resized. "It's better like this," she said. "I'm too old to be wearing a diamond ring anyway." But every now and again, when she thought no one was watching, my mother would take the ring out and admire it for a few minutes, gingerly tracing its outline before putting it back in its box.

Super Squint

BY THE TIME I was ten, street name signs had disintegrated into a blurry haze of green and white unless I was almost directly under them. I couldn't read colored words against a background unless there was enough of a contrast, and I couldn't read the aisle signs in the supermarket unless I squinted. Faces started to look the same to me, their features indistinguishable. I became anxious over my inability to recognize people as they approached, but I learned to use the idiosyncrasies of their gait and the particular way their bodies occupied space to identify them. And when that failed, I learned to look down at my feet while I walked to avoid accidental eye contact with anyone I couldn't recognize.

Eventually, as my sight worsened and my squinting powers failed me, I developed a new technique. I would push the bottom lid of my eye inward and upward to narrow my field of vision until my eyes were almost closed, but not quite. This technique was more effective than the regular squint, and for a time it worked. It was almost like a super squint.

Walking alongside my mother and father one day in a Rite Aid pharmacy, I decided to try out my new technique in order to read the signs hanging above the aisles. My father had walked ahead of us. I held on to my mother with my left hand and pushed in the bottom lids of my eyes with my right, using my thumb and index finger.

Suddenly, my mother's face was close to mine, her eyes wide as she bent down toward me.

"Kỳ Lý! What are you doing?" she whispered harshly.

"Oh, this?" I said. "Nothing, just trying to read the signs."

"Don't let your father see you," she said. She pulled my hand down and forced it against my side. "Stop pretending you can't see. Or you really will be blind. You know how your father feels about that." She glanced nervously toward my father.

"I'm not pretending, Mom. I really can't—"

"What is it?" My father had started to walk back toward us.

"Nothing," my mother said quickly, straightening up. "There was something in her eye, and we were trying to get it out. It's out now, though." She squeezed my hand, almost crushing it.

I stayed silent. I had gotten the hint.

My father shrugged and walked on.

At home, I sat in front of the mirror. My own features were beginning to blur if I was more than a foot away. The unrecognizable girl had become even more unrecognizable. I pushed and pushed at the edges of my corneas, hoping to snap whatever was broken back into place. But it never worked.

The previous year, teachers had nominated students to participate in a program known as Project Friend, an initiative to help students with low self-esteem or problems socializing. Thanks to Ms. Weisenthal, who must have noticed the many ways in which I never quite fit in with the others, I was one of those students. I didn't understand why at the time. I thought it was just a nice excuse to get out of class. Twice a week, a tall, curly-haired woman with light blue eyes, Miss Elena, would come and take me to her office. There, we played tic-tac-toe or checkers, discussing things like "confidence" and "self-esteem" while she jotted down notes on a legal pad.

"Well, Ly Ly," she'd say at the end of every session, "it's such a pleasure to have you, as always, but let's try to talk a little bit more next time. Let's talk about your feelings. Let's be friends."

I had enjoyed the Project Friend sessions when I was in fourth grade, but when I continued them in fifth grade, which was my final year at P.S. 81, they started to make me uncomfortable. Miss Elena would ask me questions about my day, how I felt about my friends, about school, about family. Our sessions became quieter, as I could not find the words to answer her increasingly personal questions. I was afraid I didn't have any feelings. There seemed to be a ship among ships within the vast unchartered seas of my psyche that I could never swim out to. And on that ship were the words I searched desperately for but could never reach.

Once, in the middle of a game of Connect 4, Miss Elena excused herself for a bathroom break. She was hugely pregnant at the time and had to take a lot of breaks. That day, she left the window open and a nice spring breeze blew into the office, ruffling the pages of her notepad. Eventually, my curiosity got the better of me, and I leaned over to see what she'd been writing in her large print.

"LT still has trouble communicating. When asked to discuss feelings, LT digs fingers into the skin of her hands. Is very quiet these days. Does not speak."

This discovery of how another person viewed me was at once illuminating and shocking. I spread my hands in front of me and noticed for the first time the half-moon marks my nails had left on the backs of my hands. I massaged the marks and wished they would disappear. Why did I do that? I thought to myself. Have I always done that? I massaged the marks until my hands were red. Then I was afraid Miss Elena would write a note on that, so I sat on them.

There, I thought. Problem solved. And it wasn't true that I had trouble communicating. I communicated just fine with the other kids. I had friends. Didn't I?

Another breeze blew through the window, but this time it felt cold against my skin, and I was aware of the emptiness of that room, aware for the first time, because of what I had seen in Miss Elena's notes, of my desire to dig my nails into the backs of my hands.

The Eldest Son

THINH AND I GREW closer in my early adolescent years, around the time I graduated from P.S. 81 and entered middle school, I.S. 93. "You were kind of like a small shadow before this," he told me. I suppose he was right. But I was growing up, had lost all my baby teeth, and wanted to leave behind the insecurities of childhood. Thinh recognized that and began to treat me as an equal—intellectually as well as in other ways.

He was six years older but seemed older still because of all the expectations placed upon him as eldest son and brother. I paid attention to everything he said and did. He was fond of Eastern philosophy and introduced me to the teachings of Mencius, Han Fei, Confucius, and Laozi. We would stay up at night and have long contemplative conversations.

"You have to be able to understand the world if you want to live a fulfilling life," he told me when he was eighteen and I was still only twelve. "And philosophy is key."

Once, when I was taking my usual fifteen-minute walk home from I.S. 93 on Forest Avenue and Madison Street, Thinh sidled up alongside me and said softly, "You know, you'd probably be more attractive and feel more confident if you walked upright instead of staring at your feet with your back bent over like that. Presentation is everything. Walking upright separates us from the chimps. Try it sometime."

Never before had I considered the importance of the way someone walked, or the idea that it was a thing that could be perfected. Never before had I considered my own being as something that could be viewed as attractive. My mother had taught me the opposite, taught me never to think about my body other than to keep it clean. But Thinh had spoken with such self-assurance that his words stayed with me. I began to consciously try to walk with straighter posture. It was uncomfortable at first, my body having gotten accustomed to my hunched-over position, but I slowly adjusted to walking with my chest out and back straight. And little by little, I began to feel at least the illusion of the confidence my new posture was supposed to convey.

Confidence was what I needed in middle school, where schoolwork was now more difficult and where friendships were not on a day-to-day basis as they had been in elementary school but something that required more continuity, more give-and-take. Veronica and I found each other again, as we were both placed in the advanced class and seated next to one another. I was so glad to see a familiar face in a new school, and so was she. To my delight, we became close friends immediately, our shared elementary school experience strengthening the bond we had. And I plucked up the courage to talk to a quiet girl named Avery one day during lunchtime when I happened to sit next to her. She was munching on a bag of Lay's chips, brownish-blond hair tied back in a ponytail, and wearing a large Pochacco T-shirt that went down to her knees. I can't remember what I said to her, but she responded enthusiastically, and we began spending time together. I was learning how to socialize, how to connect with people—what Miss Elena had been trying to teach me—and that year Veronica and Avery became my two closest friends.

Most days I walked home with Veronica and several other girls who lived along the same route. On weekends, Avery and I would meet at a playground across the street from I.S. 93, where we'd sit on the swings while we chatted and ate Italian ices. She loved music and introduced me to many of her favorite songs, and we'd sing together, her voice a lovely lilting alto and mine a passable contralto. She rarely talked about her family. But one day, in a moment of intimacy, when she must have been feeling very vulnerable, she told me how much she hated her "pops," the person responsible for her mother's limp. What he had done she didn't say then, but I filled in the blank with my imagination.

Her admission shocked me. It seemed so brave of her to voice her hatred, and something in that intensity of feeling moved and inspired me—perhaps because I lacked the ability to name my feelings for what they were. In my home, cultural norms surrounding filial piety, the duty owed to one's parents to obey them and hold them always in high regard, reigned. My natural inclination, too, to absorb and mirror others' feelings without ever knowing my own left me even more confused. I measured Avery's feelings toward her father against mine. What *did* I feel? I didn't know that one could feel anything other than love and respect toward one's parents, that it was permitted. The more I thought about it, the more I realized that the feeling I felt toward my father was perhaps not hate but fear. This was especially true as tensions between him and Thinh grew and spread throughout our home like a plague.

Thinh, at this point, was taking an interest in computers and electronics, the world just recently revolutionized by the invention of the internet. He begged my father to buy a cheap Compaq computer for him. He begged and begged, and my father finally relented. He must have thought it was how Thinh would be able to get ahead in life. But Thinh had his own ideas of what to do with that computer. He borrowed books from the library on HTML, C++, and JavaScript and taught himself programming and graphic design. He installed Adobe Photoshop and spent his time designing images of hyper-realistic water droplets and bamboo. It was a new kind of art, and he wanted to be at the forefront of it. It also meant that he spent less and less of his time helping us out with the ties and cummerbunds.

My father didn't like this. Though he had agreed to tap into our savings to buy the computer, he didn't feel the same appreciation for art, computer-generated or otherwise, that Thinh did. He thought Thinh's efforts were a waste of time and a waste of money. He'd threatened to break the computer on more than one occasion, throwing whatever he could find at the monitor, his temper unpredictable and wild. My mother would block the computer and sometimes receive the full force of the objects herself, while Phu, Long, and I cowered in a corner, watching, not daring to say a word.

The relationship between my father and Thinh grew ever more poisonous over time. The fact that we weren't getting any richer was Thinh's fault in my father's eyes. Thinh wasn't doing his share of the work on the family assembly line, and this led to increasingly vicious tirades from my father.

"He doesn't fucking get it," Thinh said to me one evening after another onslaught of verbal abuse.

My allegiance was torn. I could see that my brother was suffering but I couldn't go against my father. Though he was the cause of my own suffering, with my eyesight deteriorating and his refusal to allow me to get glasses, he was still, in my mind, the archetype of Father, a larger-than-life figure who was always to be obeyed—and more and more to be feared.

I said nothing to Thinh about what I was going through. The fact that my eyesight was worsening just didn't seem serious enough to warrant his attention. Thinh's frustrations, on the other hand, weighed heavily on me and I often watched him after his fights with my father. It dawned on me as I sat in that little back room with Thinh one evening that the pain I saw in his expression as he stared at the screen, clicking and scrolling and adjusting the shadowing of the water droplets, was what I had sensed in my mother from my earliest days.

She spent endless hours ironing the ties and cummerbunds, as well as cooking and cleaning, and my father never expressed any appreciation for her. But while my mother could not escape, or perhaps would not escape for the sake of her children—despite her declarations that she would one day run away—Thinh was determined to break free. It was only a matter of time.

And then what? I wondered. Then my father's chains would encircle Phu, then Long, and finally me. So focused was I on this imagined order of events that I couldn't detect the chains that were already keeping me captive. As I grew older I would come to understand that these were the same shackles that had kept my father imprisoned for nearly a decade of misery and despair, and that, from the very beginning, we were all haunted by the ghosts of my father's past.

Fifteen Seconds of Hilarity

ONE EVENING, AS WE awaited the next shipment of fabrics, my brothers, my mother, and I gathered to watch *Fear Factor* on the TV my father had found on the street some years before. The knobs had broken off and the antennae didn't work, so he'd wrapped tissues around the spindles where the knobs had been and covered the antennae with aluminum foil so the set would get some reception. The picture on the screen was interrupted by white horizontal lines, scrolling repeatedly from the top to the bottom, but my brothers and I didn't care. We thought my father was better than a magician.

We loved *Fear Factor*. It was a reality show where the participants were dared to complete dangerous or disgusting tasks—like jumping between buildings, walking across a beam connecting two speeding trucks, or eating live worms, horned caterpillars, or raw bull testicles—within a certain amount of time. The participant with the highest score took home a grand prize of fifty thousand dollars. I liked thinking about what I would be willing to do to win that much money, though I feared I was too squeamish and too timid to do any of the things the people on the show did.

That night we were betting on who we thought would win or lose, our voices getting louder and louder as we kept interrupting each other, when my father came out of the bedroom to see what all the excitement was about. He joined us at the point where the contestants had to eat live cockroaches. "Oh, oh!" my mother squealed, and my brothers and I joined in.

"Ly, I dare you to eat that cockroach," Long said during the commercial break, pointing to a roach scurrying across the floor beneath our chairs.

"Yeah right, *you* eat it!" My days of seeing cockroaches as pets were long past, but the cockroaches were still with us.

"Well, guess what? You just lost fifty thousand dollars."

"This is nothing," my father said. "For fifty thousand dollars? Live cockroaches? I had to eat the maggots that squirmed under my broken skin where the chains held my ankles." He rolled up his trousers to show us his scars. "Look!" he cried out at us. "Look!"

Despite my father's bouts of rage, there were still occasional moments when we had a good time as a family. I would never have predicted that one of those moments would arrive via Thinh's computer, that machine my father resented so much, but that's what happened.

It took days for Thinh to download the first video he ever showed us—such was the state of technology at the time. He left the computer on all day and night, checking up on its progress. By then Thinh and my father were barely on speaking terms. Thinh continued tinkering with his computer while my father spent his days cursing Thinh under his breath. The rest of us did what we could to stay clear of my father.

I didn't really understand what Thinh was doing. What did "download" mean, exactly? I didn't understand what the internet was or how it worked, even after Thinh tried, on multiple occasions, to explain it to me. Data, megabytes, download, upload, broadband, bandwidth, dial-up. It all seemed so abstract. I couldn't keep any of it straight. I only knew that the discordant sounds coming from the modem bothered me immensely.

But to Thinh, the promise of the internet was nothing short of magical. It was as though he had already seen what was coming, had been waiting for it all his life. There was an ever-present glint in his eyes that seemed to say, *This is only the beginning; you ain't seen nothing yet,* all his hopes rooted in some distant future. He was an avid Trekkie.

"Yo, guys, you gotta check this out," he said one day, after the video had finally finished downloading. We were done with our sweatshop duties and getting ready for bed. It was a summer evening, the air thick with heat. At Thinh's beckoning, Phu, Long, and I came into the back room, and we gathered around the monitor, which sat on the corner of the sewing room table.

The clip was short, fifteen seconds, small and grainy on the screen, and there was no sound. The scene opened on an adult chimpanzee settled in a tree, a piece of fruit in its mouth, and then the camera switched focus to a baby chimp walking a little farther up the branch and scratching its bottom. Then it sniffed its fingers and, from the shock of the smell, theatrically fainted and fell backward off the tree.

I didn't think I'd ever seen anything so funny in all eleven years of my life. And from the look of it, neither had my brothers. There was something about the way that chimp fell over, something so human about it, that made us laugh until we couldn't breathe anymore. We replayed the clip again and again, barely able to make it to the end before erupting into shrieks. I thought I would never stop laughing.

Just as Thinh moved to play the clip once again, the door burst open with a bang and my father stormed in, wearing nothing but his boxers, his eyes bleary and bloodshot.

"What the hell is all this fucking noise?" he yelled. "Go to sleep, all of you! Do you know what time it is?"

And just like that, our moment of pure glee was over. The smiles disappeared from our faces. We moved to leave the room, afraid of enraging our father even more. But Thinh didn't move. He sucked his teeth, muttering, "Oh, come on." He wasn't ready for it to end. It had taken him days, after all, to download that video. And he no longer cared enough to try to stay on good terms with our father.

In an act of defiance, he played the clip one more time, as if to say, *Man, fuck this. We're just having some goddamn fun.*

No one spoke. Fifteen seconds of nothing but the quiet hum of the computer fans, the video of a little chimp who was in for a smelly surprise, and the palpable anger of our father standing in the doorway.

Despite the tension in the air, we couldn't help ourselves. As soon as the baby chimp fell off the branch, we all erupted into laughter again. But this time, something was different. There was another sound of laughter mixed in with ours, a sound I hadn't heard in a long time. We all turned around, shocked to find that it was coming from our father, his face red, his shoulders shaking, grabbing his sides.

My father was cracking up. *"Hía, ah, Hía!"* he called out to my mother after he was able to regain his composure. She was in the living room, putting away the cummerbunds we'd made that evening to be picked up the next day. *"Bà vô đây đi.* Leave that for later. You have to come see this!"

She came shuffling into the room, wide-eyed. "What? What is it?" she asked.

Thinh played the clip again, and then we were all six of us in that little back room, either doubled over or grabbing a chair, holding on to something to steady ourselves. Sometimes each other. I looked around at my family. I took in that scene, the little chimp frozen on the screen, my brothers and my parents and I all convulsed in laughter. And I thought: Was this the power of the internet? Whatever it was, I didn't want it to end. Sometimes, I think that if I could choose one moment in time to go back to, it would be that one.

But the moment did end. The hostility between Thinh and my father returned. It was unbearable for me. Once, when Thinh stayed up late to work on one of his designs, my father broke a ceramic bowl of rice across his back, leaving a large and indelible scar. "You fucking dog," my father called him in a fit of rage. "Get the fuck out of this house."

And not long after that episode, Thinh did. The following year, 2001, Thinh started college at the Rochester Institute of Technology in Western New York. I didn't quite grasp the enormity of the change. How was it possible that one of us would be spending four years away from home, living in a dorm room with people he had never met, his worldview expanding in ways we never could have imagined? I also didn't know that Thinh would never again live with us. After graduating RIT he would move to Kirkland in Washington State and it would be several years before I saw him again. My father had succeeded in driving him away. I don't even remember saying goodbye.

Shortly after Thinh left, the World Trade Center buildings were attacked. The events of 9/11 were terrifying to us, as to so many others in New York and around the world. After school that day, I watched news of the attack on television with my parents. My mother tried to get in touch with Thinh, who was living in a dormitory at RIT, but she couldn't get through. Long-distance phone lines were overloaded by the heavy volume of calls.

"Stop worrying," my father said after my mother's sixth try. "Not being in New York City, he's safer than we are." I realized that for my father this must have brought back memories of war, of everything he thought he had escaped by coming to America. He was agitated, peering out the windows and pacing back and forth in the living room.

"But they won't get us here," he muttered. "There's nobody here for them to get. They won't get us. They can't get us."

For a long time, nobody said anything. We ate dinner in silence. My mother lit incense and poured tea into miniature cups and we all bowed and prayed before the altar.

The attacks on the World Trade Center had left me shaken and confused, and at that moment of collective grief and familial sorrow, I really missed Thinh. His absence left a huge hole in my life. I wanted to ask him about terrorism, about war, and about the evils of humanity. Hadn't Mencius asserted that at birth, we are, all of us, intrinsically good? What must it take for someone to commit such acts of violence? Why do people hurt other people? And to such horrific degrees? And how, how could it be that there was so much hatred rooted in religion?

But gone were the nights I could go to Thinh for the answers to these questions. I would have to answer them myself.

The Nail Salon Era

IT WAS LATER THAT year, in October, when we heard the news. A simple phone call to let us know that there would be no shipments of fabrics or cummerbund buckles coming in that week. "No more?" my father asked. But the man on the other line had already hung up.

By then our living situation had improved tremendously. We were eating better, canned sardines and rice no longer our primary meal. My mother was able to buy clothing from Happy Days and Kid City for us instead of relying on handouts and thrift shop purchases.

Through strict and conscientious saving from his earnings at the factory and from our home labor, my father accumulated enough money to buy a car. But first he'd had to pass the driver's license test, which took him nine tries; the day he finally passed, he went straight to a local dealership and purchased a used burgundy Nissan Altima. I couldn't believe that we had a car. It seemed to me for a long time like it was something we weren't supposed to have, like we had somehow cheated.

After the phone call, my mother and father hoped that there had been a mistake.

"Did a new shipment come in today?" my father asked every day when he got home from work. My mother would slowly shake her head.

Weeks turned into months, until, eventually, we understood. "Sweet," I remember saying. "More free time for us!" Phu and Long were silent. They knew better.

"Idiot," Long said. "Don't you know what this means?"

But even after he explained, I didn't really get it. What I did get was that shopping for new clothes was once again a pipe dream since we no longer had the income from our sweatshop labor. We depended on the kindness of our landlady to give us used clothing that no longer fit her children, and on one of my father's supervisors, a man named Jerry, who donated sneakers and jeans to our family.

My parents began to tap into their savings, which were in the form of small gold nuggets, to make rent and pay off bills. Tensions rose and they argued viciously, while my brothers and I did our best to stay out of their way. We made sure to conserve electricity, not turning on the lights until it was too dark to see. We did not turn on the television except for one half hour from six thirty to seven in the evening to watch World News Tonight with Peter Jennings on channel 7, my father's pick. We did not buy shampoo. Candy and chips were out of the question.

It wasn't much of a departure from what my brothers and I were already used to, and since we weren't the ones handling the bills, it was easier for us to distract ourselves from the reality of our situation. Long had discovered chess in school and brought home books that taught us how to play. He and I created our own makeshift chessboard out of folded paper and coins. Pennies were pawns, nickels were knights, dimes were bishops, subway tokens were rooks, and foreign coins we sometimes found, like a Canadian coin or a Chuck E. Cheese coin Phu had picked up from the street, served as our kings and queens.

For a few months, my mother stayed home with nothing to do except read *Người Đẹp* (*Beautiful People*), the Vietnamese magazine she'd get for free at temple or in Chinatown offices. There she saw countless ads looking to hire workers in Vietnamese nail salons, and an idea began to form in her mind. "We have to think of something," she told my father. "How long can we keep this up before our savings go? What will we do then?"

My parents turned to the one thing they always turned to when all hope seemed lost: their faith. A few years after coming to America, they had discovered *Chùa Thập Phương*, a Vietnamese Buddhist temple in the West Bronx. So every Sunday, that's where we'd go.

The temple was on a residential street, in a bright yellow house with red window frames and a doorway flanked by red pillars. An iron gate opened to welcome visitors into the front yard, and a large yellow flag with three horizontal red stripes flew from the roof of the building. "That's our flag," my mother told us one day. "The yellow represents the color of our skin. The three stripes represent the three sections of Vietnam: North, Central, and South. And the red color of the stripes is our blood. But that was before the war. Before it changed to a yellow flag with a Communist red star in the middle."

When we arrived, my parents would pay their respects to the stone statues of Shakyamuni Buddha and Quan Thế Âm Bồ Tát outside the temple, while my brothers and I rushed to join the throng of people in a basement cafeteria that served free vegetarian food. Fried cauliflower dipped in a coconut curry sauce, rice vermicelli served with spring rolls and mock duck meat, mushroom stew made with five different types of mushroom, and an assortment of colorful and delicious desserts. We loved temple food.

Vietnamese people from all over the city and even some from neighboring states gathered to eat and share their stories. But my father forbade us from joining the conversation. "*We* come here to pray and chant. These people come here to eat and chat," he told us. So we ate quickly, quietly, savoring every bite as much as we could. It didn't bother my brothers and me, because there was rarely anyone our age to talk to. It was my mother who suffered. A naturally social person, my mother would try to get to know the other women at the temple, inquiring about their villages in Vietnam and searching for a connection. But my father would scold and humiliate her in front of them.

"It's time to chant," he'd yell at my mother from atop the staircase leading to the main floor. "Get up here now!" And she would nearly choke on her food as she attempted to finish it as quickly as she could.

Seeing my mother humiliated like that awakened something within me. I was getting older, my understanding of the world expanding beyond the scope of my home, my sensitivity to my mother's suffering further heightened by what I was learning about feminism and women's rights in my seventh-grade social studies class. I looked around at other married couples, at the way husbands and wives treated each other, and slowly began to feel that something in our household wasn't right. It was the first time I learned to question my almighty father, the first time I recognized how irrational and out of proportion his actions were. One day, after seeing my father yell at her at the temple yet again, I spoke up.

"Wh-why can't you just tell him no?" I asked my mother. "You're not doing anything wrong." Though I couldn't disobey him as his daughter, I figured that she could do so as his wife. Her eyes widened in shock.

"Kỳ Lý, don't be disrespectful. Have you forgotten that he's your father? End of discussion," she responded. But as she said that, I saw a sad smile escape from the corners of her mouth, a tiny glimmer of appreciation. It was enough for me to hold on to.

That day, and all the Sundays after, I stayed with her while she ate, refilling my own bowl to the top so that if my father tried to hurry her, I could say I was still eating and needed her company, to which my father would throw up his hands and stomp back up to the main hall. I wanted my mother to know that her suffering did not go unnoticed, that we were in this together.

"Here, take three to each altar," my mother said as she lit a bundle of incense sticks. "Before you set them into the censer, bring the sticks to your forehead and whisper your prayer. Remember to mention your name, age, and zodiac sign."

"What do I pray for?" I asked.

"Pray for intelligence, health, doing well in school, and filial piety, the basics."

We were on the second floor of the temple, in the prayer room. Few people ventured up to the second floor. But I loved it there. It was a much quieter and calmer space than the main floor or basement. There was only one statue in the room, and it was of Quan Thế Âm Bồ Tát, the goddess of mercy and compassion, standing atop a lotus. Rays of light beamed outward from a round and blue electronic contraption behind her head, her waist-length hair and the folds of her long and beautiful white dress swept to one side as if flowing in a soft breeze.

She looked down at me from atop her lotus pedestal with a sympathetic half smile. I gazed intently at her features and imagined they moved. I wanted to believe that she was somehow alive. Her name means "the one who listens to the sounds of the world." Was she really listening? *Nam mô Quan Thế Âm Bồ Tát.* I whispered her full name three times.

"My name is Trần Kỳ Lý. I am twelve years old, born in the year of the Earth Snake. I wish to be intelligent. I wish to be healthy. I wish to do well in school. And I wish to always be pious and loving toward my father and my mother." I paused and added, "I know I already asked for good health, but please, if there is anything you can do to fix my eyes, I would really greatly appreciate it. Thank you." I brought the incense sticks up to my forehead and down again three times before I inserted them into the large censer of ash at her marbled feet.

Then I watched as my mother shook a canister of wooden sticks in front of her, a ritual reserved only for the prayer room. People entered this room specifically to ask Quan Âm a question and seek divine guidance. My mother's question on this day was whether entering the nail salon industry was a good idea since our sweatshop days were over and my father's minimum-wage income was not enough to support a family of six.

She held the canister of sticks at its base and tipped it back and forth rhythmically until a single stick slowly rose up and fell out of the canister.

It was mesmerizing. I never understood the physics behind it. I knew only that magic was at work. Each stick was inscribed with a number that corresponded to a number on a shelf adjacent to the statue. There, my parents would find mysterious fortunes written in an ancient Vietnamese dialect with a translation at the bottom that always seemed to answer their specific questions.

My mother picked up the stick but did not look at the number. She grabbed two smooth and unadorned wooden talismans from a nearby podium, painted red on one side. She brought them together, whispered a prayer, then dropped them to the ground.

"To see the answer, the talismans must show their alternating sides," she explained to me. "If they both land with the red side up, it means I must rephrase my question. If they both land the other way, it means Quan Âm is laughing."

"Why would she laugh?"

"Because she knows that we both know the question is a ridiculous one."

But this time she wasn't laughing. The talismans showed their alternating sides. So now my mother looked at the number on the stick. Number 25. She walked to a shelf in the far corner of the room and searched for the number, coming back with a small rectangular piece of paper.

Her eyes lit up. "Let's go," she said.

She didn't show me the fortune, but the expression on her face told all, as did my father's when she showed it to him. And it was decided.

Our Sweatshop Era had ended and the Nail Salon Era had begun.

Though I hardly knew what was going on, had never even been to a nail salon or considered a manicure something one might do, I could sense my parents' excitement. Their faith in this plan was absolute. Over the next few days, my father sold a few more gold nuggets and registered my mother at the Christian Nail School at Thirty-Fourth Street, in Herald Square, where she would practice administering manicures and pedicures. She brought home bottles of nail polish and hundreds of fake plastic nails.

On nights when I'd finished my homework early, I would sit with my mother as she practiced her exercises and I'd go through her growing collection of polish, taking pleasure in reading the quirky names. Some bottles had regular names like the ones found in a crayon box, "Navy Blue" or "Carnation Pink." But others had names that stirred my imagination, like "An Affair in Times Square" and "Marooned on the Subway" or "Not in Kansas Anymore." I even invented a few of my own: "Winter in a Strange Land," "No Rice Grains Left Behind!" and "Sewing Machine Oil."

I would watch my mother rub the bottles back and forth between her palms as two steel beads rattled around inside. "I'm loosening up the polish and mixing it around," she said. "Otherwise, it won't look right."

Then she would practice applying polish. Holding a beautifully curved plastic nail between her left thumb and forefinger, she would take the brush out of the bottle, drag it in a downward arc to the left, then downward to the right, then straight down the middle, until the whole nail was filled in.

Wow, I thought, impressed at how smooth and shiny the polish looked and how quickly my mother had done it.

"Can I try?" I asked.

"Sure," she said, handing me a plastic nail and a bottle of red polish. "I'll walk you through it."

I followed her instructions, though I had to bring the nail up close to my eyes in order to see what I was doing. I could tell my mother was watching me intently, but I didn't mess up, and in just a few strokes, I'd painted the nail red.

"Wa, Kỳ Lý!" my mother exclaimed. "That's perfect!"

"Really?" I looked up at her wide smile.

"Yes, really! It took me weeks to learn how to do it properly and you got it on the first try. No drips or visible brush strokes or anything!"

I looked down at the little red nail, still glistening, and beamed. I was proud of myself.

And so it went. Every weekday evening, after I'd finished with my homework, my mother would give me lessons on the different nail shapes; how to cut, file, and buff them; and how to cut cuticles, remove dirt, polish, and design nails. We practiced cutting cuticles on orange peels the way they did at her school. Sometimes, I would chase Long around the house to get him to give me his hands as canvases to work on. He feigned protest, but eventually relented. When I was done, he would point one finger to his cheek, purse his lips, and flutter his eyelashes and we would laugh and laugh.

"You're a natural!" my mother said on more than one occasion. "Look," she said to my father one day after I had finished painting on a fake nail a scene with palm trees on a beach at night, a full yellow moon rising over the water, swallows in the distance. "Isn't she talented?" I looked up at him, expecting the rejection I was used to, but this time, he nodded with approval.

"Not bad," he said to my surprise. Approval was rare.

Call Me Diane

"WHAT PROTEIN MAKES UP the majority of the nail?"

"D. Gerateen."

"Hmm, you have the right answer . . . but it's pronounced ker-a-tin. It says here that it's a protein that is found in hair and skin too."

It's a Saturday afternoon, a few months after my mother began her courses. I am holding a set of stapled papers. My mother sits across from me, scrunching her face and looking upward, as though searching for the missing word behind the furrow of her eyebrows.

"Ger-a. Ker-a. Teen?"

"No, ker-a-tin. The *k* is breathy, like the way you pronounce 'cat' or 'carrot' in English. It's the equivalent of the Vietnamese *kh* sound."

"Oh, I see. Ker-a-teen."

"No, not 'teen.' 'Tin.' Like my brother's name in English, Thinh. Ker-a-t— Oh, never mind. Close enough. Next question. An individual with onychocryptosis has which type of condition?"

"A. Diet."

"No. It's B. Ingrown nail."

My mother was scheduled to take the National Nail Technology Writ-

131

ten Examination in a few weeks. Barely able to read English, she struggled with polysyllabic words, their dips and rises counterintuitive and case-specific. "Why don't they just use accent marks?" she asked me. "How do they expect me to know that I have to stress the third syllable in 'individual' but the second in 'refrigerator'? Does that make any sense?"

I thought about this "they" from whom she demanded answers and pictured a group of bureaucrats gathered around a wooden table heaped with piles of papers and books, dictating the proper pronunciations of multisyllabic words that would be impossible for my mother to say correctly. I had no answer for her. Unlike English, Vietnamese is a monosyllabic language, and there are accent marks that dictate exactly how a word should be pronounced.

"Much more logical to do it that way," she would tell me with pride in our mother tongue. So I took to putting accent marks over her study materials to help her pronounce the words properly, and I wrote out the Vietnamese phonetic equivalent for the particularly difficult ones. It worked, for the most part.

"I did it!" she said to me one afternoon when I came home from school. It was her third attempt. She was sitting at the dinner table proudly waving a yellow certificate. She was licensed and could now find work. "I've already called several nail salons today and they all want me to stop by. I'm going first thing on Saturday. And you're coming with me."

"Me?" I asked. "Why?"

"Because you know all the steps to a manicure and we need the help financially. And you can help translate."

"But what about Phu and Long? Can't they help too?" I'd been protesting my brothers' exemption from a lot of the duties that were expected of me for years now, but I never got anywhere with my mother.

"They are boys," she said, as she always did, as if that were reason enough.

"But that's . . . that's not fair," I said, frustrated that my mother found nothing wrong with her statement, that she'd declared it with such conviction. But I hadn't yet discovered the feminist language to argue with her.

It was April. For the next few weekends, I accompanied my mother to different nail salons all over the Bronx, Queens, and Brooklyn to ask for work. We didn't even try Manhattan. You had to be an expert to work there, according to people from temple who were already in the business. It was out of our reach.

I hated that I was the only one of my siblings who had to go to the nail salon, but no amount of complaining was going to change the situation. So I consoled myself by reframing the experience as something special that I alone could share with my mother. Growing up with only brothers, and observing the way my father often treated my mother, I always felt that she and I were a team, and this was yet another demonstration of it. Besides, I thought, it was a break from the daily monotony of school and home. I got to see more of the world around me than just Ridgewood, Chinatown, and the West Bronx.

But though my mother had passed the practical exam, she didn't have the experience. Basic manicures and designs were the only things she had learned to do in the Christian Nail School. We didn't have enough money to pay for the lessons that would have taught her to do acrylic nail tips, fillings, UV gel, silk wraps, crystal gel, and eagle claw nails. Customers in the salons we visited demanded all of those, plus rhinestones, advanced three-dimensional designs, and marbling techniques.

"That's where the money's at, honey," a client told my mother in a salon in the South Bronx where she had found work for a short time. I'd told the client my mother didn't know how to do tips and that she'd have to wait for the next available technician. "Nobody gets regular manicures around here."

This was an entire nail universe for which we were utterly unprepared. So the few shops that gave my mother a chance soon let her go when they realized she couldn't do more than a simple manicure.

However, there was one salon on Broadway Avenue in Brooklyn, beneath the Myrtle Avenue train stop, that was willing to hire her. It was a brightly lit salon with salmon-colored walls. Large photos of perfectly manicured hands adorned the room. "We're really looking for someone a bit more experienced, but I can teach you what you need to learn," the owner said. He was a lanky Vietnamese man with kind, sloping eyes. He spoke softly. "Why don't you sit at the last table down there and settle in?"

It was a cold Saturday in May, the ground still covered in a thin layer of ice. I'd brought my homework with me to do in between manicures.

My mother began to unpack the tools she had been training day and night to use, grateful for the opportunity to work. I sat on the bench where customers waited for their turn. My mother sat and waited too, but it seemed like all the customers already had their go-to nail technician. "I'm looking for Kim. She's not available right now? Okay, I'll come back." The owner would indicate that my mother was free, but the clients would decline.

Finally, on the fourth day, a young woman who was new to the neighborhood walked in. She was dressed in a navy-blue suit with a pink silk blouse underneath and a polka-dot scarf tied around her neck. Her shoes and purse looked expensive. The owner shuffled after her. He was aware that my mother was the only manicurist who was free, but he hesitated, looking around to see if any of the others were close to finishing. It occurs to me now that he must have thought my mother unfit to serve such a high-class woman. When he had observed that all his techs had either just started or were in the middle of their procedures, he sighed and finally said to the young woman, "Ms. Diệp is free to do your nails this evening."

"Ms. who?"

"Diane," my mother said, standing up from her table and waving. "My name Diane." When had she chosen this name for herself? I had no idea, but I liked it. It was no-nonsense, pretty—it suited her. Later, she would tell me that she had narrowed it down to Cindy and Diane, names that were easy for her to pronounce. My father helped her choose. He broke the names down into Vietnamese phrases that sounded similar. Cindy was Xin Đì, which meant *asking for oppression*, and Diane was Đi Ăn, which meant *go eat*. Diane was the clear winner.

"Good to meet you, Diane. I want a mani-pedi today with a burgundy red polish on both." She spoke with authority and walked straight to the pedicure stations, where she sat on one of the black leather seats, placing her feet into the bowl.

"Okay, okay, I do good job for you today," my mother said. She rushed to the bowl and turned on the water. In her nervousness and excitement, she forgot to pull up the woman's pant legs, the first step.

"Uh, excuse me. My trousers are all wet," the woman snapped.

"Oh oh, I so sorry," my mother said, and began pulling up her trousers.

"And this water is too hot," the woman said, splashing the water at my mother. It was a small splash, but degrading nevertheless. "What, is this your first day or something?" I stood up but didn't know what to say. My voice was caught in my throat. The owner stared nervously at us.

"No no. I sorry," my mother said, quickly turning the water knob this way and that to see which was hot or cold.

The client, succumbing to my mother's sweetness and readiness to apologize, added in a gentler tone, "All right. It's okay. It's been a long day. My pants will dry. I guess you gotta watch the pressure on that thing, huh?"

My mother smiled, grateful for the change in attitude.

I watched her trembling hands as she scooped two teaspoons of blue pedicure crystals into the swirling water. When my mother finally sat down to do her work, she did it slowly and meticulously, not rushing like the other nail technicians I'd observed.

Still, the client insisted on scrutinizing her every action.

"You missed a spot here. You didn't take off all the nail polish."

"Oh, sorry." My mother went over it again with a cotton ball soaked in acetone.

"I need you to cut the nail on this big toe shorter. And why is this one crooked? You need to refile it. Ow, watch where you're cutting. That was my skin."

"Lý, Lý!" my mother called out to me. "What is she saying? I don't understand. She is talking too fast."

From somewhere far away, I heard her voice calling to me, but Lý didn't seem to be a name I recognized. For a second, I didn't even know where I was, where my mind ended and my body began. They didn't seem to exist in the same space. But the feeling was momentary. My mother's voice pulled me back and I returned to the scene, overcome by shame.

I wanted so badly for my mother and me to disappear, to start over. It had started out as a new adventure but I didn't want to be in a nail salon anymore. Seeing my mother, now in her fifties, hunching over the pedicure bowl, hands trembling, unable to understand, unable to communicate, was almost more than I could bear. I prayed silently for a return of the cummerbunds. Even that was better than this. At least we were all together and we had fun. Where were my brothers now? Where was my father?

"Lý!" my mother called again. "What are you doing? Daydreaming? Didn't I just ask you to come here? I need help. I don't understand what this woman is saying."

I got up from my seat and walked over, reluctantly introducing myself to the client.

"I'm very sorry. My mother doesn't speak much English, but I can translate for you." As I apologized, I felt a burning sensation in my chest. This woman would never know who we were and where we came from. We were just a couple of clumsy immigrants working on her toes, not worthy of respect. I hated her. I hated her for sitting above us on that leather chair. I hated her for thinking that it gave her power over us. I hated that it *did* give her power over us. That money was power in this world and we would never be powerful.

Still, I translated.

"Wow, your English is not bad," the woman said, relieved that she now had someone to talk to. She told me she had just moved to the neighborhood from Canada. "But between you and me," she said, "I'm not too keen on staying. The neighborhood folk seem a little sketchy, if you know what I mean." She spoke almost as if we were friends. Had she forgotten the way she'd just treated my mother right in front of me?

Stranger still was that I smiled and responded to her in an equally friendly manner, speaking in a voice I did not recognize as my own. Why was I smiling? I didn't want to smile. Why was I so sweet to her? I didn't want to be sweet. Was it that I knew instinctively it was what I had to do? I despised myself for being unable to stand up to this woman, and in later days to all the other clients who mistreated my mother, for smiling at them even as I swallowed the words I wished I could say.

The rest of the day passed in a similar way. I translated for my mother. Customers were shocked that I could "speak such good English" and I had conversations with them that took their attention away from my mother as she worked on their nails, freeing her from their scrutiny.

At lunchtime, the owner ordered us Chinese takeout from nearby, which we were grateful for. Then it was back to manicures and pedicures. Customers really began to pile in and my mother worked while I watched and translated for what seemed an eternity. At eight thirty that night, the last customer sauntered in for a quick twenty-minute manicure, and then it was time to wrap up and go home. My mother spoke in hushed tones to the owner and he gave her the money she had earned for the day, though payday was actually a few days away. She took my hand and we left for home. It was a hard, trying day, but I was immensely glad that my mother didn't have to go through it alone, that I could be of some help to her. I wanted to protect her always, to be her shield, her crystal dome.

From her four manicures and three pedicures that day, she had made thirty-seven dollars and fifty cents.

"That's all?" I asked incredulously. "There's no way that's possible."

"It's split fifty-fifty," she explained. "The owner keeps half of my earnings. That's why your father and I want to eventually run our own place, so that we can keep all of our earnings and not have to answer to anyone." She sighed and looked up to the sky. "Can you imagine it, Kỳ Lý? We would be our own bosses."

I looked up at the sky as well, searching in the stars for my mother's vision. But I saw nothing but darkness and clouds.

A Brighter Place

THAT WINTER, AFTER HAVING us read about the Triangle shirt-waist factory fire of 1911, our seventh-grade social studies teacher, Ms. Valentin, brought our class to the auditorium to show us a documentary about child labor in Bangladesh. She wanted us to know that this kind of exploitation was still happening in other parts of the world.

She wheeled out a projector resting on a dolly. Scenes of five- and six-year-olds working in terrible conditions, beaten and starved, flickered across the screen. When the film ended, there wasn't the usual chatter that often erupted from a group of middle schoolers who'd had to sit still for an extended amount of time. No one uttered a word as we stared at the blank screen. Finally, the class clown blurted out, "Yo, that's real messed up, Mrs. V."

I was outraged by what I'd seen, somehow not registering the irony of the fact that my brothers and I had been child laborers too. Cummerbund materials still littered the floor of our living room. My parents hadn't gotten rid of them just in case the sweatshop jobs came back. In the stillness of that auditorium, however, I focused only on the injustices I'd seen on that screen, on the sad eyes of the children forced to work like slaves in factories and plantations. Of course, if I'd thought about it more deeply I might have made some connection between what I'd seen on-screen and the little assembly line in my very own home. But my brothers and I hadn't been sad. We'd actually managed to make a game out of our work. It was true that the hours were long and the labor was arduous, but we'd done it as a family, and no one had kept us out of school to do it. We'd felt a sense of accomplishment too.

I couldn't say the same about my mother's work in the nail salon. That was another connection I could have made—but didn't, even though I had seen how little she earned, had helped her give manicures even though I was still a child, and had even given them myself. I had seen how people treated her, how degrading it was for her to have to put up with demanding clients who cursed her out when they were unsatisfied, who spoke to her in a condescending tone, or who didn't pay if they didn't feel like it. But all that never occurred to me while I was in school. It was probably just easier for me to look outward than inward, as it had always been.

"I wish we could do something," I whispered to Maryana, a friend sitting beside me.

"What can we do?" she asked.

"I don't know. Let's make a club or something," I suggested, half joking, half serious. She nodded vehemently. After class we brought the idea to Ms. Valentin, who supported our idea. Our homeroom teacher, Ms. Elmoznino, assisted us in crafting a vision for the club. We recruited five more members and named it the Against Child Labor Club of I.S. 93. Our mission was to raise awareness throughout the school about the exploitation of children in other countries around the world. We looked up UNICEF statistics. In 2001, there were an estimated 250 million children worldwide working in hazardous and abusive conditions. We decided our goal would be to raise as much money as possible and use that money to support a child in Bangladesh.

We held meetings before and after school. We held bake sales and raffles outside the cafeteria. We handed out brochures and flyers. I remember standing one cold December morning on the stage of the school auditorium with my fellow club members belting out the lines, "We are the world, we are the children . . ." It was the refrain to the 1985 hit song "We Are the World," by Michael Jackson and Lionel Richie. Though the lyrics of the song were originally written to raise funds and bring awareness to a widespread famine in Africa, we felt it spoke to our cause too.

But as winter came to an end, the final remnants of blackened ice in the streets melting away and fuzzy buds suddenly appearing on the tips of branches, our fervor began to wane. Soon, members stopped showing up to meetings, and we could no longer convince our fellow classmates to contribute to our weekly Entenmann's bake sales. Gone were the corny sanctimonious glances we exchanged with each other in the hallways.

I don't know what happened to the money that we raised or if it ever made its way to a child in Bangladesh as we had hoped. After some time, we stopped checking in, and our once-ambitious endeavors fizzled out. But for a brief moment, I remember thinking that despite my age and my own poverty, I too could help make the world a brighter place. And I was also excited by the realization that I'd had the ability to influence my classmates, that they'd responded to my suggestion that we form a club. Maybe, I thought, I was no longer just an outsider.

Willpower

I WAS STRUGGLING IN math, to my father's disdain. This was his domain. It was the subject he had excelled in as a child, and he demanded excellence from all of us. But the super squint was no longer working for me, even in classes where I was in the second or third row, or even the first row. I was nearing the end of seventh grade, and my grades were beginning to slip. Although much of the work was easy enough and I could figure most things out by studying harder at home, the math escaped me.

"Stupid stupid stupid," my father said one evening as I asked him for help with my homework. "This is so easy and you still don't get it? What an idiot."

"But I can't see the board in class!" I cried out in desperation. *I am not stupid*, I tried to convince myself. *I am not stupid.*

He slammed his fist down on the table. I flinched. "Not this bullshit again," he said. "Tell me, how is it that Long also 'needs glasses' but still makes good grades?"

I looked down at my tear-stained notes. I didn't have an answer. How *did* Long pull it off? Later, when I questioned Long about this, he told me that he had trouble seeing very far away, but he could still see the board with no problem. This left me even more confused.

"Eh, we all went through this," Phu later told me. "Whose class are you in this year? Pastuszka's? Yeah, she's a tough one. Don't listen to Father. He called all of us idiots. You'll be fine."

Though Phu's interest in academics at the time was waning, replaced by his love of sports, he excelled in math. He took advanced calculus classes in school and received top marks. But as much as I wanted to believe him, I wasn't fine. I had begun missing assignments because I didn't see them written on the board. I had intense headaches and felt dizzy all the time. I had no one to turn to; it never occurred to me that I should tell anyone at school. Even though I couldn't see and was aware that some of my classmates wore glasses, I did not question my father, still somehow believing that glasses were a government conspiracy. I was too afraid of my own ignorance to speak up.

Maybe I really am just stupid, I said to myself. *But if I could see, I could understand the work. I'd done so well up until this point. So that means I'm not stupid. Right? Yeah, but if Long could do the work even though he also needs glasses, what does that mean? It means that I am stupid. So Father's right after all.*

The internal dialogue never let up. I began to retreat into myself again. On the surface, I was still behaving the way I normally did, still smiling and laughing and hanging out with Veronica and Avery and other friends I'd made, but there now seemed to be an odd sensation that I was looking out at the world through a window deep inside of myself. I no longer felt connected or engaged.

My brothers, at this point, all knew about my struggles with my eyesight, as they had heard my father yell at me and threaten to beat me on more than one occasion for bringing it up. They remained mostly silent on the issue, afraid that my father might beat them too. I didn't blame them.

But before he left for college, Thinh told me a story about how

Bruce Lee, the famous Wing Chun martial artist, recovered from a spinal injury within months. Doctors predicted that he might never be able to kick again or even walk without the use of crutches. But he recovered completely.

"How did he do it?" I asked.

"Sheer willpower, Ly. Your eyesight is only a manifestation of your mind. Look up eye exercises and dedicate yourself to training. If Bruce Lee can recover from a spinal injury, you can train your eyes to see again."

After hearing that story, I was filled with a sense of hope. I ran to the library to research ways to strengthen eye muscles, such as massaging the area around the eyes to improve circulation, or alternating between focusing on a point close to me for ten seconds and one that was far away for ten seconds. I printed the instructions out and read and reread them ad nauseam, committing them to memory.

"Place your palms over your eyes. This will relax your muscles, and tension in the optic nerve will be released . . . Focus on a point close to you. Then shift your focus to a point far away and count to ten. Repeat this five times for each eye . . ."

At night, after constructing the crystal domes for everyone, which I'd gotten really good at doing, I'd lie in bed and go through the steps, pressing on my eyes and imagining their slow improvement as I completed my eye exercises. I began to lose sleep. I was afraid that if I stopped, I would never get my eyesight back. *Just a few more*, I kept telling myself.

Just a few more. And then you'll be able to see again.

But the eyestrain headaches became worse. No matter how much I squinted, no matter how many nighttime eye-strengthening exercises I did, my eyes were failing me.

"Ly, I believe I asked the class to work on the 'Do Now' problem on the board," Ms. Pastuszka said at the beginning of Advanced Algebra one day. It was May. I had been staring out the window, lost.

"Oh, sorry," I said, embarrassed. I looked at the board again, trying to make out the letters, but it was no use. It was all a blur. The boy who usually sat next to me was absent that day, so I couldn't glance at his notebook, as I had started doing. Still, I picked up my pencil and pretended to write so as not to catch Ms. Pastuszka's attention again. After some time, she clapped her hands.

"All right, folks, show me whatcha got." She called for volunteers to solve the problem. Hands shot up in the air.

"Hmm, actually," she said, "let's hear from someone we haven't heard from. How about . . . Ly?"

My heart stopped. I froze in my seat. I looked up at her, begging silently for her to let me go. *Nam mô Quan Thế Âm Bồ Tát*, I recited in my head. *Please, not me. Anyone but me.* But it was too late. She was expecting an answer.

"U-umm," I stammered. I needed to make something up, to show her that I at least tried. "Six?" I chose my favorite number. Six for six members in my family. Six for being born on December 6 in the lunar calendar, December being the twelfth month, a multiple of six. And six for the sixth letter of the alphabet: *f*, for flowers, for friends, for faith.

Ms. Pastuszka stared.

"Excuse me?" she asked.

"Six," I mumbled and looked down. Of course, if I could have seen the problem, I would have known that the answer should have been in the form of an equation. But the jig was up.

"Ly, could you hand me your notebook, please?"

I reluctantly obeyed. She stared at the notebook, at the heading on the page in neat cursive, and at the glaringly empty space underneath.

"Ly, what is going on? I thought I asked you to complete the 'Do Now' a few minutes ago. What have you been doing this whole time?"

Silence. I felt all my classmates' eyes on me. My body went numb. I felt myself going into a space where it was calm and peaceful, warm waves lapping at my feet, sunshine kissing my skin. *Where is this?* I thought, not really caring about the answer.

"I said," she repeated in a loud and staccato tone, "what . . . were . . . you . . . doing?"

I blinked and I was back in Advanced Algebra. Back to Ms. Pastuszka and back to the pain of being admonished for a problem I couldn't control. *Don't you understand?* I screamed at her in my head. *I can't see the fucking board! And the goddamned government is after me!*

But another Ly took over instead.

"I guess," I heard myself saying to her with a shrug, "I guess I just didn't feel like doing it."

"Excuse me?" she asked again.

"I said I didn't feel like doing the 'Do Now.'" My legs shook underneath the table. A collective gasp issued from my classmates.

"Go to the principal's office," Ms. Pastuszka said through gritted teeth. "Now!" she barked.

I quickly gathered my things, and though my legs threatened to buckle at any moment, they still carried me out of the classroom.

In the school hallway, I slumped against a wall, collecting myself. Then walked to the principal's office, filled with a kind of perverse pride. I felt momentarily empowered. Some part of me knew my father was wrong, but I hadn't yet learned to challenge his authority, not even in my mind. Pretending not to care about school gave me a way out. I could avoid admitting to myself and to others that my all-knowing father was, in fact, wrong about my eyesight and wrong about glasses. And I could avoid the feeling of powerlessness that would come from such a realization.

I walked on, armed with this false sense of strength, the sound of my shaky footsteps echoing against the walls of an empty hallway.

Betrayed by Our Tongues

THAT SUMMER, I ACCOMPANIED my mother to work every day. By then she had found work at another salon in Far Rockaway, Queens, where the salon owner offered her sixty percent commission instead of fifty. She jumped at the offer. My father had found Long part-time work in his factory for the summer. Phu was getting ready to go to college. He had been accepted to Pace University in the Civic Center of Lower Manhattan, which meant he would be living at home. So everyone was busy.

I was grateful to be done with the nightmare of school. Despite the deterioration of my eyesight and the misery it caused me, I had somehow survived the last marking period with only a slight dip in algebra. And I had made it into the advanced eighth-grade class. That would give me an edge on getting into a good high school when I graduated middle school, I thought, so I wasn't just relieved but thrilled.

For now, however, my focus was on practicing manicures and pedicures and translating for my mother when she needed it, which was not very challenging. But the summer was not without its own nightmares.

One hot August afternoon in Brownsville, Brooklyn, at another salon where my mother had gotten an even better deal, this one a seventy percent commission, I sat and watched her as she cut a woman's cuticle. My mother was nervous, sweat dripping down the sides of her face. The woman was severe and demanding.

"Hello?" She waved a patronizing hand in front of my mother's face. "Did you not hear what I just said? You missed this spot right here." She pointed. "I want these fingers clean."

"Yes, okay," my mother said.

"What about this one right here?" The woman pointed a long, curved nail at the finger in question. "You didn't cut any cuticle offa that one. What did I just say?" But my mother *did* cut the cuticle for that finger. I watched her do it. I opened my mouth to say something, but nothing came out.

"Okay, okay," my mother replied. The woman shifted this way and that in her chair, trying to get a good look at my mother's handiwork, bringing her fingernails close to her eyes every time my mother made a cut, making it doubly difficult for her to do her job.

"Hello?" the woman said loudly again. "Is this your first time or something? You ain't doing nothin' for these fingers. You speak English? Excuse me, can I get somebody else to do my toes after this? This bitch don't know shit."

"Okay, okay, I do for you. Don't worry," my mother said, her eyes pleading.

"Mom," I whispered in Vietnamese, shaking. "Just stop doing her nails. She can't talk to you like this. She's saying bad things about you."

The woman glared at me. "Hey. You talking shit about me?"

"Okay, it's okay. I do for you, don't worry," my mother said again. Then, in Vietnamese, to me, she whispered, "Lý. Don't make this woman angry. I can take care of myself. We need the money."

"But, Mom, she can't—"

"Whatsa matter? You got a problem?" The woman glared at me, her eyes bold and menacing. "She don't like me?" she asked my mother. I wanted to say something, but again I couldn't find my voice. I was only thirteen years old and she frightened me.

"Kỳ Lý!" my mother hissed. "Go home now. You are no help to me." She turned back to the client and smiled widely. "Sorry," she said to the woman. "My dawduh go home now. I do for you, don't worry."

The dismissal lodged itself in my throat like a sideways pill, the bitterness lingering no matter how many times I attempted to gulp it down. I grabbed my things in quiet indignation and left.

I heard the woman's voice trailing behind me as I closed the door. "Dammit. This one here still got some shit on it."

Outside, a light summer rain was falling on the graffitied storefront buildings across from the salon. Dope addicts sheltered beneath store awnings, bent over like horseshoes, their arms hanging limply, almost touching the ground. The humidity made my hair stick to the sides of my face. I made my way to the train station with leaden feet, gripped with anger and humiliation. A manicure was only five dollars. Why didn't she stand up to that woman?

It occurred to me that my mother's weak command of English may have helped her withstand the insults of her clients. If she didn't understand what they said, she wouldn't feel the humiliation of it. For her, ignorance truly was bliss. I mulled this over as I sat on a wooden bench in the Sutter Avenue train station waiting for the Manhattan-bound L train. There were two men nearby who were also waiting for the train. I barely noticed them, preoccupied with my disgrace and a small fly buzzing nearby. After some time, the Canarsie-bound train arrived and one of the men climbed the stairs to the platform while the other stayed, pacing back and forth.

We were now the only two people in the station. The sudden intimacy made me notice the man's odd appearance. His head was completely shaved, and he had large silver earrings along the rims of both ears. His face was haggard, though he appeared to be only in his mid-twenties. He was tall and skinny, wearing a black logo shirt and black parachute pants that starkly contrasted with his pale white skin. As though sensing my attention, he stopped pacing back and forth and looked directly at me, a grin spreading across his face.

I lowered my eyes and kept my head bowed, hoping he would go away. My heart began to pound in my chest. After what seemed a long time, I picked my head back up to see where he had gone, but the station was empty. I breathed a sigh of relief and sat back on the wooden bench, this time focused on a stain on my jeans above the knee.

But after a few minutes, I felt something next to me and glanced up. It was the same man, who was right in front of me now, this time with his genitals hanging out through a slit in his parachute pants, a few inches away from my face. I froze in terror, unsure what to do. He moved forward and pressed the pink flesh to my cheek and then over my mouth. I pushed it off and quickly stood up. I wanted to scream, but I couldn't find my voice. My heart pounded even more loudly against my chest, my knees shaking violently beneath me.

The man backed away with the same menacing grin on his face and began advancing toward me again. I ran as fast as my legs could carry me past him, toward the turnstiles and the station attendant's booth beyond them, waving to the man in the kiosk. But even in my terror it didn't occur to me to go *through* the turnstiles and exit the station altogether. It would have been a waste of a MetroCard fare.

"Excuse me, sir," I croaked as loudly as I could to get the attention of the station agent, since he was at least ten feet away from me.

He took some time to respond, turning a page in his newspaper before he looked up. The seconds crawled by and I dug my nails into my hands to keep from breaking down. "Yes, miss, what is it?" he said into the speakerphone.

"I—that man—he—" I couldn't speak. How could I put into words what had happened? What exactly could I say?

"Excuse me?"

I whirled around to point the man out, but he was gone.

The station agent stared at me briefly, asked no questions, and simply shrugged, returning to his newspaper. Defeated, I walked back to the wooden bench and sat down again, tears pooling in my eyes. A loud beeping from above signaled the arrival of the Manhattan-bound L train. Stunned and weak-kneed, I walked up the stairs to the platform, relieved to be going home.

But as the train pulled into the station, the man suddenly appeared in front of me again, this time with his hands jerking inside his pants. I opened my mouth to scream, to say something, anything, but again, my voice eluded me. People were coming out of the train, but no one appeared to notice what was happening. He had pressed his whole body up against me, my back against the platform wall. After a few moments of struggling, I managed to get away and made a run for it. His arm lurched out and grabbed at me, but I wriggled free and ran back down the stairs toward the turnstiles. Again, ever careful about wasting a subway fare, I didn't exit, but I figured I was safe because I was in a place where I would be visible to the station agent. Although the man was now nowhere to be seen, I couldn't risk going back up to the platform, so I stayed where I was, crouched down by the turnstiles.

Once I felt physically safe again, in view of the station agent, I didn't want to replay the scene in my head to try to figure out what had happened. I didn't want to know. I didn't want to believe that there were sick people in this world and that I had just encountered one or that it had happened because my mother worked at a nail salon in a dangerous, crime-ridden neighborhood, and my brothers weren't with me and neither was my father. I wasn't angry. I couldn't afford to be. What would that anger do? Even as I sat there, somewhere in the recesses of my mind, a door swung shut on that experience and the key was thrown away, not to be found again until much later in my life.

Instead, I drifted off to a world where I lived a different life, a world where I could see, where we had enough money, where rude women didn't insult my mother, where my brothers were with me, my mother was with me, my father was with me. And we were all happy. I don't know how many hours I stayed there, daydreaming. I stayed until night fell, until my mother arrived to catch the train home from the nail salon. She found me still crouched in a corner by the side of the turnstile.

"*Ủa?* Kỳ Lý? What are you doing here?"

I looked up feebly. "Waiting for you," I lied.

"What? Why would you do that? You waited all this time? That was hours ago. Look, you're so pale. You must be hungry. Come on, let's go home." She took my hand and led me up to the platform. It felt nice to hold her hand.

At home, I couldn't hold down anything I ate. I was running a fever, so I went to bed early.

"Lý, why did you wait for me in that train station? Look at you now, sick. Medicine is not cheap, you know." She sat down on my bed, sighed, and stroked my hair. "That woman today was so mean, wasn't she? In the end, she made me do all that work and then left without paying me. I should have listened to you." She clicked her tongue and stroked my hair. "But what could I have said anyway? My English is too weak."

I lay in bed, defeated, tears sliding out of the corners of my eyes. Each of us had been betrayed by our tongues, a voicelessness from which neither of us could escape. I wanted to reach out and hold my mother. I wanted to tell her that everything was going to be okay, that we were going to make it, that we were so close to reaching the American dream, to big backyards and white picket fences, to fancy clothes and fancy dinners out, to never having to lower our heads and bite our tongues.

But I couldn't. Because I knew it would be a lie.

Part III

Summer 2011. Pitkin Nail Salon

Thank the Buddhas

I WAS BEGINNING TO feel growing pains, an aching in my knees, the first signs of puberty taking place in my body, but my metamorphosis was slow. By the time I was in the eighth grade, I'd been listening to the girls in my classes talking about periods and pads for at least two years. I never joined that conversation because I thought any discussion of bodily functions was dirty and refused to listen. My parents had opted out of sex education for the four of us every year. It was not a mandatory class and my parents' vehement opposition to it made it clearly taboo. As a result, I had no idea that I, too, would eventually menstruate. No one ever told me.

This was also why I didn't really understand what had happened to me in that subway station. When the man exposed himself to me, I knew it was bad—something "dirty," something terrible—but nothing about what it meant. Sex and sexual urges were completely foreign territory to me, sexual harassment and assault even more so.

In the locker room before gym class most of the girls were already in bras and they would change into their gym clothes in front of each other. I changed in the bathroom stalls, embarrassed that I was both unable to afford a bra and lacking the chest to fit into one. A handful of other girls did the same. When our gym teacher became aware of this, she decided to take points away from anyone caught changing in the stalls. I imagine she thought she was aiding in the development of a healthy self-esteem, but instead it was just yet another instance in which I felt I was being punished for something I had no control over. Panicking, I went home and asked my mother to buy me a bra so I could start changing in front of the other girls too.

"That's nonsense. You don't need one. You don't even have a chest," she said. But, sensing my distress, she handed over one of her old bras. It was a yellow and frayed C cup.

"What is that?" Some of the more well-endowed and not-so-nice girls pointed and snickered when I took off my shirt to change, revealing my mother's bra dangling over my small, flat chest.

After that, I always wore my gym clothes underneath my regular clothing. I was insecure about the way I looked, about the way my body was developing. Since my parents still couldn't afford to take me to a hair salon, my father cut my hair, just as he'd been doing since I was a toddler. The "style" was always the same, short and uneven, trimmed at the back with a razor, not that different from the haircut he gave my brothers. I was feeling less and less like a girl and more like an awkward stick with arms and legs and a pimply face.

Neither could I join the girls in school when they talked about their crushes. I didn't know what it was like to have a crush, having never had one of my own nor allowed myself to think about boys or girls in that context. In any case, I had to devote most of my energy to trying to figure out how to see again, my myopia leaving me a very small and oppressive space in which to navigate the world.

On the rare occasions when one of my brothers wasn't rushing me to get out of the bathroom, I'd stand in front of the mirror, press my face to it, trying to measure every inch of the girl I saw, to make sense of her somehow. She had the same ugly and uneven bobbed haircut I had, her face round and pimply, her body scrawny, her chest flat. But something just didn't add up. Was the whole of my existence summed up in this reflection that I couldn't recognize as my own? Pressed so close against the glass, I could only see one part of myself at a time, and never the whole. The mirror wasn't broken, but the result was the same.

And as my vision became further impaired and the headaches increased, not only did I not recognize the girl in the mirror—I could barely see her.

I joined a chess club in school to distract myself. Mr. Dechongkit, the chess club adviser, would sometimes take a group of us to a nearby pizzeria and order us food. We would talk about anything and everything. Mr. Dechongkit made learning fun and made us feel like he was one of us. He had a great sense of humor and our group meetings were always full of laughter, especially my own. Those days, once I got started laughing, I couldn't stop—something I seemed to have inherited from my mother—which caused others to erupt into laughter as well.

Chess was the perfect escape, something I was halfway decent at, and something I could share with my brothers too. There was an order to the game, rules that I could understand, a board I could see, and moves that I could make to ensure a desired outcome. My favorite piece was the knight. Its movement was awkward, and its power different from that of the other pieces, as it could jump over pieces in a strange L-shape and sneak up on the opponent unnoticed.

Long and I had a tally pinned onto the wall, a scorecard of our chess games together. We played a lot of chess those days on our paper-and-coins board. At first, Phu was also on this tally, but we began to see less and less of him, as he started spending all his evenings hanging out with his many friends or playing in handball tournaments throughout the city. It was his way of escaping, his way of defining himself in the world without the pressure of my father's incessant admonitions and Thinh's shadow looming over him. And then it was just Long and me and our chess games.

All the while, I was looking forward to high school. It would give me a chance to start over. New beginnings always gave me hope. Maybe my eyes will be fixed by then, I thought, as I prayed obsessively to Quan Thế Âm Bồ Tát. At night, I was still massaging the area around my eyes and doing my eye exercises. I still believed that if I did them enough times, my vision might improve.

That fall, I took a test to apply for the specialized high schools of New York City, which included Stuyvesant, Bronx Science, and Brooklyn Tech. Thinh, Phu, and Long had all taken it, unsuccessfully, and now it was my turn.

"Don't bother," my father told me. "Your brothers didn't make it in, and they're boys." Maybe he was just trying to steel me against disappointment, but I couldn't shake the resentment of being considered lesser than my brothers simply on the basis of my sex.

Though I had little faith I could prove him wrong, I knew that these schools accepted students solely on the basis of the test score, and since I doubted that my grades alone would be good enough to get into any of the other schools of my choice, I'd decided that the best way to keep all my options open was to take the test.

That day, I walked nervously into the exam room, silently chanting the names of all the different Buddhas and bodhisattvas for guidance. It was a difficult test, particularly the math section. My limited vision had made it hard for me to absorb much of the math I'd been taught for the last two years, and I soon lost hope. By the end of the test period, I had run out of time to complete the final section. There were twenty-three questions left that I had yet to answer when the proctor called time.

"Okay, pencils down, everyone! Time's up."

Everyone else put their pencils down. I felt ready to cry. Somewhere in the depths of my mind, I heard a voice saying, *Don't leave any questions blank. If you don't know, better to bubble anything in.*

Against the rules, I picked up my pencil and quickly bubbled *B*'s and *C*'s into the rest of the Scantron form.

"Hey, didn't I say pencils down?" I heard a voice say loudly. "What are you doing? I could disqualify you right this second." I looked up to see the proctor standing by my desk, glaring down at me. He yanked the Scantron from beneath my pencil.

But he was too late. I had already bubbled in my answers. My hands trembling, I tried to look as innocent as possible, as though I hadn't heard the time call. He shook his head and rolled his eyes as he walked away with a pile of Scantrons and test booklets in his hand.

I put my head down and cried. It was over. There was only that one chance, and I had blown it.

I suppose there was a benefit to the way my parents approached our academics. No one at home was counting on me to get into the specialized high schools, so no one was particularly disappointed when I told them I probably hadn't. Aside from sleeping and eating, the only things that mattered were making money, saving money, and keeping ourselves afloat financially.

One day in mid-March, my mother came home from work with a big smile on her face. She began lighting incense sticks for the altar.

"Kỳ Lý, we're going to be business owners!" she told me.

"What do you mean?"

"Lisa wants to sell me the space." Lisa was the owner of the Brownsville salon where my mother had been working since August.

"Sell you the space? Really? Why?"

"Tired, I guess, and I don't blame her. She's in her sixties, after all, and just wants to go back to Vietnam. Anyway, she told me she'd sell it to me for twenty thousand dollars, equipment included."

"Twenty thousand dollars? Do we have that kind of money?" I asked, bewildered by my mother's calmness.

"Trust me, twenty thousand dollars is nothing. Your father has eight thousand saved up, and the rest she said we could just pay her with our earnings from the salon. Your father has already sold all the gold, deposited the cash, and given her a check."

I was stunned. Just like that, we had become business owners. The feeling I had when my father first brought home our car washed over me once again. I was incredulous. Business owners? That kind of thing didn't happen to people like us. When my mother had talked about being her own boss a few years earlier, the dream seemed so out of reach. And yet, here we were.

After my parents had finalized the transfer of the salon from the previous owner to us, I accompanied my mother to our first day as business owners. Was this our big chance? I thought on the way there. Were we finally going to get ahead? Of course, I'd already seen the salon the previous summer when I tagged along to learn the trade and to help translate for her, but I'd completely forgotten what it looked like. It was someone else's salon then, so I didn't care as much to take in the details. But when we arrived at the salon, my heart sank as it dawned on me that, of all the salons in the world we could have had, this was the ugliest, dirtiest, and most run-down salon I'd ever seen. I stood there in embarrassed silence while my mother busied herself with cleaning the place up.

"Can you believe it?" my mother said. "Our very own salon!" She was sitting on a metal stool by the pedicure stations, resting one elbow on a knee, chin in hand, knuckles straining against the thin translucent latex gloves she'd put on.

Though the details were lost on me, edges and colors bleeding into one another, it was easy to get a sense of the place. As I followed the path of my mother's gaze—from the dilapidated manicure stations to the peeling sky-colored walls and down to the floor, covered in a buckling dark gray carpet full of discarded nails, cuticles, and cotton balls—I didn't share her awe at our good fortune. I was repulsed. *This* was ours now?

Behind her, a black leather massage chair loomed above a soapy pedicure basin. She swiveled around on her stool and pushed a button on the side of the basin to activate the jets. Clouds of foam instantly formed, bumping into each other as they eddied on the surface of the water. Despite the lavender soap she'd pumped into the water, the stuffy odor of dead skin still hung in the air.

"We'll do this every morning," she said aloud to herself, making a mental checklist. "We're going to keep it clean." Then she shot me a look. "Well, don't just stand there. Help me out! Grab a broom! Stop daydreaming."

Thin tubes of fluorescent light pulsated above me, flickering occasionally. As I searched for a broom and more details came into view, my disgust only grew. There was truly nothing to recommend the place. It was small and narrow. Three battered and polish-stained manicure tables were lined up against one wall, with a fourth facing the entrance. The glue beneath their veneer had long since lost its adhesive power, so that if you walked too close, a panel would snag your pants before releasing you and snapping back. An irregular-shaped sheet of wood, cracked and haphazardly painted, served as a partition between the tables in the front and two pedicure stations at the back. And right at the dividing line, the dull carpeting gave way to a gray-and-white linoleum floor missing a few tiles.

It was clear that no attempt had ever been made to hide the salon's hideousness, that it had never been loved, could never even euphemistically have been described as having "character."

But to all this, my mother seemed immune. I wondered briefly if I should say something, if she could see what I saw, but I kept my mouth shut. If she didn't notice, I reasoned, it would be cruel to point it out. And if she did, even more so. *It's only the beginning*, I tried to tell myself for her sake. *Give it a chance. Things will get better.*

I found a broom and dustpan by a sink in the back. My mother paused in her cleaning to watch me as I struggled to sweep dust, cuticles, and nail clippings from the floor. The clippings caught on the nap of the carpet and jumped in different directions.

"Don't press the broom so hard into the carpet," she chided. "That's why they're scattering all over the place. Lightly sweep them into the pan. That's it. There we go." She sighed and shook her head. "You need to keep practicing. This is a woman's duty. People will laugh at you when they see a girl who doesn't know how to properly sweep a floor. Or worse, they'll laugh at me for not teaching you properly. Is that what you want?"

I sighed. "No, I don't want that," I said. And it was true. As much as I dreaded being there, I still wanted to be the girl who knew how to sweep. I still wanted to be the girl who made her mother proud. Lightly, lightly, I told myself.

A thick, familiar scent drifted through the room. My mother had begun to burn incense for a makeshift shrine to Quan Thế Âm Bồ Tát.

"This is the beginning of our answered prayers," she said softly to herself. "Here, child." With one powerful wave of her hand, she put out the flames and handed me three sticks of incense, their tips glowing orange. "Pay your respects. We have much to be grateful for."

I climbed up on a brown metal folding chair to reach the shrine, then inserted the sticks into a plastic cup of rice grains on a wooden shelf. Behind the cup hung a framed illustration of Quan Âm, dressed in flowing white robes, standing atop a pink lotus blossom. I observed her closely, but without the deference I once had.

There was a time when I believed that she would keep me safe, but my faith had waned. Where was she last year? Or the years before that when I called out her name again and again, I thought, as I stepped back down to the floor. I could almost hear my mother scolding me for having lost my faith. I looked over to her, tidying bottles of nail polish on a shelf on the wall, determined and proud.

I returned to the task at hand. Lightly, lightly. I was getting the hang of it. The carpet was looking much cleaner than before, my little dustpan filling up with debris. The more I swept, the more I began to feel little glimmers of my mother's hope seep into me. Yes, even if it wasn't the most luxurious salon in the world, I supposed we could make it work. "Business owner" had a nice ring to it. Both Thinh and Phu were in college now, and Long would be next. We even had a car. We were almost there. Almost American.

"This is it, Kỳ Lý," my mother said as she wiped down the inside of a plastic drawer with a wet towel. Her sleeves were rolled up, her forearm muscles tensed. "You'll be working for me from now on. How do you like that?" She looked over at me and smiled. "You're going to have to take care of the customers when I can't. No more training, okay?"

I nodded obediently, not wanting to let her down.

"Good girl," my mother said.

Later that spring, a raspy voice announced over the loudspeaker that the results for the specialized high school entrance exams were in and that the letters deciding our fates would be handed out momentarily.

"Yo, Ly, heard the results were in today. What score you got?" Long asked when he came home from Brooklyn Tech that afternoon. Though Long had not made it into any of the specialized schools when he took the test, he'd scored high enough that school officials at Brooklyn Tech allowed him to take a summer "discovery" program. The deal was that if he did well during the summer, he would be granted admission. Long was just as ambitious as Thinh was academically, and he knew how important a good education was. So he'd worked hard that summer and Brooklyn Tech had accepted him in the fall.

I took out the envelope I had received from my teacher, which I hadn't had the nerve to open. Long grabbed it from me before I could see what the letter said.

"Oh, shit. Sorry, man, you didn't make it."

I felt my heart sinking. My father was right. I tried to take the letter back from Long, but he held on to it. "Yeah, man, your score was way low."

"Shut up," I said. "Give me that."

Then he burst out laughing. "Yo, you should see the look on your face! It's fucking hilarious. I'm just kidding, man. Congrats! You did it!" He gave the letter back to me. There was a graph showing my score and the different scores needed to get into each of the specialized high schools. A single line was highlighted.

Somehow, I had made it into the Bronx High School of Science. Long held out his hand and we did the silly secret handshake we'd come up with years ago. It was an elaborately choreographed sequence of moves that involved shaking hands, then sliding them apart and balling them into fists that we bumped up and down against each other, up and down, before ending in the classic knuckle-to-knuckle fist bump. I couldn't believe it. That I'd made it into a specialized high school was something to be proud of. That I'd made it into the Bronx High School of Science, which required a score higher than Brooklyn Tech, was a feat. But that I was a girl and the only person in my family to have done this was nothing short of a miracle.

"Pure luck," my father said.

"Thank the Buddhas," my mother said. "You couldn't have made it in without their blessing."

They Call Me the Tattoo Man

IT HAD JUST FINISHED raining, an afternoon sun shower, sudden and quick, lasting only about fifteen minutes. East New York and Brownsville were now refreshed, their energy livelier, the heat momentarily abolished by the rain. A greenish light fell on the glistening streets as people wove in and out of homes and shops, ambling through the streets with a renewed sense of being.

Inside the nail salon, my mother ripped sheets of paper towels in half, twisting the halves into coils that would later be used to separate freshly cleaned toes so that the toenails would not accidentally brush up against each other and ruin the polish.

It was June, a few months after we had gotten the salon, and business was still slow. Clients did not yet recognize or trust us. I had been cleaning a set of my tools with rubbing alcohol when a stocky man appeared at the entrance, peering in as if unsure this was the right place. I gestured for him to come in. Drops of water slid off the man's inked arms and glistened in the waves of his gelled black hair. He had a distinct look. He was light-skinned and heavyset, with a square jawline and a goatee. Three silver earrings adorned each ear.

"Man, that rain came from outta nowhere!" he said loudly, disrupting the silence of the salon. "Mind if I get some paper towels to wipe this shit off?" he asked. "My daughter's right behind me. She wanna do her nails."

My mother nodded to me from the back end of the nail salon, where she was done twisting the Bounty halves and had moved on to washing one of the pedicure basins. A roll of paper towels on a metal stick attached itself to the right corner of each of the manicure desks. I ripped a few sheets off a roll on the desk I was sitting behind and handed them to him. He thanked me and sat down on one of our metal fold-up chairs.

I watched as he wiped the excess water on his hair, face, and arms. He wore dark blue overalls attached only on one strap so that the other flapped down over a black tank top, which showcased the work done on his burly arms. His left arm appeared to have an oriental theme: Twin geishas decorated his biceps. Red-and-white floral fans spread across the bottom half of their faces, shrouding them in mystery. They stood with their backs against each other, donning delicate colorful robes. The blue-and-green scales of two large koi fish encircling one another provided the background for the geishas as other variegated patterns unfolded into the scene like origami paper, covering his entire arm.

His right arm was less elaborately illustrated. The background was not as colorful or patterned, mostly just a blackish blue filling in the spaces. Midway between his biceps and triceps, there was an image of a girl with a big head of short black curls and a small body, scantily clad in a red tube top with red heels.

"You know Betty Boop?" he asked me, tracing my gaze to his arm.

"Uh, no," I said, quickly looking away, embarrassed that he had caught me staring.

"You don't know Betty Boop? Everyone knows Betty Boop. That's her," he said, pointing at the little seemingly half-naked girl on his arm, flexing as he did so. "That was my first. I had my girlfriend hold a mirror up to my arm to do it. Her face is a little lopsided, Betty Boop's, I mean, but still, not bad for a first, eh? Then came this one," he said, pointing to a dancing skeleton in black with a pirate's hat on top of his skull.

"You did all that yourself?" I couldn't help asking.

"That's right, honey," he said as he leaned back into his chair with an air of pride. "They call me the Tattoo Man. I got my own business and everything. Wish I could give you a business card and shit, but I'm all out."

Just then a girl walked in who very much resembled the Tattoo Man. Her arms and neck were covered in tattoos. She wore a red plaid button-up tucked into her ripped blue jeans, with the sleeves rolled halfway up her forearms. She came right up to my desk and sat down in the chair facing me, making a loud thump as she sat.

Her presence was like her father's. It seemed to take up the whole salon. Though the rain had stopped, beads of water appeared on her nose and forehead. She was fanning herself with an advertisement card she had in her hand and breathing heavily. Her green eyes reflected the light in such a way that they looked wet, and she wore a messy auburn bun tied loosely at the nape of her neck. I turned on the fan a few feet away and set it blowing in her direction at the maximum speed.

"Thank you . . . so much. You . . . have . . . no idea . . . how good that feels . . . ," she said in between gasps of air. "Pops . . . you walk too fucking fast. I told you . . . to slow down."

"And I told you to lose weight. Ain't my fault you fat."

"Ay, shut up, stupid," she said as she reached over and slapped him on the arm.

"Girl, do that again and Imma beat you," he said, showing her the back of his hand.

"You see that?" she said to me. "Fucking child abuse, right?" They both burst out laughing. "Nah, just playing, just playing, me and Pops is best friends . . . Right, Daddy?"

I smiled at the strange scene. I'd never seen a daughter and father interact that way.

"Yeah, whatever," he said and rolled his eyes. "Listen, you got a card for the girl? We was talking about the business and I'm outta cards. I'll call Oscar for some more."

She took out a card and handed it to me.

"So can I get my nails done?" she asked after catching her breath. "Just filling and design. I don't think I need a new set of tips. Whatchu think?"

I looked over at my mother, who nodded to let me know that I could take on this customer. I examined the girl's long nails and decided a filling was okay for right now. I wiped off her cracked nail polish with a cotton ball of acetone. The polish was caked on thick and it took several cotton balls to take off all the polish. I didn't mind. I enjoyed their company.

Father and daughter bantered back and forth. Warming up to me, they included me in their conversation and I was happy to be a part of it. They were Puerto Rican. He told me that when he first came to America, he was a teenager and took on a few delivery jobs, but when his bills were too difficult to manage, he decided to go into the tattoo business with a friend of his, which paid better and meant he could work from home. Then he met his wife and had his daughter and two boys. Now he was teaching all of them the art of tattooing.

"Yeah, he always be experimentin' on me when he gets new ideas. See this one?" She lifted up her shirt to show some kind of blue flower that peeked out from the folds of her belly flesh. "He messed it up, 'cause he was drinking and smoking at the same time, so it came out mad weird-looking. He thinks it's, like, abstract or whatever the hell." She cracked up and dodged a few balled-up paper towels her father threw at her.

Grateful for their stories, I wanted to return the favor. I searched my dusty catalogue of memories and thought of the first time my father discovered Starr Playground on Onderdonk Avenue, about fifteen blocks from our apartment. It was our first summer here in New York, and my father was adamant about taking his children outside. "We have to take them somewhere," he told my mother. "They'll die staying in the house all day." For my father, even the smallest preoccupations existed in the realm of life-and-death. So my mother called Mrs. Six and asked if she knew of any nearby parks she could take the children to. *Công viên* Starr, she told my mother and gave her the directions.

When the six of us arrived after what seemed like a particularly long journey (it was the first time we had ventured somewhere outside the vicinity of five or six blocks), my brothers dispersed quickly onto the playground, climbing onto the rocking bridge and sliding down the slides. I wanted to play with them too, but my mother said I was too young. Seeing my disappointment, my father walked me over to the swings. He picked me up and put me in one that was made for toddlers. "Get ready," he said and gave me a hearty push.

A big rush of wind against my face, I found myself high up in the air. The upward motion was exhilarating. But I stopped at the apex of the swing, and began to fall backward very quickly. Frightened, I cried out for my mother. "No," he said to her as she rushed over. "Don't worry," he said in a gentler voice to me. "Look, it's fun. Don't you think it's fun? I'm right here. I won't let you fall." He continued to push me. "There we go. Don't be scared."

In the air, I looked down and saw both my parents' faces, on them an expression of utter delight. I heard the peal of my brothers' laughter on the jungle gym. They were happy. And I was no longer scared.

But so much time had elapsed since that moment of happiness, of affection, and it was such a small, intimate memory, it didn't seem like something that could possibly be of interest to my customers. I stayed quiet as the Tattoo Man threw another ball of paper at his daughter, which she skillfully ducked at the expense of one of the designs I had been painting.

"Whoops," she said, laughing. "His fault. Don't worry about it. Ain't nobody gonna see that smudge anyway. It's a little thang."

As she was done drying her nails underneath the two mini-fans on my table, he paid me and handed me a two-dollar tip.

"Yo, this design is dope." She spread her fingers wide in front of her father's face.

"Girl, you betta get them shits outta my face if you know what's good for you." The Tattoo Man swiped at her fingers, then turned to me. "If you ever want a tattoo, you know who to see." He winked. "Let's go, Jess. Hurry up. We gotta go pick up your brother."

"I'll be back, Miss Ly," she called out as they were leaving. "Peace!"

I looked down at the card, crushed and wet from the rain. It was black with the words "THE TATTOO MAN" emblazoned across the front and a number on the back. For a moment, I considered: maybe a simple outline of a turtle. Or a small elephant on some discreet part of my body.

"Don't even think about it," my mother called from a corner of the salon.

Back on Track

GALILEO SOLEMNLY PLACES HIS hands on a globe. To his left, Archimedes, in a toga and sandals, brandishes an oversized screw. Behind him, Newton holds an apple in one hand and a rolled-up scroll in the other. All the way to the right, Marie Curie examines a small vial in her left hand. Telescopes, microscopes, prisms, and skeletons fill the background. Three robed men representing the Sciences occupy the middle ground as a central godlike figure wearing a blue robe reigns over the whole scene.

The sixty-three-foot Venetian glass mosaic mural, called *Humanities Protecting Biology, Physics, Chemistry*, is the work of Frank J. Reilly, and it looms large over the entrance lobby of the Bronx High School of Science. At the base of the mural, encircling it, is a quote from John Dewey: "Every great advance in science has issued from a new audacity of imagination."

It was July, my first time on campus, my first time traveling all the way to the Bronx by myself. I stared up at the mural in awe. As I entered the building, a security guard at the front desk directed me to the auditorium on the main floor, where the incoming students would be given their schedules.

As I sat waiting for my name to be called, I glanced around nervously. The other students looked so much older than me. Everyone seemed better dressed, more relaxed, comfortable with where they were. Some were seated with a group of friends, while I saw no one familiar. A few had taken out books to read. Others were catnapping in their seats. So bold! I thought.

I had received a letter a few months before that invited new students to take summer courses if they wanted a head start on their freshman year. Aside from perfecting my skills as a manicurist, I had nothing else to do, so I signed up to take Health and Music Appreciation. I wanted to be as prepared as possible in the fall. It was a new beginning, and this time, things would be different. I was going to have my feet planted firmly on the ground and not let anything deter me from doing well in school, not even my failing eyes.

Thinh had come back that summer for a visit and we were all together again for the first time in what seemed like forever. I told him proudly about my acceptance to Bronx Science and he was pleased to hear the results. I wanted his approval almost as much as I wanted my father's. His presence brought warmth and color back to the family as we gathered around the dinner table. My family was complete again.

"High school is way harder than middle school," Long warned me. "It's a lot more work. You better be ready for it." Of all of us, Long had become the most accomplished academically, surpassing even Thinh.

"Eh, don't listen to him," Phu said. "It's not that bad." Looking at him across the table, and comparing him to Long and Thinh, I realized I hadn't noticed how big he'd gotten. He was working out every day, his body striated with well-defined muscles. He was captain of nearly half a dozen teams at Grover Cleveland High and brought home huge trophies every year from his sports tournaments. But he didn't care much about academics, so I was more interested in Thinh's opinion about high school. Like Phu, Thinh didn't think I had anything to worry about. He advised me to just do what I had to do and I'd be fine.

"Nah, they're just saying that 'cause they didn't go to better schools," Long said. Having managed to get himself into Brooklyn Tech, he'd become a bit of an elitist, which Thinh and Phu did not take to kindly. But I didn't doubt that Long was right about the coursework being more challenging. This was a specialized high school, after all, and I was determined to give it my best shot.

I went to my classes every day, motivated to do well and get ahead. I trained myself to focus on listening to every word that came out of my teachers' mouths. It didn't matter that I couldn't see the board. I took copious notes, and I vowed to myself that I would speak up this time and ask classmates for their notes, not to copy but to see if I had missed a crucial piece of information. I was surprised at how kind they were, how willing to share. I got to know a number of students that way, and over time I got better at note-taking myself. Sometimes, people even asked to borrow my notes, which made me feel proud of myself and gave me the confidence to think that I might be able to get through the rest of school despite my world growing ever more dim and murky.

My efforts paid off. I soared through those summer courses with near-perfect grades.

As a result, the first day of freshman year was not as daunting as it might have been. Hundreds of students lined up in the courtyard waiting for the doors to open.

"Ly!" A group of kids I recognized from my summer Health class waved me over. I waded through the crowd to get to them, grateful to be remembered and included. Then I noticed another familiar face in the crowd, a boy with freckles and braces and a head full of curly hair. It was Michael, a classmate of mine from middle school. Though we hadn't been close, he waved to me and I walked over.

"Hey," Michael said. "I was looking for you."

"For me?" I asked. "Why?"

"Because we're the only ones from 93 who made it here. We gotta stick together, man."

I smiled. Already, the year was shaping up to be a good one. I was starting to make friends. Michael and I were in geometry class together and we were seated right next to each other. And all my classes, though challenging, were manageable. Because I had taken the summer courses, I had two free periods that fall, which allowed me to focus on assignments that required more time to complete. Teachers were impressed with my performance, and my winning streak continued for the rest of the semester. I was succeeding. The tides were finally turning.

A Thing or Two to Learn

SCHOOL WAS OUT FOR spring break and I had joined my mother in the nail salon. We had owned it for almost a year by now. Although I was initially nervous about taking on my own customers, I'd gotten pretty good at manicures and pedicures and fell into a nice rhythm of work as I practiced my small-talk etiquette with customers.

One afternoon, we were saying goodbye to a woman who had been coming regularly for tips and fillings every two weeks.

"Call me Red," she said to us. "Errybody call me Red. I had red hair once. Dyed, you know, and it just kinda stuck. At first I didn't like it, but then I realized you never gonna have power over what people call you or how they see you. You gotta go wit da flow."

She stood in the doorway rummaging around for money in her black snake-embossed purse, her hair, now blond, shaved close to her scalp. "Dang, I ain't got no tip money today. I'll get you later, Diane," she said as she put a cigarette in her mouth and walked out the door into the brisk spring air.

My mother was cleaning her tools, oblivious to the woman's departing remarks. It was rare for customers to tip us. But we didn't mind.

Tips were a luxury. It was hard enough getting properly paid for our work, let alone getting tipped for it. There were many times when, after my mother or I had finished a set of nails, a customer "didn't have enough money" or "damn, I left my pocketbook at home" or "shit, could you wait right here while I go out to the car and get some change? Imma be right back . . ."

"Don't worry, Kỳ Lý," my mother would tell me when a customer walked out on us. "Don't dwell on it. Their lives must be that much harder than ours."

That day my mother was feeling good about the way things were going. She was now averaging three to four clients a day at Pitkin Nails, with three or four times as many over the weekend, when I pitched in to help. My father would often join us as well on the weekends. Though he didn't know how to do manicures or pedicures, he would have a client sit at one of the stations while he took off their nail polish. That way, he could stall for time while my mother and I finished up with our clients.

We weren't making much money, but with my father's wages from the factory we were able to get by. "There'll be more, Kỳ Lý, don't worry. You'll see."

As she did every morning, she lit incense sticks and prayed to the framed picture of Quan Âm on our makeshift altar. "Please send us kind customers today," she'd say softly under her breath, holding three incense sticks in both hands as she brought them up and down, up and down, in prayer, the long yellow-and-pink sticks sending thin swirls of smoke and waves of scent through the air of the salon.

This was always her prayer, and sometimes it worked. We had lovely clients on some days. My favorite was a regular named Sheila. She was the very first client my mother had when she started working for Lisa. A diabetic woman in a wheelchair, Sheila needed someone who was careful and gentle to do her manicures and pedicures. After my mother worked on her, she swore she would never go to anyone else ever again. For Christmas, she handed us both twenty-dollar bills.

"This too much," my mother protested.

"Bet you never seen this kinda tip before, have you?" Sheila said with a twinkle in her eyes. "Ah-ah, I'm not taking that back. Don't hurt my feelings now, you hear? I want the two of you to buy yourselves a nice Christmas gift this year. You hear me? Y'all deserve it." My mother and I both cried.

But other times, the prayer didn't work.

After Red left, a woman walked in wearing a hot-pink tank top tucked into tight blue jeans. Her large breasts spilled out of her bra, outlined beneath her shirt, and she had a blond wig with bangs that reached the top of her eyelids and moved with every blink. She looked at the laminated pricing chart we had hung on the wall beside the door, then sat down in front of my mother and held out her hands across the table.

With an icy glare, she said, "Full set."

Enrique Iglesias's song "Hero" had just come on the radio. My mother was excited. She loves Enrique.

"You like song on radio?" she asked her client. "I like very much. He good singer."

But the woman stared at her, lips pursed and jaw clenched. It was a look that my mother sometimes received when she tried to engage with her customers. It was a look that bothered me immensely. Whenever I discussed this with her, she would say, "What look? I didn't see anything. You think too much, Kỳ Lý." But I couldn't stop feeling outraged. How dare she look at my mother that way? Would it be too much to have a brief conversation with the woman directly across from her?

Just then another customer walked in.

"Manicure!" the customer sang softly. "Remember me? I was here three weeks ago. I think a woman named Diane did my— Oh, there you are! Well, you seem busy today and I'm in a bit of a rush, but how about you?" She directed her gaze in my direction.

I gestured her toward the chair in front of my table as I stood up to prepare a soak bowl for the manicure. When I returned, she was on the phone. I took the unoccupied hand. She smelled like lilacs in the summertime and had honey-smooth skin and long, elegant nail beds. She spoke quietly on the phone as if she were telling a secret to the person on the other end.

I was happy to work in silence, content to listen to Enrique on the radio and focus on what I was doing. Her hands were easy to work with since they were regularly manicured. Over at my mother's table, however, her client was giving her a hard time.

"This isn't even."

"Can you cut this a little more?"

"Now you've cut it too short!"

"Can you pass the file over on this side one more time?"

"Okay, okay, no problem," my mother said.

Oh no, I thought. I silently wished, as I often did those days whenever my mother had a difficult customer, that we could switch. She had suffered enough in her life. She was already abused at home. Why did she need to be treated poorly at work as well? It wasn't fair.

My client, done drying her nails under the little fans on my table, stood up and reached slowly and carefully into her purse so as not to smudge her nails. She pulled out a dollar between her thumb and forefinger and placed it on the table. Then she winked and left silently, still listening to her phone. I moved toward the back end of the salon to wash and sterilize my equipment, while observing my mother's progress from a distance. The woman was silent now, simply staring out the door as my mother designed the last of her nails and began to apply the top coat. I began to feel sleepy, the lull of the late afternoon tempting me with a nap. After I had placed my tools in the sterilizer, I climbed onto the nearby pedicure chair and closed my eyes.

But the reverie did not last. I again heard the woman's voice criticizing my mother's handiwork.

"I don't like it," she said after my mother had applied the last coat of nail hardener. I opened my eyes and peered over. I wished she would just leave already.

"Okay, I do for you again," my mother said, reaching for a cotton ball and the acetone bottle. She took the woman's hand into her own, but the woman quickly drew back.

"Get offa me!" she yelled, and knocked over my mother's bottle of acetone. She jumped up. So did my mother. Hearing the commotion, I leaped from the pedicure chair, nearly slipping on a wet spot on the porcelain. The woman stood over my mother, glaring, one hand on her purse and the other clutching her car keys. The color had drained from my mother's face, her lips ashen. Wisps of gray hair fell across her lined forehead. My mind was racing, but I didn't know what to do. I didn't know what to say. My voice was caught in my throat, but then I found it.

"Wait," I said, walking up to the woman to examine her nails. "What don't you like about them? Just let us know and we can fix it for you. I'll redo them for you, no charge."

I studied the beautiful nails my mother had just finished for her. It was a full set of long acrylics that she had already spent an hour or more to complete. The woman had requested two colors on each nail, hot pink and a metallic royal blue, a process that required my mother to paint each nail completely blue, then paint a layer of hot pink over half the nail at the tips, which she had done with great precision, her lines perfectly straight with no sign of blue showing beneath the pink. A white wispy design with golden glitter shimmered across each nail.

"Fuck you," the woman spat. "Y'all can't do nails for shit. I'm getting the fuck outta here."

My mother stood her ground. "You-you no pay, I call police!" she managed. She grabbed the phone from inside her desk drawer and held it up as evidence of her resolution.

The woman took one step backward, knocking over her chair. Then in a fit of spite she hurled the bottles of polish that lined the wooden tiers on my mother's manicure station to the ground, accidentally brushing three of her nails across the white laminated wood and leaving it smeared with traces of hot pink, blue, white, and a sprinkling of glitter.

"Fuck!" she muttered, and finally made her exit. My mother stared at the nail polish bottles on the dusty carpet, one of which hadn't been properly closed and was now spilling out into a tiny puddle of hot pink. I took a paper towel from the roll on my mother's desk and bent down to retrieve the bottles and clean up the spillage.

"*Không sao đâu, Ý,*" I began to say from under the table. "It's okay, Mom. We—"

"Lý, call the police," my mother said. "I'll follow her while you dial."

"What?" I asked, incredulous. "No, just let it go, Mom, please." But my mother was not about to let it go. She was already halfway out the door with the phone still in her hand.

"If you don't call, I will," she said and walked out.

I stood up, replaced the bottles, and followed my mother out the door. I instantly spotted the woman a quarter of the way down the next block. She was leaning through a car window chatting with the man inside, completely oblivious to us. It clearly never occurred to her that we might pursue her.

"Lý, Lý!" My mother tugged on my arm. "Look," she said, pointing to a nearby deli, "there are two police officers in that store. Go ask them to help us."

I stared down at the ground, visions of cummerbunds and ties flashing across my mind. I wished again that I were back home with my brothers, sitting on the linoleum floor turning those ties outside in.

"Go now," my mother insisted. "Before she gets away."

With leaden feet, I walked into the deli. The police officers, a man and a woman, were by the counter, finishing up their purchase.

"Excuse me," I said in a feeble voice. "My mother and I need help."

They looked down at me and said in unison, "What's the problem?" Though they looked intimidating, they both had warm smiles.

"We work in a nail salon up the block, and that woman," I said as I led them out of the deli and pointed to the woman across the street, "that woman didn't pay us after my mother did an hour's work on her nails."

"Oh, another one of these," the policewoman said with a roll of her eyes. "All right, all right, let's check it out."

They walked over with us and the policeman whistled at the woman.

"Come over here a second," he said, his voice booming. "We wanna talk to you."

The woman glanced up nonchalantly, then, realizing that she was at the receiving end of the command, immediately soured her expression. "Oh . . . fuck, what they tell you?" she said, ducking out from under the roof of the car.

"This young lady here says you didn't pay for those nails," he said.

"Oh yeah? She told you that?" She glared at me. "Well, that's right. I didn't pay 'em 'cause they done fucked up," she said, holding up the hand with the smeared nail polish for the officers to see.

"I don't know . . . ," the policewoman said. "That looks like an easy fix. The rest of it looks nice." I felt my spirits soar. I looked over at my mother, who stood with her hands crossed over her chest, indignation written across her furrowed brow. I wanted to hug her and tell her it was going to be all right.

Suddenly, the man in the car got out. Standing with his legs shoulder-width apart, arms folded across his chest, he nodded to the police officers. Moments later, others joined the scene, a small crowd of twentysomethings with gold chains, do-rags, and baggy shirts. They nodded at the policeman with gravity, and he nodded back. He bent and whispered something to the policewoman. She nodded. It was a domino effect of nodding. She abruptly turned to us and said, "Hey, listen, her nails are clearly messed up. You can't expect her to pay now, can you?"

"Yeah," the policeman said. In speaking to us, both the police officers turned their backs to the bystanders, as if to shield us from the group. "Just let it go. I know you worked hard on them, but some battles you just don't want to fight. How long you guys been in the neighborhood?"

"Almost a year . . . ," I said, still trying to process what was happening.

"Yeah, you got a thing or two to learn about Brownsville. Some situations you're better off steering clear of. You know what I mean, don't you?"

"Lý, what is he saying? I don't understand."

"Let's just go, Mom," I said. "They can't help us."

"Why? You are police!" My mother voiced what I could not bring myself to say. Her eyes flitted back and forth between the officers, her hands spread out in front of her. "You no help us? Why?"

The policeman stared at her blankly. "What did she say?" he asked his partner. She shrugged. And with that, they turned and left. The woman and her posse also left.

Later that night, when my father came to pick us up, my mother and I relayed the story to him. But rather than sympathizing, he shouted at us: "What is wrong with the two of you? Are you stupid? Why are you causing trouble? You call the police and who knows what will happen! They'll throw all of us in jail! Idiots, both of you!"

My mother looked over at me in shock and confusion.

Then a bitter smile spread slowly across her face, and she threw her head back and laughed.

The Blood Bowl Sutra

THE VENERABLE AND PIOUS Mục-Kiền-Liên, one of Buddha's closest disciples, uses his powers of worldly transcendence to search the realms for his deceased parents' souls. He finds his father's soul resting peacefully in the heavens, but he cannot find his mother's soul. When he finally asks the Buddha for guidance, he learns that his mother's soul is trapped in the depths of a special hell made for women. Shattered by the thought of his beloved mother suffering, he journeys to hell to save her.

When he arrives, he finds his mother sitting on a bed of nails, shackled to the ground with a bowl of blood balanced on her head. He tries to feed her a ball of rice, but the rice turns to flames before it reaches her mouth. When the Lord of Hell raises the platform on which she sits, the bowl of blood tips over, drenching her.

Mục-Kiền-Liên weeps for his mother. He looks around at this dark underworld and hears the anguished cries of countless other women condemned to the same fate.

"Why?" he asks the Demon Lord of Hell. "Why are there only women here, and no men?"

"Because," the Lord of Hell explains as he again raises the platform, "women alone soil the earth with their unclean blood, which leaks monthly into the rivers and streams and eventually into the ceremonial tea that good and spiritual men prepare for the gods. Women must suffer for their defilement. It is their fate."

Hearing this, Mục-Kiền-Liên begs the Demon to forgive his mother, to allow him to take her place. The Demon refuses, but is so touched by a son's love for his mother that he allows Mục-Kiền-Liên to perform a thousand merits on her behalf. This will free her from her bloodied damnation and allow her to be reborn as a man.

"But what about the other women?" I asked my mother as she once again recited this story, a story I'd heard many times before.

"What about them?"

"He only asks for his mother to escape her fate, but what about the other women? Shouldn't they escape as well? They don't deserve that either."

"Oh, Kỳ Lý, but we do. We're inherently dirty. That's why you must wash your undergarments by hand. That way, you don't soil your brothers' clothes. Look, I wash my undergarments by hand too," she said, pointing to a rack where she had hung recently washed underwear to dry. "Before, you were too young, so I washed it for you, but now that you are getting older, this is what you have to start doing. Besides, you have just started menstruating. Now you are dirty."

I was fourteen, sitting in the bathtub, both mortified and frightened. Moments before, I had confessed to my mother that I was going to die.

"That's not something to joke about, Kỳ Lý," my mother had said, at which point I burst into tears and showed her several pairs of bloodied pants.

She examined the pants with an amused look on her face that left me puzzled. How could she smile when something so horrific was happening to me?

"My little girl," she said, putting her arms around me and laughing. "This is nothing. You're not dying. You're just menstruating. Wow, at so young an age too! I was eighteen when I first started menstruating. I thought I'd have a few more years before I talked to you about it, but I guess it's all this American food you're eating."

And it was then, as I sat there, confused by what she had just said but no longer thinking I was going to die, that she told me the story of Mục-Kiền-Liên—the same story she'd told my brothers and me countless times to remind us of what it meant to honor one's parents. But this time, for obvious reasons, she emphasized the blood. In some versions, the women are even forced to drink their own menstrual blood or demons will come to tear their limbs apart.

Today, I wonder how many women (and men) have passed this story down to their little girls through the ages—a story originating in twelfth-century China that has stood the test of time despite everything we now know about the role of the menstrual cycle in reproduction. It's fascinating to me that such a story could ever have been believed to be true, even more fascinating—and depressing—that there are people in this world who still believe it, and that one of those people happens to be my own mother.

Later, in high school, when I took biology and finally learned about the reproductive cycle (which, of course, all the other girls had already learned about in the sex education courses my parents didn't allow me to take), I would use this language of science to challenge her, and her brow would furrow under the strain of conflicting ideologies. One made more sense, but the other had the advantage of existing in the realm of the parables and fables that guided so much of my mother's life. And she had lived too many decades with this belief to give it up. For me, the science easily outweighed the power of myth.

And yet, as I sat in the tub that day, the word "dirty" reverberated through my mind like a ripple across the pond of my tenuous identity. It would be a long time before I was able to separate myself from it.

Hey, Beautiful

I SUPPOSE NOT BEING able to see affected my ability to perceive beauty. From a young age, what made things beautiful—what made a girl pretty and a boy handsome, what made an outfit stunning and a hairstyle cute—was lost on me. All I could see were blurry shapes and faces, so I thought beauty was nothing more than an artificial construct. In that, I was supported by the Buddhist notion that nothing in the physical world exists, that all things in this three-dimensional realm are illusory. So when friends asked me if I thought someone was hot or sexy, I didn't know what to say. At some point, people started calling me asexual. Which bothered me, mostly because it was just proof of yet another thing that I lacked.

But I couldn't escape thinking about it. Working in the nail salon, I was surrounded by women and men who spent a lot of time and paid a lot of money to be beautiful. Beauty was something to strive toward, something to possess, something that could elevate one's position in life. Was beauty something even I could possess? I asked myself. When there weren't any customers around, I would examine myself in the mirror, standing so close I would fog it up with my breath. I wondered about what others saw when they looked at me, and I wished that I could see myself through their unbroken eyes.

By now, the summer after my freshman year at Bronx Science, our nail salon was overflowing on weekends: mothers and daughters, boyfriends and uncles, grandmothers and grandchildren, career women and partygoers, all crowding into the cramped room.

Seeing how overwhelmed we were as the only manicurists in the salon, even my father started to help us with a few mani-pedis, though having received no formal training, he wasn't very good at it.

On one busy Saturday afternoon, I was working at the second manicure desk from the entrance, my father at the first. He was carelessly slapping thick layers of acrylic onto his client's nails. His glasses had started once again to slip off his face because they were held up by only one temple arm, the other having broken years ago. So he had positioned himself in a way I'd come to associate with him—face up, chin jutting out, to try to keep the glasses on his nose. The girl he was working on turned around to her friend to mouth the words "What the fuck?" as she gestured with her other hand in my father's direction.

Meanwhile my mother was at the pedicure station working on someone's feet, the nails turned upward with a thick yellow layer of fungus between the nail and the nail bed. All ten of her toenails were infected.

"I want you to fix my toes," the woman said with an accent thick and slow as molasses. She wiggled a set of ten very long and elaborate fingernails my mother had done for her the previous week, showing off. She was a regular.

The condition she had on her toenails was a mix of nail psoriasis and a fungal infection. It was painful and unsightly, and not uncommon in our salon. The fungus often spread via use of unsterilized equipment and unclean pedicure basins. I knew from working with my mother at other salons that sterilization was often not a priority for them, because it was all about how many customers you could handle and how fast. Sterilizing meant slowing down. But that never influenced my mother.

Her ideas of honor and justice were too ingrained, and she never once abandoned them despite the enormous amount of pressure and competition from her coworkers. When we finally had our own space, she taught me to be vigilant about sterilizing the equipment. "It doesn't matter if you have several clients backed up. Make them wait. Don't let money make you forget how to be a good person," she reminded me.

But despite our strict sterilization efforts, fungus was unavoidable because other salons did not adopt the same practices. Clients would arrive at our door and ask us to fix the problem. But the damage was already done. Our job was to clean and cover it up as best we could with nail polish. We were beauticians, not podiatrists.

In truth, I preferred working on damaged nails. I reveled in the process of transformation. There wasn't any sense of accomplishment in working on a set of perfect fingernails or toenails. Though she found this odd, my mother welcomed it, since she herself disliked working on fungus-ridden feet. Normally, it would have been I who was doing the pedicure on my mother's customer that day, but because I was already in the middle of working on someone else when she came in, I couldn't.

Once I'd finished the manicure and sterilized my tools, I walked back to my station and beckoned to the next client. It was someone I recognized. He was a regular biweekly client whose name I have blocked from my memory, although he was someone I once thought of fondly.

Tall with waist-long dreads that he tied back using two of the locks, he wore an oversized graphic tee over baggy jeans. He had smooth sepia skin and light hazel-brown eyes that shone with an intense curiosity.

"Oh, hello!" My mother waved to him. He flashed an exuberant smile and waved back. Always cheerful, he had endeared himself to my mother, who made a point of personally offering him water on hot days.

"Hey, Beautiful," he said, sitting down at my table.

I smiled at the compliment. That was his line, "Hey, Beautiful," and he never failed to say it.

"Nice to see you again," I said. "The usual?"

"You know it," he said, and spread out his fingers. A car mechanic, he hated having dirty nails, and he had been coming to us steadily for the better part of two months after discovering our salon.

I prepared a soak bowl for the manicure, using warm water and a few drops of soap to loosen the dead skin. I went through the steps silently, as I normally did, speaking only when necessary or when spoken to. I understood that the salon was a place of refuge for many, a place where they could retreat within themselves. I wanted to give my clients the choice about whether to initiate conversation. During past manicures, the man had shared stories about himself and relayed some of the local news from the neighborhood. He also sometimes asked me questions about what I was learning in school and other, more personal questions like how many siblings I had, what my hobbies were, and if I had a boyfriend. Today, however, he was quiet and watched my movements intently.

All around us, people chattered on, telling each other about the latest celebrity gossip—*Can you believe they still be talking about Janet Jackson's wardrobe malfunction?*—about Cecily's new baby—*Cute lil' pumpkin weighs eight pounds!*—and what they were going to wear to Junior's upcoming birthday bash. Babies cried, hyperactive toddlers were yanked by the collars of their shirts and told to sit down and stay still. The radio was loud, and some clients requested that we turn the volume even louder, yelling above the music at each other, bobbing their heads up and down to the beat and drumming their fingers on their thighs or the tables.

It was a hot summer day and I was wearing a pair of jean shorts and a sleeveless black T-shirt. Our air conditioner didn't work, so we had purchased two oscillating pedal fans and turned them to the highest setting, aiming them at our customers. Still, the heat was stifling and oppressive.

Suddenly, I felt his hand brush against my thigh. Thinking nothing of it, I apologized and moved backward in my chair. I continued to snip away at his cuticles. Again, I felt a light touch. I giggled nervously, hoping it was just another accident, and moved my legs again. This time, I felt his hand caress my upper thigh, just where my shorts ended. I looked up, startled, still half smiling. But his gaze made me uneasy, and I understood then what was happening. My smile disappeared. I didn't know what to do. I tried to move my legs completely out of the way, but a firm hand kept one of my legs in place. I began to sweat profusely.

I looked over at my mother, her back still bent over the woman's toes. I thought of calling out to her, but felt the need to protect her from the scene. I didn't want her to know what was happening. I looked over at my father, beads of perspiration dripping down the side of his face as he struggled to see what he was doing. He was having a hard time too. I looked back at the man, who was staring intently at me, his hand firmly gripping my thigh.

"Stop," I said softly.

"What?" he said. "What's wrong? I'm not doing anything." The question made me doubt myself. Was I imagining this? He flashed a toothy grin that revealed something lustful and sinister that I had never noticed before. He released his hold on me. I felt the blood flow into my face.

I caught a glimpse of the picture of Quan Âm on our makeshift altar out of the corner of my eye. And I prayed silently for the man to keep his hands off me. I worked as quickly as I could.

"Please wash your hands," I said quietly after administering the final step. He grinned, got up, and walked to the sink. I breathed a sigh of relief. It was over. I watched him warily as he walked back to the table. He seemed like the same person he had been for the two months I had known him. Again, feelings of doubt crept into my mind. Maybe there was nothing wrong. Maybe he was just being friendly.

"How much I owe you, Beautiful? Ten?"

I nodded.

He took out a ten-dollar bill and five singles, rolling the singles up. "And this is for you, Sugar." He winked. "See you all next week," he said to my mother and father. My father nodded. My mother waved goodbye and called out a thank-you. And just like that, he strolled out of the salon.

I stared at the clump of singles in my hand. It was the biggest tip I had ever received, aside from Sheila's twenty-dollar bill that one Christmas, and I didn't know how to feel. Though every fiber of my being had writhed in misery just moments before, I was also thrilled by the money. I was even more confused when I saw the expressions on my parents' faces after I handed over the dollar bills.

"Wow, five dollars? Good girl!" they said. "You must have done such a good job!"

I wondered what they would think or do if they knew the reason behind the tip, but I didn't want to cause them any pain or trouble. If I could preserve their happiness by staying silent, I thought, then I should.

Months passed, during which the man continued to make his biweekly visits. I tried to anticipate his visits so that I could brace myself. On days when I expected him, I started wearing long trousers or jeans as a matter of self-protection. And I tried to sit as far away from the table as I possibly could without interfering with my ability to do my job. I was still friendly, because I didn't know how else to be. I didn't know how to show anger.

Anyway, I'd decided there were worse things. At the end of the day, who was more objectionable—the women who would shout insults at me and my parents, and would not pay the amount they owed, let alone tip, or this man who treated me well, paid me compliments, and tipped me? Never mind the inappropriate touching. He wasn't harming me physically, I reasoned. And I came to regard my ability to withstand his touch as a test of strength. In my distorted perception of reality, I had achieved a delicate reversal of power.

Some days, the man wouldn't do anything at all. He was the same pleasant person I remembered before the incident, and he would tip me the same generous amount at the end of the manicure. This further confused me. It made me question whether I had imagined the looks and the touching. And then when it happened again, I didn't know what to do or how to feel. My mind would go blank.

Eventually he stopped coming, though I never knew why. For some time, he remained in my memory, not as a bad person, but as a valued customer. Despite the repeated violations, despite his apparent assumption that he had command over my body, I still thought of him with something like affection. I'd conjure up the man I knew before the touching began, the one with the warm smile, the one who always called me Beautiful. If I could force myself to only remember him this way, then I could forgive the bad times. That is, I could forget the bad times.

And it worked.

Soon it was as though I had forgotten him entirely. The memory lay buried deep within, not to be revisited until much later—until the first time I gave someone permission to touch me.

Falling

THOUGH THE CONSCIOUS MIND forgets, the body remembers. These violations confused me, made me doubt my own reality. And they made me more uncomfortable than ever with any sense of my own sexuality, less able than ever to imagine that I myself might one day be in a romantic relationship with anyone. The man in the salon had called me beautiful, but had he meant it? Was his touch the price one had to pay for beauty? I recoiled from the thought.

And yet, I was beginning to care about the way I looked to others. "Presentation is everything," Thinh had told me. And I believed it. But when I looked at myself, looked at the way I "presented" myself, with cheap and baggy outfits, hand-me-downs from my brothers, donated clothing, which never escaped the scrutiny of my peers, I felt trapped and insecure. I had never chosen my own clothing, never experimented with style, and never had a haircut besides my father's botched, uneven creations. I knew that it set me apart from others, and I was embarrassed for it.

In an act of rebellion, and to my father's chagrin, I began to grow my hair out. At least that was something I could afford to do. But there was also the fact that my vision was worsening by the day, and my courses were even more challenging than they were before. There were more notes to take and more homework. Completing just one assignment took so long that I had no time for the others. I'd stay up all night, plagued by headaches and staring at incomplete notes. I started showing up to school sleep-deprived and disoriented.

"Unprepared again?" my teachers would say, marking the negligence in their grade books. I tried to explain the situation to them, but the well of compassion had run dry. "Ask someone for notes," they said simply.

"Hey, mind if I copy your notes again?" I asked a few classmates.

"When are you going to get glasses?" one said, exasperated.

"Sorry, my notes are a little all over the place. You might be better off asking someone else," another said.

I got the hint. Not wanting to inconvenience anyone further, I stopped asking.

The only class that spoke to me through my fog that year was English. Ms. Liu was a fierce force in the classroom who both terrified and inspired me. She was a brilliant teacher, clear, efficient, and strict. Though her assignments were demanding, I knew it was because she cared deeply about what she was teaching and I didn't hold it against her. Nor did I think she was being unfair when I handed in assignments late and she reprimanded me for it. Though I felt embarrassed, I recognized that she was simply doing her job, and there was no way for me to explain what was going on at home, in the salon, and in my mind.

However hard it was for me to complete my assignments, it was in her class that I fell in love with words. Reading Toni Morrison's *The Bluest Eye*—I could still read books if I held them a few inches from my face—moved me to tears. It was the first time a book had ever spoken to me so directly. Pecola Breedlove's quest for a different set of eyes, though for reasons different from my own, was my quest too. And Soaphead Church's granting her the eyes at the cost of the destruction of her already fragile sanity, though wicked, was some-thing I could understand. If I could live in a dreamscape where I could see clearly, I thought, even if it meant giving up my sanity, I would choose that.

But it wasn't just the story. It was the way Morrison wrote it, the poetry and power in every sentence. I savored each one. Reading her work was a way for me to cheat my condition. I'd never been able to see so clearly. But in the everyday world, the one I had to live in, if I didn't have a book pressed almost to my nose, I was seeing less and less. Walking down the street was becoming a challenge. I'd stumble on things that I didn't see on the sidewalk, never had a sense of where I was because street signs were so hard to read, and often didn't recognize people if they greeted me from too far away, all of which added to my insecurities and anxiety.

"Ba," I pleaded one evening. "Please, I can't see the board. I need glasses." We were seated around the table for dinner. There were only four of us that night. Thinh was in his last year of college at RIT, and Phu, although he still lived at home, rarely joined us for dinner. I looked at Long for support, but he said nothing. I didn't blame him. My father just continued eating as though he hadn't heard, though I could sense his anger bubbling beneath the surface.

"Kỳ Lý, not this again," my mother scolded me. She looked ner-vously at him, then back at me, pursing her lips and making a face that commanded silence. "Finish your dinner."

Later, she took me aside and whispered, "Stop bringing this subject up. You know what your father's answer will be."

And she was right. My father did not budge. Long's ability to see the board and do well in school despite having been told he needed glasses was proof to him that if I wasn't doing well, it was due to a lack of intelligence and nothing else. He also remained convinced that we were simply succumbing to a "glasses hysteria" that had been fostered by the government and further fueled by our foolish desire to assimilate to American society and be "cool" like other kids. But I no longer bought into these ideas. My faith in my father's infallibility had been crumbling for some time, ever since he'd yelled at my mother and me for contacting the police that day in the nail salon, and the fact that he continued to think that glasses were a government conspiracy consolidated my skepticism about him.

I began to harbor a deep resentment toward my father, for his craziness and his ignorance, and against my mother too, for failing to stand up to her husband and failing to protect me. How could she abandon me like this?

Around this time, Mr. Dechongkit, my eighth-grade chess club adviser, reached out to me. He had known that I needed glasses but didn't know how badly until Michael, my middle school classmate who had also made it to Bronx Science, told him. Michael had seen me struggling to copy notes in geometry, and one day, when he asked me what my issue was, I told him the truth. That I wasn't allowed to wear glasses.

"This is ridiculous, Ly," Mr. Dechongkit said after he found out. "You need to see."

"I know, but my father won't allow me to get glasses," I confided in him. I figured since he was no longer my teacher, there was no harm in telling him. He was the first adult outside my family I ever told. I was desperate.

"I have an idea," he said. "I'll buy you glasses. You don't have to tell anyone. Just keep the glasses in your locker at school. Your father will never find out. But you have to be able to see. You can't go on like this."

He and I met outside an optometrist's office in Ridgewood one winter afternoon. And he bought me glasses.

"Whoa," I said the first time I put them on. I stared at the gnarled roots of a tree outside the office, momentarily absorbed by the complexity and beauty of its lines. But almost immediately my stomach clenched and I took the glasses off. Seeing the world so clearly was a sensation so overwhelming that I couldn't allow myself to feel it. *I don't deserve to feel this way*, I thought. *I am a disobedient child.*

But I thought about what it would mean to be in class and be able to see the blackboard, to walk down the street and recognize my friends, and I allowed myself to feel gratitude. Immense gratitude. I gave Mr. Dechongkit a hug and asked how I could repay him.

"Don't worry about it," he said, shrugging. "You don't owe me anything. Just do well in school. That's all."

Though I was nervous about this new step I had taken, I thought that my prayers had finally been answered. But the mind works in funny ways. I found myself reluctant to wear my glasses. Despite the fact that I knew my father was wrong, his words echoed loudly in my mind every time I put them on. And so I tried to use them as little as possible—until my grades were suffering so much that I eventually braved the guilt I felt in defying him. Maybe, I reasoned, if I continued to wear them, my eyes would remember how to see again, and then I wouldn't need glasses anymore.

But the opposite happened. The headaches didn't end. I felt more tired and less focused than ever before. And one day, I noticed that even with my glasses, the edges of things had started to blur again, that words on the board and street signs were getting fuzzy. Before I knew it, I seemed to be right back where I started.

Am I just cursed? I asked myself. Or was my father actually right? Maybe wearing glasses *did* make my eyes get worse. Maybe this *was* a ploy from the government all along, to get people hooked on glasses so that they would become forever dependent on them, get higher prescriptions every year until they were blind. Or maybe this was karma from a previous life.

"You just need new glasses," a friend who also wore glasses told me.

"New glasses? But I just got these six months ago."

"Yeah," she said. "Sometimes that happens. Your eyes keep changing. I remember one year I had to get a new prescription three times."

I couldn't believe it. *Just my luck*, I thought. My grades continued to slip. I couldn't catch up anymore. I thought about reaching out to Mr. Dechongkit again, but how could I? He had paid all that money to buy me a pair of glasses and this was how I repaid him? I imagined the look of disappointment that would appear on his face. The thought was unbearable. I felt so ashamed of myself. All he'd asked for was that I do well in school, and I had failed, just like I always seemed to do.

At the suggestion of a couple of my teachers, I began to meet regularly with Madeline Walsh, the school guidance counselor for my grade. She was tall, with wispy blond hair and a heartwarming smile. She worked with me on the self-esteem issues that were surfacing again because of my school troubles, and allowed me to skip classes to chat with her, writing notes to my teachers saying that I was excused for the day.

"So what's going on with your classes?" she asked me one day. "Why are your grades slipping?"

"Oh, you know. My vision. I'm just waiting for Medicaid to kick in, that's all." I figured Medicaid was the kind of excuse no one would pry into, but Ms. Walsh saw right through it.

"Ly, it's been two years now, and you're almost a junior. You're telling me Medicaid hasn't kicked in in all this time?"

"It's complicated. My parents forgot to renew my Medicaid, and then we lost the prescription, so I had to go back to the eye doctor and then wait for the Medicaid again. It's your turn, by the way," I said, gesturing to our chess game. She was playing the white pieces.

"I see," she said, pausing to think before she continued. "It's just . . . your teachers are very concerned about you. Your grades have not improved and you've been cutting a lot of classes. What's going on? What happened to the glasses you had a few months ago? I don't really buy this whole Medicaid story. I can help you if this is a money issue."

I sighed. What could I say? She knew. There was no use hiding it.

I reluctantly explained to her the truth about my father, the traumas of his past, and the prohibition against glasses. And I told her about what was happening to my eye sight. She listened with a compassionate ear.

It felt good to be able to confide in Ms. Walsh the same way it felt good to confide in Mr. Dechongkit. But after I left her office, I felt that sinking feeling in my stomach, regret and shame burning me up inside.

I had once again betrayed my father.

When I received my report card for the second marking period of the year, I was crestfallen. Though I had already made the calculations hundreds of times, I still wasn't prepared for material proof. It occurred to me then that if I continued down this path, I wouldn't graduate high school, wouldn't get to go to college, wouldn't be able to find a good job, and would have to spend the rest of my life confined to the nail salon. I imagined myself at my mother's age, stooping over a pair of feet. My mother had an excuse. What would mine be?

"Ba," I said when my father arrived home from work that day. I had spent the train ride home from the Bronx rehearsing my lines. Doing well in school, I thought, was the only way to escape the fate I'd just imagined for myself. I had to try again. Taking a deep breath, I forced myself to say, "Ba, I need glasses."

He was sifting through a stack of mail he'd just retrieved from the mailbox, reading by the early-evening light that poured in through the living room window.

He looked up. "This again?" he said in a deceptively calm voice.

"Can I please get glasses? I-I really can't see. Please," I begged him.

I can't exactly recall the sequence of events that occurred in the next few seconds. All I remember is that it was swift and loud and that a ceramic bowl was hurled to the floor, where it broke into smithereens.

"Đụ má mày," he cursed in Vietnamese. "Not this again. What did I tell you? Huh? What did I say?"

In a fit of tears, I ran up the stairs to the rooftop. I couldn't take it anymore. My father's lack of reasoning, his refusal to budge, and my own powerlessness over the situation. None of it made sense. And none of it was fair. I felt so hopeless, so helpless.

"Where do you think you're going?" I could hear my mother screaming after me.

On the roof, someone had placed a metal folding chair with a foam seat and backrest. Not knowing how to express my rage and frustration, I ripped the fabric of the chair open, bits of it jamming under my nails. I pounded on the asphalt of the rooftop until my knuckles bled. I felt my skin ripping open and my hands swelling until the pain was unbearable. I'd hoped that the physical pain would eclipse the psychological. But it didn't. I just felt worse.

I walked over to the edge of the roof and looked down. I imagined the fall, bones breaking, my head smashed open on the concrete of the driveway below.

I heard a noise behind me. My mother.

"What do you think you're doing? Get back down here right now. How dare you walk away from your father while he's talking? You know he only cares about you. You know—"

She noticed my bloodied knuckles. Her eyes narrowed.

"You stupid girl. You stupid, disobedient, unfilial girl," she said. "Why can't you just listen for a change? You know what the outcome will be. You have no one to blame but yourself." And with that she walked back down the stairs. The fact that she was still siding with my father made everything even more unbearable.

"Holy shit, Ly," Long said softly when I finally came back down and he saw my hands. "What the fuck did you do to yourself? What's wrong with you?" I understood that there was no judgment in his words. It was more a statement of sympathy than anything else. I had no response. I saw anguish in his eyes and realized how powerless he felt too.

"Why didn't you tell me about your grades?" he tried again. "I could have helped."

"I've been telling you all for years now," I said. "I can't fucking see. How many times do I have to tell you that? I haven't been able to see since the third grade, remember?" I broke down in sobs. "Oh, what's the use? It doesn't matter anymore."

Long said nothing. There was nothing he could say and he knew it. But for the first time in my life, he put his arms around me and gave me a hug.

The Fe Maidens

THAT SPRING, THINH GRADUATED from RIT, came home for another brief visit, and almost immediately landed a job as a programmer at Microsoft in Seattle. It happened so fast I didn't even process the fact that he'd left for good until he was already gone.

He was the first to leave us, the first to dream of a life beyond Ridgewood, the first to escape. When it finally dawned on me that he was moving on, I felt betrayed. In my mind, he was supposed to come back and help out at the nail salon, or tell my parents to get a different salon because this one was too dangerous, too ugly, and we weren't making enough money. He was supposed to come back and convince my father to get me glasses. He was supposed to help me figure my life out. But instead, he was busy living his own life. Everyone was—my father at the factory, Phu and his dedication to sports, Long going to class and studying in all his spare time.

I was beginning to accept that there was nothing anyone else could do. I must have been an awful person in my past life to be born into this one, I thought.

After school let out, I returned to work at the nail salon full-time, twelve hours a day, seven days a week. That summer, our place was swarming. My mother and I couldn't handle the increased volume of clients, so she hired a few people. Once again, it seemed like our fortunes might be changing.

But as competition increased in neighboring salons, we had to keep lowering our prices. What used to be a ten-dollar manicure was now a seven-dollar manicure, and then it eventually became six dollars with a free design. Pedicures were ten dollars, but we offered a mani-pedi special for fourteen dollars, design also included. And because those prices meant that our workers couldn't earn a livable income, my mother started steering many of her own clients to them, which meant less money for us. "They need to eat too," she said. Even so, our turnover rate was high. But unlike most of the nail salon owners she herself had worked for, not only did she offer all of her employees a sixty-forty split on commissions, but she supplied every new hire with gloves and tools. She bought everyone lunch when she could afford it. And for those who were just entering the profession, she taught them the whole trade and shared with them tricks that other technicians usually didn't share, like marbling techniques or three-dimensional acrylic designs or tips on how to hold the brush to apply the perfect layer of polish.

"Your mother was the best owner I ever worked for," Xuân, one of our hired techs, later told me. "I still feel bad for leaving, but there just wasn't any money coming in. The neighborhood was too poor and too dangerous. It had nothing to do with her, I hope you know. I'm forever indebted to her. Your mother taught me everything I know."

The following fall, when school started again, I once more vowed that things would be different. My hair was getting so much longer now, a mark of improvement, I thought. Things were changing. I'd be a better student; I wouldn't let my vision take me down. *You are the light*, I whispered to myself.

"Ly, you need to join a team if you want to go to a good college," Long reminded me. He himself was a senior in high school and had just started the college application process. He had become a national Lincoln-Douglas debate champion, taking home trophy after trophy every year. His grades at Brooklyn Tech were stellar and his SAT scores were exceptional. He knew exactly what he was talking about. I admired his success and wanted to go down the same path he did.

But with sports teams out of the question because I would never have enough time to practice, and in any case couldn't see well enough to play anything, I didn't have a lot of options. So I joined the robotics team, which was the only team that accepted members regardless of their level of skill. Though I knew nothing about electronics or the construction of robots, the community was welcoming. It was full of charming misfits and geeks, an acceptable and even cool thing to be at the Bronx High School of Science.

I fit in immediately despite being one of very few girls on the team. Having grown up with three brothers, I was perfectly comfortable in an almost all-male group.

Shop turned out to be very rewarding, and a great escape from my feelings of inadequacy. I learned how to operate different kinds of machinery: drill presses, band saws, circle saws, metal lathes, mills, and drills. To my surprise, my poor eyesight was only a slight hindrance. I discovered that I could make careful measurements on the metal parts of the robot, then calibrate the machinery accordingly. Once the pieces were clamped down, the machine took over, and all I had to do was supervise the oiling of the lathes and make sure the machine was producing the shape I wanted.

I spent so much time with them and liked them so much that I came to think of the people on the robotics team as my family. Thomas, a gentle giant, was the team captain, and his mother, Dena, attended team meetings and often supplied us with dinner and snacks while we worked long hours after school on building robots for the annual competitions. Over time, she became something like a second mother to me, to all of us. She was our beloved Team Mom. There were only two other girls on the team, Alex and Antoinette, and they became some of my closest friends as we spent almost all our time together working in the shop. Alex, who was also on the swim team, wanted to be an astrophysicist and Antoinette loved drawing cartoons and wanted to be a veterinarian. Unlike them, I didn't know what I wanted to be or what I liked. But I was glad that they accepted me and also that I wasn't the only girl on the team.

One day, Mr. Levy, the assistant principal, approached the three of us. There was a movement at the time to encourage girls all around the country to enter STEM fields, so his idea was that we start our own team. An all-girls team.

"We're the Bronx High School of Science, after all," he said. "And we wouldn't be much without all you wonderful ladies making your contributions. What do you girls think?"

Alex, Antoinette, and I looked at each other and responded with a resounding yes. So together we founded the Fe Maidens—Fe as in the atomic symbol for iron—and when the season began and we started constructing our own robot, we named the abundantly riveted robot Rosie the Riveted.

Best of all, working on the robot after school meant spending less time at the nail salon. "She has to do this for college," Long told my parents. He had been accepted to the school of his choice, the prestigious Macaulay Honors College at Hunter, and moved into the Brookdale dorms in the Kips Bay neighborhood of Manhattan that year. He was getting a full-ride—a laptop, free dorm room, and grant included.

"Girls don't need to go to college," my father said. But he backed off. Some part of him knew better.

The Fe Maidens won the Rookie of the Year award in the NYC

regionals that year, which qualified us to attend the international FIRST Robotics Competition held in the Georgia Dome in Atlanta, Georgia. We were ecstatic.

Again, it was Long who convinced my parents to let me go to Georgia, though surprisingly it wasn't too difficult. They didn't ask many questions. In previous years, Long had traveled to California for his own championship tournaments, so I suppose they figured this was what high school students needed to do.

"How long are you going for?" they asked.

"Four days," I said.

And that was the extent of their curiosity. I tried to explain to them what we had been working on all those months, but gave up halfway, sensing their lack of interest.

So I packed a small backpack and met the team at Bronx Science on the day we were scheduled to leave. It would be my first time traveling overnight on a bus, and my first time traveling to a different state. I was nervous and excited. The drive down to Atlanta took more than fourteen hours, but when I saw the vast exhibition space where the competition was to be held, I forgot all about the long, exhausting drive. I'd never been inside a space that grand, never been exposed to students from all around the country and even from places all over the world. There were teams who'd flown in from Brazil, Europe, even New Zealand and Japan, and some of the US teams were so good they'd been sponsored by NASA and MIT.

Our team colors were green and purple, so Alex and Antoinette and I bought green and purple dye to spray our hair and clothes. I had green hair for days. Radio station anchors arrived to interview all the teams and I was awestruck by the magnitude of the event. It was wild. I felt so free in that big, roaring stadium. And when I saw the complexity and sophistication of many of the other robots, I felt simultaneously intimidated and thrilled. I couldn't believe that our Rosie the Riveted had been selected to compete among them.

The competition lasted three days. On the final day, after the last match had taken place and it was time for the awards ceremony and closing remarks, Sergey Brin, cofounder of Google, took the stage to deliver a speech, behind him an enormous white projector screen. The video that accompanied his talk was all about the amazing progress being made in science and technology—about robots that would walk and run and jump and turn into vehicles, robots that could potentially rescue people in times of disaster and need, about breakthrough advancements in nanotechnology that could be the key to curing cancer, etc. "All of you, right now, right here in this stadium," Brin told us after the credits had rolled, his voice echoing across the vast space, "you are the future." And the crowd erupted in cheers.

In the end, our team didn't win any prizes, but I was proud nevertheless that we'd made it that far in our very first year as an all-female robotics team in a male-dominated field. When we got back to school, even students who had no clue what robotics was congratulated and high-fived us in the hallways. We were, for the moment, celebrities. Of the nerdiest variety. I soaked it all in. My grades were still suffering, but my achievements with the Fe Maidens made me feel like I might be able to do something with my life after all. I was moving forward somehow.

That summer, I was in good spirits and hopeful. In between manicures and pedicures, I made an effort to study for the SATs. As I filled out college applications, my clients watched with amusement.

"Dang, she still be on that thing? When you finally gonna go to college, girl?" Sheila teased me.

A Lazy, No-Good Daughter

DESPITE MY MOMENTARY OPTIMISM, once I was back at school and beginning senior year, I couldn't turn things around. My will alone wasn't enough to change the fact that my eyesight was still compromised. I was in a perpetual daze and found it hard to concentrate. After seeing my grades continue to plummet, Ms. Walsh took matters into her own hands and made a phone call to the Administration for Children's Services (ACS), reporting a case of child neglect.

To my horror, the ACS came knocking on our door early one morning in the form of a slim young woman with long black dreadlocks and a lanky young man with a thin scar on the side of his cheek. I saw the looks of confusion on my parents' faces, which gave way to fear as they slowly understood what was happening. The government really was after them, and it was my fault.

The ACS caseworkers looked around, and I knew how things must have appeared to them: a roach- and mouse-infested household, where an aging Vietnamese couple and their adolescent daughter lived. My father stood there in his tattered trousers and his stained T-shirt, stunned.

"No, I treat my dawduh goot, very, very goot. This my family, you see?" He gestured to the one family photo we had in our apartment, on top of a radiator. "We sleep here, and we eat here. Very, very goot."

The ACS officials jotted down notes.

"Are you happy?" they asked me.

"Yes, I'm very happy here!" I said as brightly as possible. I was trying to recover from my shock at the invasion, because I knew I needed to put on a show. I had to make things right. I looked over at my father and could see his face reddening. I could feel the pounding of his heart, could almost hear his frightened thoughts.

"Where do you sleep? Can you show us where you sleep?"

Two sets of eyes stared at me, waiting for me to answer. I pointed to a cot on the floor of the living room. After Thinh and Long moved out, there was no need for the jury-rigged bunk bed situation, so my father broke it down. My parents slept in the front bedroom, Phu slept in the back room, and I slept in the living room.

They jotted down more notes.

"I know it's not much," I told them. "But it's all we have. We're immigrants. My father doesn't make much."

"I see," one of them said, nodding to the other. "And what about the glasses?"

My father's eyes widened in understanding. His English was still limited but he had heard the word "glasses" often enough from me to know what this was all about. "She—"

"Don't say anything to them," I barked at my father in Vietnamese.

I turned to the caseworkers and tried to explain: "We've been waiting for Medicaid to kick in."

They took down more notes.

"Your guidance counselor gave us a different story."

"I don't know what she's talking about," I lied. "I'm telling you the real story right now."

"Okay, miss," the woman said, exchanging glances with her colleague. "We understand. We'll be back here in two weeks' time."

With that, she gave me her card and they shook hands with my father. My mother stood petrified, tears threatening to erupt from her eyes. I could feel the fear radiating from them both, spilling out into the empty space between us, an unbridgeable distance.

They turned on the lights of the altar, put their hands together, and bowed their heads. They didn't say a word to me; nor could I offer them any kind of meaningful apology or words of comfort. Their confusion, their fear, their anger, mixed in with my own shame, were loud enough.

That night, my father woke up screaming from his nightmare, calling for my mother to take the kids and run. It had been a long time since he'd had an episode, and I knew it was all my fault this time. I lay in bed crying silently, praying for the nightmare, both his and mine, to end.

After I got out of my morning classes the next day I stormed into Ms. Walsh's office without even knocking.

"Why did you do that? Why didn't you say anything to me before you went to the ACS? Why didn't you discuss it with me? Do you know what you've caused?" I spoke as loudly as I could. But my strength gave way. "How am I going to fix this now? How am I going to fix this?" My voice tapered off into a whisper. Students, teachers, and guidance counselors stopped what they were doing to stare at me through the open door.

"I'm sorry, sweetheart, but I am mandated by the law to report any kind of neglect or abuse that I suspect is happening to the kids I deal with. It's protocol."

"Protocol? You just ruined my life because of protocol? You didn't even try to understand. It's not my father's fault. He spent almost a decade in prison. He isn't right in the head. He was never trying to hurt me. He just doesn't know any better."

Ms. Walsh stood behind her desk, mouth slightly agape. Then, with sudden strength, she declared, "I don't regret it. If I had to do it again, I would."

I understood that she wanted to comfort herself, that she wanted to feel justified in her decision. And later, I understood that it was the right decision for anyone in her position. But I, too, wanted to be comforted. I wanted to know that it was all going to be okay, that my parents wouldn't suffer because of me.

But there was nothing I could tell myself that would be a source of comfort. I was full of regret. If *I* had to do it again, I thought, I would have never ratted my father out. I would have worked harder. I would have been a better student. I would have been a better daughter.

Part IV

Winter 1972. Ba in uniform, South Vietnam.

Re-Education

I CALL MY FATHER "Ba." In Vietnamese, that means "Father." There was no room for friendship in this relationship.

As I struggled to reach my father in the days that followed ACS's visit, to somehow repair our relationship, to reconcile my fear and resentment of him with my love for him, I thought about his past. I thought about what I knew of it from stories my mother revealed or from the rare moments he was open with us.

He was born in 1952, in Tam Bình, a small town in Vĩnh Long City, across the Mekong from Trà Ôn, the village where my mother is from and where I would eventually be born. Both his parents were Teochew, like my mother's. Having moved from China to South Vietnam as adults, they could not read Vietnamese or speak very much of it. At a young age, he had to help his parents navigate a country they couldn't understand, and as the eldest, he took care of his two brothers and five sisters. In elementary and middle school, he was at the top of his class. He sang and danced in school musicals. He had beautiful penmanship.

"Go back to China," the kids in the neighborhood said when they heard him speaking Teochew to his parents and siblings. "Haven't your kind been here long enough?" The Chinese and the Vietnamese had history. One thousand years of Chinese domination and tyranny over Vietnam had fostered within the Vietnamese a hatred of anyone who spoke the language or had Chinese ancestry. It didn't help that my father was also awkward and socially inept, laughed too loudly and made inappropriate jokes. He had a weird gait, involuntarily moving his head from side to side as he walked. The neighborhood kids mocked him. He had few friends.

After class was over, he would run in his white-and-navy-blue uniform to a hill a few roads away from his family's hut and climb to the top. There he would sit and pick at the grass in the quietness of the afternoon until, without fail, he heard the loud, rhythmic sputtering of the Huey helicopters. He'd get up and chase them, waving his arms furiously as they flew overhead. Then he'd go home and memorize different aircraft models.

"It was exhilarating. I thought they were the future. I thought, one day I would own and fly one myself," he told me on one of the nights he took me up to the flat asphalt rooftop of our Ridgewood apartment to look for helicopters or airplanes. He loved to be able to identify them. "Look, look!" he'd cry out, arm outstretched and pointing in the sky. "That's a Boeing 747." I was nine or ten years old and was developing a fear of insects, swatting at them in the dark, feeling an itch first on my arm, then on my leg, much more preoccupied with these tiny abominations than interested in my father's revelations.

But it was in these moments that I might have glimpsed remnants of my father's childlike innocence, peeking out from beneath the years of war and strife that had long ago encased him, the innocence that was compromised in 1968 when, at the age of sixteen, he was drafted into the war.

He could solve complex equations in his head very quickly and was promoted to lieutenant at the age of seventeen. His job was to plot coordinates for bombs.

"Math is everything," he used to tell me and my brothers. "If you have a solid grasp of math, you will be all right in life." What he meant was that it had saved him from going out onto the battleground and getting shot.

Looking back, I realize that must have been why he was so mad at me when I was failing in math. His obsession with our learning it went back almost as far as I can remember.

When Long was six and I was only four, he made us recite the multiplication tables while we cut fabrics and pleated cummerbunds on the floor of our living room. In later years he'd beat us when we didn't understand our math homework. He'd give us equations to solve before we went to bed at night and test us on them in the morning. It wasn't just a question of understanding numbers. He was trying to save our lives.

After the fall of Saigon on April 30, 1975, my father knew that it was the end for everyone who had fought for the South Vietnamese. He was stationed on an army base in the Quảng Bình Province north of Central Vietnam when he heard the news. Running outside, he saw American helicopters, dozens of Hueys, in the sky, and he waved his arms wildly, running after them, along with dozens of his fellow soldiers. "Hey!" he yelled. "Over here! Come back!" But it was too late. The Vietcong had surrounded the base. They rounded up the troops, shackling them together and shooting anyone who resisted. "I kept looking for them in the sky, but they never came back for me."

My father was one of almost two and a half million South Vietnamese soldiers who were captured and sent to the "reeducation camps," where they were forced into backbreaking and often dangerous labor, sweeping minefields, digging wells and latrines, cutting down trees. They called the camps *trại học tập cải tạo*, meaning a place where you could be purified of your sins, offered a chance to re-create yourself through labor that benefited the community.

"They told us we only had to attend for about a week and a half, just until they sorted out the paperwork. Then they whipped and electrocuted us. They fed us once every few days, sometimes weeks, part of a potato." My father served a ten-year sentence.

He never talked much about his time in the camp. The story of the turtle, which he told us many times, is one of the few exceptions. Otherwise he mostly kept his memories to himself. Who could blame him? But whenever he raised a hand to us and we ran crying to our mother, she would say, "One day, you will forgive him."

As I searched for a way to ease his pain, I wondered if I could trade my forgiveness for his. But I was torn. I remembered looking at him through tears as a child, seeing his crazed, bulging eyes that I'd inherited, white in an almost purple face, while he beat us, yelling obscenities and threatening to throw us out of the house. How could I forgive that? Later, I would liken his expression to the look of Saturn devouring one of his sons in the Goya painting, blackness all around him, his son's bloodied body clutched tightly in his two hands, the head and right arm already gone. But I felt sorry for Saturn, somehow. I felt his pain and his despair. For my father, I could feel nothing.

In school, I was an emotional wreck, suddenly bursting into tears wherever I was. In class, on the stairs, or in the hallways, unable to hide my anguish. Friends offered their support and sympathy, and teachers were understanding. Alex, who served as cocaptain with me on the robotics team, met me at my locker one day and presented me with a large stuffed turtle. "I hope this makes you feel better," she told me. "I won it at an arcade, and I know how much you like turtles."

I could barely speak, I was so touched by her gesture. As I held the turtle in my hands, I thought about why it was that I liked turtles so much. It had become such a part of my identity that I'd forgotten its origin. I revisited those nights, years ago, sitting on tattered couch cushions on the floor and listening to my father tell us about his time in prison. He was trying to make us understand what war was then, and what it meant to be a prisoner.

After my father rescued the turtle and the warden saved my father from being shot and ordered his release from prison, relatives found him not far from the camp area. All seventy-two pounds of him. He had collapsed from exhaustion, dehydration, hunger, and pain before he could make his way home. It was over—seven years of "re-education." But it wasn't really over. He'd been sentenced to ten years, and the remaining three years of his sentence would be served as the government saw fit. His sisters brought him home with them. They fed him. They clothed him. They nurtured and consoled him. Many of his friends were dead. You are lucky, his sisters told him.

Two years later, he married my mother. He was thirty-one. They had four children: Kỳ Thịnh, Kỳ Phú, Kỳ Long, and Kỳ Lý—each of us named after the military communes he was stationed in during the war. But the Vietcong were still not finished with him. Soldiers would come by each day to take his earnings, as was the custom of the new regime. They showed up with rifles. They also sometimes stopped my mother on her way to delivering merchandise and confiscated the goods.

Standing in the hallway of Bronx Science, clutching that turtle to my chest, I felt so sorry for my father and even more ashamed of myself. I knew what doing well in school meant to my father, even if he didn't have high hopes for me. Back in Vietnam, when Thinh and Phu were old enough to go to school, the principal rejected them because they were the sons of a traitor. They sat together holding hands in front of the school and wept until neighbors told my father. He sent them to school every day for three years, fruitlessly, hoping they would be given a chance.

But my father's time being "re-educated" eventually did prove as transformative as the Vietnamese name for the camps suggested. One day, he heard on the radio about the Humanitarian Operation, a subprogram of the Orderly Departure Program of 1979. Its mission was to resettle former South Vietnamese prisoners of war and their immediate families in the US. My father applied. Six months later, he left Vietnam with his wife and four children. On a Boeing 747. Yes, lucky was what they called him.

Lying

I SAT IN A drab room on an uncomfortable metal chair. Rectangles of fluorescent light flickered rhythmically above me, the carpeting beneath my feet was stained and gray, and the walls were hung with bad art in tilted frames. One other person was there, a chubby, blond, blue-eyed boy in a tracksuit, leaning back on his chair with legs spread wide apart, staring blankly at the floor. He looked to be about twelve years old. I wondered what I looked like.

I was in the office of the Administration for Children's Services in Jamaica, Queens. After the caseworkers' visit to our apartment, I knew I had to find a way to fix the situation. I had to make my father believe that the government was not after him. And I had to make sure that my parents did not suffer in any way because of something I had done. If I could get the ACS case closed, maybe they would forgive me. I took the train one evening after school to 165-15 Archer Avenue in Jamaica, the address on the back of the card that the visitors had given me. A woman in the reception office had taken my name and led me into this dreary office space.

"Offices are closing in fifteen minutes," she notified me.

Aside from the boy, I saw no one. Somewhere, a clock ticked loudly. After what seemed an interminably long time, the woman who had visited us emerged from one of the cubicles and beckoned me toward her. The name on her cubicle door was "Adobe." Had she told us her name when she was in our apartment? I didn't remember.

"Lie, right?" she said when we sat down. I simply nodded. I was used to people mispronouncing my name and it didn't seem worth the effort to correct her. She checked the time on her watch, took a deep breath, and exhaled sharply, as if to say, *This better be quick.* She leaned forward. "What is the reason for your visit today?"

"Well," I began. I hesitated, unsure what to say. My thoughts flashed back to the shock on my father's face when he understood what was happening, a look of heart-stopping fear and panic. I forced myself to continue. "Well, I . . . I just wanted to know if maybe it was possible for you to close this case?" I focused my attention on the colorful stick-figure drawings Adobe had pinned to the walls of her cubicle. A framed photo on her desk showed her sitting on a blanket in what looked like a park with a man's arms around her and a little girl on her lap—no doubt the artist who had created the drawings.

Adobe began to rummage around in a green metal filing cabinet filled with Pendaflex folders. "Close the case, what do you mean?" she muttered as she searched, a question directed more toward the cabinet than toward me. I waited, unsure whether I should answer, digging my nails into the backs of my hands, silently repeating the name of Amitabha Buddha in my mind. She moved on to a different cabinet. "Now, where did I put that file?"

When she finally found it, she turned back to me. "Now, where were we? Oh, right, reason for your visit today?"

I repeated my request. She nodded, flipping through the notes in her file. She chewed on the back of a pen.

"See, here's the deal," she said, putting the file down. "I can't do that. We're scheduled to come back to your apartment in two weeks to continue our investigation. If we're satisfied with what we see, there's nothing to worry about, you understand?"

My thoughts began to swirl. I dug my fingernails further into my hands. Foolishly, I hadn't thought far enough ahead to know what to say if my request was rejected. I suddenly had the urge to straighten out the files on her desk, reposition the drawings on the walls, and even rearrange the stick figures in the drawings. *The child's feet should land on the grass, not float away like balloons. And those flowers have too many petals. The sun should be colored in all the way, and outlined properly.*

"W-well," I stammered, "but there really isn't any reason to do an investigation. My parents, they don't neglect me. And they try very hard to do everything they can for me. I'm always well fed and clothed and—"

"It says here that your guidance counselor reported a case of child neglect because your father refused to get you eyeglasses, which has led to your depression and poor performance in school. Is this true?"

"Actually . . . no, it isn't," I said slowly, trying desperately to think of something. "I only told my guidance counselor that so she would get off my back about my grades. I made up that story."

"Made it up?"

Adobe grabbed a legal pad from atop the cabinet and began to jot down notes. Seeing this, I kept ad-libbing my way through more lies, living up to the name she'd called me. I told Adobe that I had gotten a pair of glasses a few years ago, but broke them on purpose to get out of doing work in class.

"I mean, seriously, who likes school? It's so-o-o boring," I said. "I just don't care about doing well in school. So I figured if I told Ms. Walsh that I wasn't doing the work because my father wouldn't buy me glasses, that would explain everything. I never thought she'd follow up on that."

I stopped talking to allow her to finish her notes. She did, checked her watch again, and looked up at me. Her features were just a blur to me, so I couldn't tell what her expression was, but I imagined it was one of exasperation.

"Is that all?"

"Yes," I said, hoping this was enough to get her to close the case.

"Okay, I'll have to discuss this with my supervisor. But you'll hear from us soon. Thanks for coming today, and if you have any questions or need anything, remember to call the number on the card."

"But are you still going to come back to my apartment in two weeks?"

"I don't know," she said, shrugging her shoulders. "Hard to tell."

With that, she stood up and held out her hand. I shook it, thanked her, and left. I walked through the dark corridors, pushed against heavy doors, and stepped out into the open air. Outside, the sun had set completely, the sky a deep blue. The streetlamps were lit, casting a rusty glow on the sidewalk. A cold wind whistled through my cheap, thin coat, still two sizes too big for me and by now it seemed unlikely I would grow into it. My bones ached. I felt as though they would crack from the cold.

I had no idea what was going to happen next. I was nervous and scared for my parents. Would they be charged with neglect and sent to jail? Or would I be taken away and sent to another home? But I was too exhausted to dwell on these thoughts. They passed through my mind like gray clouds on a windy day as I made my way home.

Surviving the Riptide

A WEEK LATER, IN the middle of my astronomy class, I was called into Ms. Walsh's office. A tall, muscular man in a tight navy suit with a striped tie sat in her office. His hair was blond and cropped close to his head. A large man, he had an even larger presence, and I felt very small next to him.

"Ly, have a seat." Ms. Walsh motioned to the armchair next to the man. "I want you to meet Dr. Hayes."

The man leaned forward in his chair and held out his hand. "Hi, Ly," he said in a soft but strong voice. "I'm Dr. Hayes. How are you?" I shook his hand warily.

"I just got off the phone with Adobe," Ms. Walsh said to me. "She told me about your visit to her office last week. And she has agreed to close the investigation on the condition that you see a state-mandated psychiatrist for the next two years."

I looked at the doctor, who nodded solemnly.

"Now, I've told Dr. Hayes a little about you and about our relationship, but he's going to take over for me from now on, okay? Of course, you're still always welcome to visit me during your free periods." She paused and looked attentively at me. I felt her eyes roam over my face, trying to read me. "How do you feel?" she asked deliberately.

I couldn't speak. It took a few moments to process what she had just said. I felt an avalanche of weight begin to slide from me, and then an immense feeling of relief. *Nam mô A Di Đà Phật.* My father was safe. Adobe had believed the story I'd concocted.

"Um," I said hesitantly. I didn't want to keep Ms. Walsh in suspense, but I was afraid that if I sounded too ecstatic she might think I was happy to be leaving her. "I think I'm okay."

"Ly, look, I know you've had a rough time," Ms. Walsh said. "I'm so sorry for all of this. But we all just want to help you. You know that, don't you?"

I assured her that I did.

She sighed so deeply and looked at me with such sympathy I thought she might cry.

Dr. Hayes stood up. "Well, shall we, then?"

"Oh, right." Ms. Walsh collected herself. "So Dr. Hayes will be setting up his office in the room next door. That's where you'll be meeting with him every week. I don't want to eat into any more of your time. But if you have any questions, you know where to find me!" To the doctor, she added, "Take good care of her, okay?"

"Will do," he said, winking at me.

I met with Dr. Hayes twice a week. It took a long time for me to feel relaxed around him. I was wary of saying anything that might get my parents in trouble again. As a result, many of our sessions were filled with long, uncomfortable silences. He wrote notes down on a legal pad and asked me questions, to which I usually gave short answers, never sure of what would be all right to say.

One of the rare times I did try to open up to Dr. Hayes, I told him about the relationship between my father and Phu. In those days, I rarely saw Phu, who resented our parents because they put so much pressure on him to live up to Thinh's example. He avoided my father as much as he could, going to his classes at Pace, staying out late on the handball courts with friends, slipping into bed after my parents were asleep, and often leaving before they woke up. But when he couldn't escape being around my father, the two of them would often end up in a screaming fight about where his life was headed. Sometimes, the fights would even get violent, I explained to Dr. Hayes. Once, my father picked up a chair and threw it at him. My mother got in between and the chair hit her instead, sending her staggering to the floor. In a perverse way, I said, I was grateful for Phu's hostile relationship with my father, because I felt it gave us something we could bond over.

"And how does all of this make you feel?" Dr. Hayes asked. "I've heard you intellectualize a lot about your father's motivations, about why you think he acts the way he does, but let's talk about your feelings."

The minutes crawled by, my anxiety spiking. My feelings? I thought I *had* been talking about my feelings. But the more he probed, the more my mind drew a blank. Was this what my mother had warned me against when I was a child? Had I ended up swallowing my words after all?

Dr. Hayes diagnosed me with dysthymia, or high-functioning depression. It's a depressive disorder that can sometimes accompany high achievers who are able to mask their depression well, he explained to me.

"Based on what you're telling me, I think it's safe to assume that you've suffered from this for many years now," he said. "You've been able to do well, relatively speaking, making it to such a prestigious high school despite your circumstances, and getting decent grades up until recently, but I have a hunch that there's a lot going on beneath the surface. Making sense of your feelings, naming them, will help you tremendously."

I ransacked my brain for the words with which to name my feelings, but came up short. I had nothing to say. It was yet another failure, another lack, another form of blindness.

At home, my relationship with my parents had gotten much worse. Although I'd told them about going to the ACS office and getting the investigation called off, hoping they would appreciate what I'd done, it didn't help. My father's fears had been realized. Because of me, the government had finally come after him, after all these years. There was nothing I could do to gain his forgiveness. I couldn't reach him at all.

I watched him one afternoon, sitting by the living room window and staring out at the setting sun. I could hardly see the features on his face, let alone his expression, but I could feel his pain. I wanted badly to tell him that I was sorry. That if I could I would take away all the horror and trauma from the war and his time in prison. I would make him whole again. But how could I tell him that? I had never once told my father I loved him. I had never once apologized to him. I wouldn't even know how to begin.

As he slipped into an abyss of fear and anxiety, I slipped further into my depression. I began to skip days at the nail salon, where I'd been working most weekends, which only exacerbated my parents' feeling of betrayal. Unable to contain his rage, my father kicked me in the head one morning as I slept. I was too lost within myself to even react. I was shattered. I was ashamed.

Soon after, Phu graduated from Pace and got a one-year contract to work at Nike headquarters in Beaverton, Oregon, as a business systems analyst. Finally, what he'd been waiting for had arrived: his ticket out of Ridgewood. I remember watching him from the window of our apartment as he walked to the train station on his way to the airport, rolling a suitcase and carrying a duffel bag. I stuck my head all the way out the window, counting his steps until he disappeared around the corner.

Gone. My brothers had all abandoned me, Thinh for Seattle, Phu for Beaverton, Long for the dorms at Hunter College, where he'd lived since enrolling as a freshman the previous year. Now I was the only child left at home.

Around this time I stopped showing up to some of my classes. Before, I had skipped only occasionally, but suddenly it didn't make sense to attend class at all if I couldn't see anything. I befriended a group of boys who smoked pot and played with fire and did other dangerous things. I rode the trains back and forth with no destination for hours. I drifted. Somehow Ms. Walsh managed to explain the situation to my teachers. I don't know what she told them exactly, but they were sympathetic and generous with their grading.

When the year eventually came to an end, I managed to squeak through, barely passing all my Regents Exams, the mandatory standardized subject tests specific to the state of New York. This meant that I could actually graduate with the rest of my senior class. And I was stunned to discover that, with the help of Ms. Walsh, my college adviser, my teachers, and the recommendation letters that they wrote for me, I had been accepted to the Macaulay Honors College at Hunter College, where I would join Long.

Not only that, the college provided a full-tuition scholarship, a free dorm room, a free Apple laptop, and a Jack Nash Scholarship of twenty-five hundred dollars every semester based on my maintaining a GPA above 3.5. That was enough that I would even be able to help my parents if needed and still have money to pay for my meals and school supplies.

I couldn't believe it. How was it possible that I'd made it in? I felt like I'd been caught in a violent riptide, beaten by waves again and again, on the verge of drowning, then slammed back to shore, choking and gasping for air, incredulous that I'd somehow survived.

A Graduation Gift

I ASKED MY PARENTS to come to my high school graduation.

"And miss a day at the salon?" they replied. After owning the salon for five years, we were still struggling financially. Competition had increased tenfold and customers were leaving us for better-looking and better-staffed salons with lower prices. Unable to break even, we were losing money rapidly.

"Come on, guys," Long said. "It's her graduation. You should go."

"Okay, we'll go," my mother said.

"Nonsense," my father said. "She doesn't need us to go." My mother reluctantly agreed.

I had already anticipated their response, had already steeled myself against the pain of rejection. "You're right," I said. "I don't need you to go."

Thinh had come back from Seattle to visit, so he and Long agreed to come to my graduation in their place. Phu had just begun his job at Nike and couldn't make it. The events of that day are a blur to me. But I remember that it was nice having Thinh and Long there. Thinh had bought a horn to blow into when they called my name, and I could

235

hear that horn as I walked across the stage. They didn't say it, but I think they were proud of me.

There was one problem, however. I was certain college would be even more difficult than high school, and I still couldn't see.

"Still?" Thinh asked when I mentioned it to him. He'd been so busy with his own life that he'd forgotten all about my eyesight problem.

"Yeah, I don't think it's the sort of thing that gets better with time," I told him. "And I did those eye exercises you told me about but they never worked."

A few days later, Thinh took me to an optometrist.

"Your sclera seems bruised," the optometrist said. "Have you suffered any injuries to your eyes recently?"

"No, not that I know of," I replied. "I mean, sometimes I push really hard on the edges of my eyes so I can see better. Kind of like a super squint when regular squinting doesn't work."

The optometrist stared at me. "Yeah, um, don't do that," he said. "You can cause severe, irreparable damage to your eyes if you do that."

Too late, I thought. I'd been doing it for the last eleven years of my life. Besides, my eyes were already irreparably damaged.

"How bad is her eyesight?" Thinh asked.

"It's not bad at all," the optometrist said. "It's just regular myopia with slight astigmatism."

"But she says she can't see anything."

"Well, of course she can't, without proper corrective eyewear. My vision is better than hers and I would still be hopeless without my glasses. What was her prescription before this?"

"We don't know," my brother said.

"Well, give me her glasses, then. I can figure it out."

"She doesn't have glasses. It's a long story. But actually, I was wondering if she could get contacts." I looked up at him. Contacts?

"Yeah," he said to me in Vietnamese. "So Mom and Father won't find out."

I couldn't believe it. I'd felt so abandoned, but Thinh had come back to help me after all.

The first time I tried the contacts on in the store, the optometrist called me a natural. "Usually it takes some time for people to get used to these," he told me. "People never just pop the contacts into their eyes like you did." Maybe wanting to see as badly as I did facilitated that process for me.

It was exhilarating to finally be able to see. There had been a brief period of clear-sightedness when I put on the glasses Mr. Dechongkit bought for me. But other than that, it had been more than a decade since I had seen the world in such crisp lines and bright colors. Looking at Thinh, I realized I could recognize him from a few steps away instead of inches. I could even see the pores on his face.

"Your graduation gift," he said, handing over the box of contacts. "Don't tell anyone." I cradled the slim little box in my hand as though it contained a precious treasure. Which it did. They were expensive, but Thinh had done well for himself while he was away. He now owned a house and a BMW, the car he'd always talked about having when we were younger. He was doing it. He was living the American dream.

When I stepped out of that store into the bright June light of that summer day, the possibilities seemed endless. *This is when my life finally begins*, I thought. *I can see!*

Of course, I had to be careful to hide the contacts from my parents until I could move to the dorm in the fall when school began. At night, I waited until they were asleep to go to the bathroom and remove the contacts. Before doing so, I would always take a few moments to carefully examine the girl I saw before me. She was a little taller now, and her hair had grown out into a bob. But the face was still the same, still my father's face, with two large eyes looking out at me. *You're a liar*, the eyes seemed to say. *A fake. I know your secret. You're still blind.* And sure enough, she was right. As soon as I took off my contacts, that crisp, clear world faded away, hazy and out of focus. Then I would tuck the case that contained them into the waistline of my pajamas so that if my mother or father intercepted me on the way out of the bathroom they wouldn't notice anything. Sometimes, I would be so worried they might discover my secret that I just slept with the contacts. They were biweekly contacts, so I figured that if I left them in for the whole two weeks I would have to deal with the anxiety of being caught only twice a month. And that way, I could live longer in the illusion that I was seeing with my own two eyes.

Soon after I got my contacts, clients at the salon, where I was once again spending a lot of my summer, were surprised at the improvement in my work. Until then I had had to bend down so close to the nail I was working on that my nose would sometimes graze the wet polish, and I'd have to polish the nail all over again. And there were sometimes inconsistencies in the designs of the nails because I couldn't see more than one nail at a time, which made it hard to match them exactly. Now that I could see what I was doing and the results were so much better, some clients even requested that I do the designs on their nails after my mother or father had done their tips or manicures. My parents were pleased, though I knew my father would have been furious if he'd known the reason for my sudden breakthrough.

Mad Cheap

"YOU'RE GONNA NEED A blanket and a lamp," Long said. He thought about it some more, then added, "And maybe a small trash bin, but that's about it." He'd been a minimalist since his earliest years and was just as frugal as my father. In their eyes, few things were essential. Anything beyond essential was luxury. And luxury was not meant for people like us.

It was a mid-August afternoon in 2007, and I was scheduled to move into the dorm the following week. Long and I were standing in an air-conditioned Bed Bath & Beyond looking for dorm room essentials. Two minutes in and I was already overwhelmed, but Long was quick and focused. He knew exactly which section to go to.

"All right, let's get you a blanket first," he said, zipping through the aisles. I wanted to look around a little more, to try to get my bearings, but there was no chance of that. He was a no-nonsense kinda guy, in-and-out-in-less-than-thirty-seconds kinda guy. I trailed behind him, trying to keep up while at the same time trying to take in as much of the store as I could. It was so bright and spacious, and everything had that brand-new smell.

Then, as though we had hit the brakes on a car, we stopped suddenly in the bedding section. "Okay, which one?" he asked.

I looked around, dumbfounded by the huge variety of things on display. I had no idea what I was supposed to choose. This wasn't a section just for blankets, which was the only word I knew, other than pillows, that was relevant to bedding. I didn't know what sheets were or comforters or quilts or duvet covers. We used thin blankets at home, and slept on plastic straw mats atop naked mattresses, the crisscross pattern of the straw leaving red marks across our backs as we slept. It was all I knew.

But here, the options were endless. Down comforters, down-alternative comforters, microfiber duvet covers, sheets and pillow-cases with different thread counts, mattress covers and mattress pads. The packaging had card inserts depicting perfectly made beds with everything matching.

Wow, I thought. *Could my bed really look like that?*

"All right, you stay here and pick something," Long said, already itching to move on. "I'm gonna go find the lamp section."

I looked at the vast selection before me, my little flame of hope extinguished by the reality of decision-making. My head began to pound and I started getting nervous. I hated shopping. I hated not knowing what the answer was.

Okay, Ly, you can do this. It's just a freaking blanket. I picked up each item gingerly and tried to make sense of it all. Quilt or comforter. Down or down-alternative. The 300 thread count or 500 thread count. What the hell's the difference? What on earth was a thread count? Then I noticed the prices and panicked. If I was going to get one of each item so that my bed could look like the bed on the picture, the total price would be astronomical. I let out a loud groan.

"Need help?" a sales associate standing nearby asked.

"No," I said. "I mean, yes. I mean, I don't know." I hung my head in shame. Why was this so difficult?

"Well, are you going dorm room shopping?" she asked, assessing my age. "Or looking for something specific?"

"Oh, right, dorm room shopping," I said. "I, um, I need bedding." The idea that I was going dorm room shopping immediately distracted me from the situation. Yes, that's right. I was going to be in a dorm. I was going to have my own room for the first time in my life. Who cared if I didn't have proper bedding?

"Okay, then you might want to consider our all-in-one bedding sets," she said. "They're just three aisles down that way and to your right." I followed her directions, and sure enough, there they were, all-in-one bedding sets conveniently color coordinated so I wouldn't have to expend the mental energy of trying to make everything match. Now it was just a matter of choosing one of the dozens of sets before me.

Long appeared by my side and let out an exasperated sigh. "Ly, come on, do you really need all this?" he asked.

"Well, I don't know," I said. "Don't I? What about you? Don't you have something like this?"

"Does it look like I would?" he said, annoyed. "Of course not. I just brought that blue blanket I had from home."

"Oh," I said. I felt guilty that I wanted more, that I wanted my bed to look like the one on the picture. Long never wanted more than what he had. He was very practical. I guess it was better that way. There'd be no dashed hopes, no foolish dreams.

"Oh shit," he said, pointing at a price tag. His mouth was agape and his eyes were almost as big as mine.

"Yeah, I know," I said. I didn't even bother to look. I knew it would be out of our range and had already moved on to thinking I could just bring the straw mat and the blanket I'd been using all these years. Long was right. I was silly for wanting so much.

"These are mad cheap, actually," he said. "They're on sale. You should get one."

I looked up. Did he just say what I thought he said? I took a closer look at the price tag. It still seemed expensive to me, but compared to the items I'd been looking at in the other section, it was way cheaper. And since Long was paying, it was his call. The sale appealed to his frugal side.

"Yeah, really," he said. "All right, come on, let's go. We're wasting time. Just pick your favorite color or something."

That wasn't hard. I thought about trees and plants and turtles, like the one that protected my father all those years ago. Green. My favorite color was green.

I picked up a set and lifted it off the shelf. It was heavy. The comforter was green, and the bedding was cream-colored with green stripes.

"This one?" I asked Long.

"Yeah, sure, whatever," he said.

I clutched it tightly to my chest. I couldn't believe I was going to have my own bedding set.

"Wait, what about you?" I asked. "You don't want one too?" I thought about the little blue blanket I knew so well. There were large dark blue flowers on it. It was tattered and pilling all over. He'd had it for as long as I could remember.

"Nah, I'm good," he said, not even looking back at me, not even pausing to think about it. And then it was on to lamps and trash bins.

Welcome to a New You

NOW THAT I WAS equipped for dorm living, my next priority was to set up a bank account. When I graduated, Dr. Hayes had moved our sessions from the high school to the Mount Sinai Adolescent Health Center. There, he introduced me to Pamela van der Meulen, a legal advocate for adolescents, who would help me with opening a bank account and other practical matters. "Pam's great," he said. "You're going to love her. She's a real mom type, very nurturing. You'll see."

He was right. Pam was warm and caring. We chatted for hours in her office. She asked me personal questions about my life while sharing details about her own. It was different from the conversations I had with Dr. Hayes. Talking to her was easy. She jotted everything down on a notepad, and I made an appointment with her for the following week. Not only did she help me with the bank account, but a week later she also helped me move into my dorm room at the Brookdale Campus Residence Hall at Twenty-Fifth Street and First Avenue, six subway stops away from the main campus at Sixty-Eighth and Lexington.

Long had left for Costa Rica to study abroad that semester, so I was

243

on my own. Not that I minded. After being known as Long's little sister during elementary and middle school, I didn't want to have to take on that identity again. I wanted to reinvent myself, to establish a reputation as Ly Tran, nothing more and nothing less. I would have liked to have had new clothes for the new Ly Tran, but there was no money for that.

When Pam and I arrived at Brookdale on a breezy late-summer afternoon, she helped me carry my possessions—the bedding set, the lamp, a bag of clothing, and a few other essentials such as towels and a shower caddy. My room was on the third floor. After we unpacked, she took me out to a Greek diner on the corner of Twenty-Third Street and Second Avenue. It was the first time I'd ever had an omelet. Broccoli and cheddar cheese. I loved it.

Once Pam said goodbye, after giving me hugs and wishing me luck, I walked back to the dorm, back to my new room. I looked around and took everything in.

My room was ten feet by twelve feet and furnished with a wooden desk and chair, a dresser, a nightstand, a single twin-sized bed, and a built-in closet. There were no holes or peeling paint on the smooth white walls, the wood floor was clean, and for the first time in my life, I had a place to hang my clothes. I ran my fingers along the furniture, then sat down in disbelief, stunned to think that this was where I'd be staying for the next four years.

I decided to make the bed right away. It was positioned beneath the windows, which looked out over a courtyard, and after a few minutes of trying to figure out what went where and in what order, I made it look almost like the bed in the picture. Once I was done, I took a few steps back and nearly cried. It was only a bed, but it symbolized hope to me, my feeling that things were about to change.

How different it all was from my life back on Bleecker—the lack of any space I could call my own, the makeshift bunk beds my father made for us, the rough sheets of wood we found on the streets that functioned as our worktables. This was *my* room, *my* bed, *my* work desk and chair, *my* closet, and *my* walls. And best of all, it was clean. Not a single roach in sight.

I climbed atop the bed and pretended to be a princess in a palace. Pressing my palms together, I sent a prayer out to the goddess of compassion.

"Nam mo Quan Thế Âm Bồ Tát," I whispered. "Thank you for this gift."

I was so happy when I fell asleep that night. It all seemed too good to be true.

The next few weeks were a whirlwind of orientation events, classes, meet-and-greets at the dorms, and Friday-night Shabbat dinners hosted by Hunter Hillel that anyone could attend. Dena, our Robotics Team Mom, who was now a dear friend of mine, came to visit and helped furnish my room with a green papasan chair and lamps. I immersed myself in these experiences, convinced that I could leave my troubled past behind and become someone new. With my adviser, I finalized my schedule, taking on a load of six honors courses, including a literature course on William Blake for seniors and a psychiatric diagnosis course for juniors. I didn't really know what I wanted to major in, but my growing preoccupation with the way the mind worked, *my mind* in particular, made me want to study the mechanics of the brain. I'd been broken, and now I wanted to fix myself.

I needed special permission to enroll in the advanced classes since I was only in my first year, so I reached out to the professors to make my case and they let me in. I was determined to do well. This was my opportunity to prove to everyone, and most of all to myself, that I was capable.

I was busy making friends too, meeting a lot of new people in the dorm and in my classes. I also reconnected with old friends from Bronx Science. Pooja, a girl I'd known only casually in high school but who turned out to live right next door to me at Brookdale, became a close friend. She often visited my room unannounced, bursting through the door the way Kramer did in *Seinfeld* and sitting down on my bed for a chat. I loved that.

Other friends would knock on my door to invite me to go out and we'd explore different parts of the city—Union Square, Gramercy Park, the East and West Villages, and Tribeca—many of which I'd never seen before, despite living in New York City for more than fifteen years. We would eat in Thai, Indian, Japanese, Italian, and Greek restaurants, all of which thrilled me. Some of the upperclassmen would even buy alcoholic beverages for us and bring it back to the dorms, and I discovered that I really liked the taste of whiskey.

Someone introduced me to Guille, a handsome gay exchange student from Spain who prided himself on a great sense of style. One day, when a group of us were hanging out in my room, Guille perused my closet, going through my pathetic wardrobe and frowning.

"Oh, *honey*," he said in a beautiful Spanish accent and with dramatic flair. "We've *got* to do something about this. I can't let you go around in these clothes. What are these jeans? Are they boys' jeans? And these shirts are way too big on you. With a figure like that, you need something more formfitting."

He didn't hold back, and I wasn't offended. In fact, I appreciated the way he so freely offered his criticism. He had the unique talent of doing so without making a person feel bad about it.

"I have an idea. Let's you and I go shopping!" he said. It was his favorite thing to do.

The scholarship that I'd received from the Honors College had just been deposited into my account earlier that week. This was my chance, I thought. I could finally learn how to have my own style. So I agreed. The very next day, we went shopping at stores like H&M and Forever 21, stores I'd never been to. When Guille asked me what it was that I liked to wear, I told him I had no idea. He asked me if anything on the rack stood out to me, and though I could now see with my contacts, I had no clue what to choose.

"Okay, how about this?" he said. "How about you give me a budget and I'll pick out all your clothes for you? You'll be my doll. I won't lead you astray, I promise. And we won't get anything you're uncomfortable with."

Again, I readily agreed, excited that, for the first time in my life, I would have clothes that fit me properly, that would define me somehow the way they seemed to define others. Guille and I zipped through the stores, in and out of changing rooms, buying this, returning that, figuring out what colors would look best against my complexion and what shapes would look flattering on my frame. We came home with at least five new outfits, skinny jeans, dresses, colorful and patterned tops, flats, and a belt, all of which Guille carefully instructed me on how to wear. He made me promise to either donate or throw away all my old clothing.

"Welcome to a new you," he said, turning me around to look in the mirror after I finished changing into one of the outfits. I couldn't believe how different I looked. I felt like I was seeing my own body for the first time. Even the girl in the mirror looked surprised. *This isn't you*, she tried to say, but her voice was beginning to lose its strength. I twirled and twirled around in my new outfit with a huge grin on my face. Guille wrapped me up in his arms and gave me a big kiss on the cheek.

Was this what life was supposed to be like? I thought. Easy and free, full of delicious meals, new discoveries, new clothes, and wonderful new friends? I couldn't believe how drastically my life had changed in just a few months' time.

I thought of my parents and wished desperately that I could share a slice of it with them. Since I was so busy at school, I no longer had time to help at the nail salon. A wave of guilt would wash over me every time

I passed a salon on the street, but I quickly brushed it away. It was just a matter of time, I thought, before my education would enable me to give them a better life. This was the beginning. I needed to escape first, but I swore I would come back for them.

Living in such close quarters with so many new people was a completely different experience for me. I was so intrigued that, in my spare time, I began to write lengthy profiles of the friends I'd made. I observed them all—their habits, their idiosyncrasies, their manner of dress, their gait, their scent, and even (not surprisingly, I suppose) the way their nail polish was applied—with an intensity that now seems very strange to me. Every night, when I returned to my dorm room after an evening out with friends, I would immediately jot down notes about them. I spent countless hours in furious examination of the lives of others.

But who was I? What unique characteristics did I possess that set me apart from everyone else? My own profile was blank, the girl in the mirror still a mystery. It was as if I were seeking to delineate myself through my observations of others. If I could understand them, and the ways in which I was and was not like them, maybe I would be closer to the mystery of who I was. But no matter how hard I tried, that girl seemed determined to remain unknowable.

Though I no longer had to worry about hiding the contacts from my parents, I continued to skimp on changing them. I would stretch biweekly contacts to monthly contacts, and eventually, I kept them in for months on end. They didn't seem to affect my eyes other than to dry them out a bit. But that was nothing compared to not being able to see for so long. I could handle a little dryness.

And with the ability to see for the first time in years, I was invincible. I got straight As my first semester. I loved my psychology courses and considered becoming a psychiatrist. I made a lot of friends. I got a job working as a part-time peer educator for the Asian and Pacific Islander Coalition on HIV/AIDS (APICHA). There I met Douglas Nam Le, a public health specialist at NYU who asked if I wanted to be cofounder of an initiative geared toward spreading health awareness in the Vietnamese community. It was called the Vietnamese Community Health Initiative. Of course I did. I was on a high and I wanted to do everything.

Douglas nominated me for NYU's Center for the Study of Asian American Health 2007 Youth Leadership Award for my outreach efforts in the Southeast Asian communities of New York, and to my surprise, I won. A part of me that I thought I'd lost forever, the part of me that started a club against child labor in middle school, that made me think I could have a positive impact on the world, had miraculously returned.

By the end of my fall semester, I'd taken on three more roles. I couldn't seem to stop. I was an ambassador for the Honors College, event chair for the American Cancer Society's annual fundraiser Relay For Life, and I was also part of CRAASH, the Coalition for the Revitalization of Asian American Studies at Hunter. In public I was confident, polite, attentive to the moods of others—and driven. If I kept busy enough, I wouldn't have to obsess about that girl in the mirror, wouldn't have to feel guilty about my parents. But no matter how many activities I threw myself into, the guilt was there. The girl in the mirror was there. Always there.

My mother would sometimes call and ask about school.

"It's great," I'd tell her. "I'm doing well. I'm getting really good grades. And how's the nail salon?"

"Oh, you know," she said. "Same as always. The heater broke the other day, so your father and I have been using propane burners to heat the store."

Since there was nothing I could do to help, conversations like this one would upset me so much that I began to distance myself, returning my mother's calls only occasionally and getting off the phone as soon as I could. It felt wrong that I was having such a good time while my parents toiled away, earning so little money and getting mistreated. I would try to brush the guilt away, remind myself that being in school was the best thing I could do to eventually find a way to help them. But then I'd imagine my mother and father standing over propane burners to warm themselves or returning to their cockroach-ridden apartment after a long day at the salon, and the feeling that I had abandoned them would keep gnawing away at me. I felt like a failure no matter what I did. This would soon become a self-fulfilling prophecy.

Though I somehow managed to ace my first semester, my success was short-lived. I began to have nightmares—scenes of my mother sitting on a pedicure stool scrubbing someone's feet as they hurled insults at her, scenes of my father finding out that I had betrayed him again by wearing contacts and going on a rampage against me. At first, it was just one or two nightmares here and there during the week, but as time went on, the frequency increased and I started to lose sleep.

I told Dr. Hayes, whom I was still seeing weekly, about my guilt and the nightmares I'd been having, and he prescribed Lexapro, an antidepressant, and Dexedrine, a stimulant to help me focus.

"This is completely understandable," he told me. "You've probably been depressed for a long time, but you're a highly functioning depressed person, which is how you've managed to do so well despite your condition. But it makes sense that the symptoms would show eventually. I suspect you may have a bit of ADD as well, so the Dexedrine may help with that. We'll start with a low dosage and see how it feels. If we need to increase it, we'll increase it."

When the spring semester began, I again took on a full load of six courses, aimed toward a premed track, but this time, everything was different. Even with the medication—or maybe because of it, I wasn't sure—something strange was happening within me. Though on the surface I still seemed to be thriving, I felt like I was disintegrating. My perception of reality and my sense of self started to fragment. When I was with friends and colleagues, I could still sometimes appear happy, energized, charismatic even, but in the solitude of my room, I felt utterly helpless, sometimes sobbing uncontrollably for hours on end.

I felt as though I were splintering into many identities, splinters that did not cohere into a whole.

"It was like you were different people," Chui, a dear friend from Bronx Science who also attended the Honors College with me, told me years later. "In high school, I only knew you in one context. But in college you always seemed to be different depending on who we were with, so I always had a weird feeling that I didn't know who you were. I began to seriously question whether the Ly I knew was the real Ly."

And then there were moments when time suddenly didn't seem to work the same way anymore. It expanded and contracted, leaving me disoriented. What seemed to me to be only seconds were hours in real life. I drifted into my inner world and stayed there for longer and longer periods. I stopped answering my mother's calls. I began to sleep for twelve hours at a time, even more some days. Holed up in the confines of my room, I didn't want to leave because I was afraid of what I might find on the other side of the door and afraid of what others might find within. I was paranoid that friends would finally figure out who I really was, someone who didn't belong anywhere, not in the prestigious Macaulay Honors College, not among her smart accomplished friends, and not even in her own home.

———

Trying to maintain some semblance of normality and routine, I would make my way to the shared dormitory bathroom on my floor to wash my face and brush my teeth so I could go to class. But turning on the water—the old problem of going from dryness to wetness—was as frightening as it had been when I was a child. A voice in my head would repeat, *Just do it and get it over with*, as I hovered above the sink, frozen with fear. Sometimes, I couldn't bring myself to do it, so I would drag myself back to bed and stay there until the next time I could muster enough courage to go back and try again. Other times, I was successful and did manage to start. And then an even bigger challenge arose.

I couldn't stop.

Stop it right this instant, I'd say to myself. *Stop moving your hand. Come on, Ly. You can do this. Take the toothbrush out of your mouth. Come on, you idiot. Stop it!*

Often it wasn't until someone walked into the bathroom that I would be able to stop. When, sooner or later, one of my fellow students came in, this would allow me to act normal. It was as though by watching another person's movements, I could borrow their agency for the moment.

Friends began to worry about me because I would disappear for days on end. They would march into my room in the mornings and try to wake me up. I'd wake up long enough to assure them that I was going to class. They'd wait outside my room until I got dressed. But as soon as they were certain they'd done their job and left me to do the rest, I slumped back down onto my bed. The bed that was supposed to represent a new beginning was now a reminder that escape was futile, that no matter how hard I tried, I would never possess the strength to overcome the circumstances of my life.

Eventually, I developed a conjunctivitis infection. I'd stopped taking my contacts out at night, partly because I didn't care enough anymore and partly because I was hoping that the contacts would simply fuse with my eyes and I would wake up one day with perfect vision. It was magical thinking. It was self-sabotage.

I woke up one morning barely able to open my swollen eyes. *Good*, a voice within me said. *That's exactly what you deserve.*

A Danger to Myself

DROPLETS OF WATER DRIPPED from my hair as I held a pair of broken sandals in one hand, clutching a fistful of magnolia blossoms in the other. My bare feet caked with mud and my dress soaking wet, I must have been an alarming sight to Dr. Hayes as I walked in for my appointment.

"Ly!" he said, his tone of voice betraying how surprised he was, although he quickly caught himself and managed to get his voice under control. "Come on in." He hesitated, then pulled down a roll of paper towels from the top shelf of his desk and handed it to me. I apologized for my appearance and wrung my hair out with the towels. Then I sat down and placed the magnolia blossoms in my lap.

A few hours earlier, two friends from the Honors College, Katie and Leo, had invited me to go to Central Park with them after class. It was a warm late-April day. The sun was out and trees were blossoming all over the park. We bought ice cream and wandered around, soaking in the sun. It felt good to be outside. Winter had been unbearably long, and I'd spent much of it in bed. But I never missed my appointments with Dr. Hayes.

That day I had mustered enough energy to make it to class before my appointment, with a little trip to Central Park in between. But once we were in the park it began to rain unexpectedly—a downpour, and I was wearing flimsy sandals. The rain muddied the dirt paths we walked on, and my sandals fell victim to the suction of mud and rainwater. The straps broke off one sandal and threatened to break off the other as well.

It seemed silly to wear just one sandal, so I took them both off and walked around barefoot. It didn't bother me. And it never occurred to me to try to get to a store to buy another pair of sandals or at least a cheap pair of flip-flops after I left Central Park. It certainly didn't cross my mind how bizarre it would be to show up shoeless in Dr. Hayes's office. I felt more alive than I had in months, grateful for the rain and the sunshine and the promise of spring. It made me forget the guilt that I had been feeling for betraying my parents, my shame over my failures in school, and my fear that maybe school really wasn't for me.

"You look like a little wood nymph," Katie said.

"Yeah, wild child," Leo said.

I laughed and bent down to collect the beautiful pink-and-white magnolia blossoms that had fallen off in the downpour.

Back in Dr. Hayes's office, I was still on a kind of manic high.

"Are you okay?" he asked.

"More than okay," I said. "I haven't been this happy in a long time."

"Oh? And why is that?" he asked, jotting notes down on his pad. He eyed the blossoms on my lap.

I took a deep breath. "I haven't been doing well," I finally told him. "I'm scared that after all this progress I've made, I'm just going to fail again. I had a 4.0 last semester, but I don't know how I'll get through this one. I haven't been able to get out of bed. I haven't been going to some of my classes and I haven't been turning in my assignments." I held up a magnolia blossom, feeling a pang of guilt in my gut for whining. "But I'm doing better today," I quickly added, forcing a big smile.

"I went to Central Park with my friends and had a great time. Here, this is for you."

"Thanks." He smiled but didn't take the blossom. Instead, he wrote more notes in his pad. "So, Ly," he said slowly as he finished writing. "This is completely new information for me. Why didn't you tell me you weren't going to class and that you weren't handing in assignments?"

"I'm sorry," I said. "I just keep thinking that I can turn things around, and if I can, then no one needs to worry about it. But now it's almost the end of the semester. I'm doing fairly well in two of my classes, but the other four . . ."

"Have Lexapro and Dexedrine been helping at all?" he asked.

"They've been helping a bit," I lied. I didn't want to tell him how bad it really was, about my episodes in the bathroom and the sensation of falling out of time. But he seemed to pick up on the fact that something was seriously wrong.

"Are you having any suicidal thoughts?" he asked.

I thought about the question. Suicide? How interesting. I never considered it. But if I did, why would I tell anyone? I was mulling the question over in my mind when I realized that I might have been taking too long and Dr. Hayes was waiting for me to answer.

"No," I said. "No suicidal thoughts."

"Okay . . . ," he said, jotting down more notes. "Well, how about this? How about we increase the dosage on your medication, see if that will get you out of your funk. You're clearly very depressed and this isn't good. But as for your grades, don't worry. You're not going to fail. I can fax over a medical note to your school, and we can get you medically excused from the classes you aren't doing well in, and for the ones you are doing well in, maybe you can take a few incompletes. I'll talk to your adviser. We'll work something out."

Really? It was that easy? I thought. Fantastic! Things were going to work out after all. But then I thought about my parents and felt

suddenly like I was falling off a cliff. My heart soared and plummeted, soared and plummeted, until I hardly knew what I was feeling. I don't even recall the rest of that conversation with Dr. Hayes.
I left the room numb with exhaustion from the ceaseless ricocheting
of my emotions. I didn't even notice that I'd dropped my magnolias
on the way back to my dorm room until I arrived and saw that they
were gone.

The following day, I woke in the late afternoon to three loud knocks
on my door. It sounded like there was a commotion outside my room.

"Come in," I shouted. But the visitors continued to knock. I slid off
my bed and opened the door. Two security guards and the director of
the Brookdale dorms stood gravely outside. Static streamed from their
walkie-talkies.

"Ly Tran," the director said, which was odd because we knew each
other. I didn't know why she had to say my last name as well. "You have
to come with us immediately. We're taking you to the hospital."

"The hospital?" I asked. I wasn't aware that I was sick.

"Ms. Tran," one of the security guards said. "Please gather a few
essential items, nothing more than that, and we will escort you to the
Mount Sinai psychiatric ward."

"The psych ward?" I asked, my voice barely a whisper. My mouth
was dry, my heart rate spiking. What was going on? What had I done?

"Yes, we have reason to believe that you are a danger to yourself."

"Wh-what?" I stammered. "But I don't— There must be some kind
of mistake. M-may I call my psychiatrist?"

"You can call him on the way," they said. "But we have to leave now.
And don't bring more than what you need. Unessential items will be
confiscated." So I gathered my things as instructed, a toothbrush and
toothpaste, my cell phone, and the stuffed turtle Alex had given me.

They looked questioningly at the turtle but didn't say anything. I was glad for it. Though it wasn't a real turtle like the one that saved my father so many years ago, I wanted to believe it could protect me. It was all I had.

Several students had come out of their rooms to watch the spectacle. I wanted to disappear.

"Are you okay?" A friend silently mouthed the words to me.

I smiled weakly, nodded, and waved to them as the elevator doors closed. My knees threatened to buckle under me.

"It's okay, sweetheart," the director said to me in the elevator. "It's just a temporary thing. I know it's hard now, but it'll get better." I remained silent.

Outside the Brookdale dorms, she hailed a cab, and we both climbed in. One of the security guards walked up to the car door and looked in.

"You're gonna be all right?" He was addressing the director, not me.

"Yeah, I'll be fine," she said. "Just do me a favor and make sure my office is locked. I'll be back in a bit."

Meanwhile, I used my phone to call Dr. Hayes, but my call went straight to voicemail. I didn't leave a message.

"Anything?" the director asked.

"No, he didn't pick up," I said and looked down at my lap in confusion and defeat.

Then I noticed the pants I was wearing. I was so scared that I'd forgotten to change out of my pajamas.

After I was dropped off, an identification bracelet was slapped onto my wrist and all my belongings confiscated, including my clothes. I had to change into a hospital gown.

"You'll get these back when you leave," the nurse told me, holding up a clear plastic bag of my things.

"But what about my cell phone?" I asked. "How will I get in touch with anyone?"

"There are communal phones in the ward," she said. "When you get settled in, you can call whoever you like at the scheduled times for calling. In the meantime, I need you to sit here and wait until you hear your name."

I did as I was told. I sat in the waiting room for hours, nurses walking back and forth ushering people in and out. To make matters worse, my period had arrived, and I was leaking.

"Could I please get a pad?" I asked a nurse. "I have my period."

"Sure thing, baby. Just sit right there."

But she never came back. Another nurse approached me to weigh me and take blood samples. I repeated my request. She told me she would come back with a few pads for me. Hours went by, and my gown was beginning to get drenched. I called out to a few other nurses, who said they would tell someone to come by. I eventually went to the bathroom and wedged brown paper napkins between my thighs. Then I returned to my seat and drifted off to sleep.

Finally, sometime around midnight, someone shook me awake.

An elderly Filipina nurse peered down at me.

"Lie Tran?"

I nodded, not having the energy to correct her pronunciation. Lie seemed apt. I was nothing more than that.

"Come with me."

I shook my head. I was too embarrassed to get up from my seat. I knew I had soiled it.

"What's the matter?" she said.

"I-I'm, I have a—" I stammered, ashamed of myself. "I have a leak. I'm leaking." My eyes welled up with tears.

"Okay, get up, please," she said more forcefully. So I did. Her eyes widened. "Oh my God, honey. We need to get you out of this gown." She called to another nurse. "Hey, can you bring me a box of menstrual pads ASAP? And can you get someone to take this seat out of here?" She turned to me and walked me into a nearby examination room. "Why didn't you tell anyone?" she asked in an admonishing tone.

"I-I don't know," I said. "I'm so sorry."

Why didn't I say something to someone? I asked myself. Or did I? I couldn't really remember. I didn't know what was going on anymore. I was so unsure of myself, of everything. What had I done wrong?

After giving me a box of wipes to clean myself up and a new hospital gown, orderlies led me to a room with three other patients, two of them diagnosed with schizophrenia, and a third with bipolar disorder, as I would later learn.

"H-hello," I said to my roommates when the orderlies left. "My name is Ly."

One of them hissed at me, probably because it was close to 1:00 a.m. by then and my arrival had awakened her. Another smiled weakly and gave a small wave. And the third simply said, "That's your bed." She pointed to one in the corner of the room. I walked over to it and sat down. The room was dimly lit and smelled like someone had just thrown up. There was a bathroom for all of us to share, but the door had broken off from one of its hinges and did not close all the way. The overhead light flickered on and off.

I lay down. I wanted to cry but was too confused to even do that, so I drifted off to a fitful sleep. Strange sounds coming from other rooms in the ward erupted in the middle of the night, waking me every now and then. The sounds frightened me, and I groped around in the darkness for my turtle. Where was it? Didn't I have it with me? Did I lose it or was it with my other belongings? I couldn't remember if I'd given it to the nurses when I first arrived. Thoughts swirled nervously in my mind, but I could no longer fight against my exhaustion. I eventually fell into a deep sleep.

The next morning, a nurse woke me up and handed me two pills. She knelt beside me with a glass of water. "Show me your tongue," she commanded after I'd taken the pills. I didn't understand why, but I stuck out my tongue. Later, I discovered it was to make sure that I had swallowed the pills.

"Good girl," she said, getting up. "All right, ladies. Let's go. It's breakfast time!"

My roommates left the room and the nurse directed me to a cafeteria across the hall where I'd be taking all my meals. I sat down at an empty table and ate my breakfast quickly, silently, with my head down. After the meal, we had the option of going back to our rooms or going to a lounge where we could watch television or play board games. I chose to go back to my room, not knowing what else to do.

Doctors and counselors showed up at various times during the day to question me.

"Do you know why you're here, Ms. Tran?" one of them asked. I thought she was a doctor but wasn't sure. She'd come into the room with several other people, maybe students or interns, maybe counselors. Since no one introduced themselves to me I didn't know who anyone was.

"No, not really," I said.

"We've been trying to get in touch with your psychiatrist, Dr. Hayes, and have been unsuccessful," she said. "We need to talk to him to know why you're here before we can move forward with a plan for your treatment and release. So please bear with us until then."

"Okay," I said.

"How do you feel?" she asked.

"I don't know," I said.

"Are you suicidal?"

"No," I said. It was the second time in two days someone had asked me. Why did they think that? "But if I were," I added, "I wouldn't tell anyone anyway."

I'm not sure what inspired me to say that. Glances were exchanged. Notes were taken. Little flashlights were shone into my eyes. Then they left.

"Oh, um, excuse me!" I called out after them. "W-would you happen to know where my turtle is?" I asked.

"Your turtle?" They jotted down more notes.

"I . . . I brought a turtle, a stuffed one, with me, I think, when I came."

"Oh, it must be with your confiscated belongings if you brought it with you," one of them said. "I can grab that for you."

She came back with it a few minutes later. Though I knew it was silly for an eighteen-year-old to need a stuffed animal, it brought me immense relief. I felt safe. At least I was no longer alone, I thought. Besides, I'd never had any toys or stuffed animals when I was growing up. I was making up for lost time.

Then one of my roommates, the one who had told me where my bed was the prior evening, came into the room. She was a middle-aged black woman, thin, with her hair shaved close to her head. She held herself in a regal manner, her movements both elegant and imposing. She pointed to the turtle.

"What is that?" she asked, her eyes narrowed in suspicion. "Why do you have it?"

"It's my stuffed turtle," I said. "A friend gave it to me." Although it wasn't a real turtle, like the one that protected my father all those years ago, it still comforted me and reminded me of my parents. I wondered what they were doing in that moment, wondered what they would think if they knew where I was, if they would be ashamed of me.

"Fine. A turtle is fine," she said. "As long as it's not a snake." She eyed me, as if inviting me to inquire more. I took her cue.

"You don't like snakes?" I asked.

"No, I don't," she said. "And I'll tell you why. They're the vilest creatures on the face of this planet. They're an abomination against nature, against God. It's the devil himself. You know that, don't you?"

I shook my head no, but she didn't seem to notice. She told me that she had had a dream once while she was studying at Dartmouth College, one in which a snake had wrapped itself around her, whispering in her ear to follow it. Then she launched into a long, elaborate story about how it would never leave her alone and was always trying to make her do evil things she didn't want to do. I listened intently and observed her every gesture. Her story fascinated me. I suddenly wanted to know everything about her, what she majored in at Dartmouth, how she ended up in the psych ward, what her illness was. It occurred to me then that being here might not be all bad. I'd been studying psychology and psychiatric diagnoses at Hunter, and this would be a chance for me to learn on the ground. I could think of it as research. I was desperate for some kind of coping mechanism, and this was what I seized on.

"What are you looking at?" she suddenly asked.

"Oh, n-nothing," I said. "I'm just listening."

"Well, how come you don't say anything?" she asked. "You scared of me?"

"No, no, that's not it," I said. Though a part of me was scared, most of me was curious. "Your story is just interesting. That's all. I want to hear more."

She sat down on her bed, facing me. "I'm Jane," she said. It was more of a declaration than an introduction.

Then she smiled. It was a wary half smile, but a smile nonetheless. I smiled back. Jane suddenly didn't seem so frightening anymore. She took some getting used to, but I realized that she was just lonely. She spoke to me whenever I was in the room, cautiously at first, but once she decided I wasn't a threat, she was able to relax. We became friends.

Over the course of the next several days, I got to know Jane well. She was a poet, and she recited her poems aloud to me. They were mostly about the snake devil, but I liked them. There was a good cadence to her words and she was always so impassioned as she spoke. She told me she suffered from bipolar disorder and had forgotten to take her pills. She'd become manic, so she checked herself into the psych ward. I wondered if what I had exhibited was manic behavior. Was that why I was here too? I thought.

But then it was time for Jane to go. She said she'd been there for a week already, and the doctors decided she was stable enough to be released.

"Take down my number," she said. "Let's meet again on the outside."

I was sorry to have lost my friend, but grateful that I'd made one at all. Most of the people in the ward had occasional visitors or phone calls from friends and family. I had no one. I didn't want my parents to know where I was, and I was too ashamed to reach out to any of my friends and ask them to visit. With Jane gone, I began to look for other people I might be able to connect with.

I still ate my meals alone, but sometimes I would go to the lounge to see what the other patients were doing. I watched them play games like tic-tac-toe or Connect 4 and would sometimes be invited to play myself. These were games Miss Elena had played with me during our Project Friend sessions, and I was grateful to be invited to join. Though many of my fellow patients suffered from disorders that would occasionally lead to psychotic episodes, they didn't seem dangerous to me. I began to sense the pervasive and profound loneliness that afflicted them. It was a loneliness I could feel in myself, and I wanted to understand them the way that I wanted to understand myself, the way I wanted to be understood.

I found computer paper in the lounge and started to sketch the patients, recording my observations of them beneath the sketches. Every day, the head psychiatrist would find me and inform me that they still hadn't heard from Dr. Hayes. Counselors would whisk me away to private rooms and ask me the same questions they asked me every day, mainly: How was I feeling and was I suicidal? They also asked me to explain the events that led to my hospitalization, but I didn't really know how to answer that. Had I missed something? Did Dr. Hayes tell me I would be sent to the hospital? All I could tell them was that after a semester of straight As, I was in danger of not passing my classes that spring because I couldn't wake up in time to attend them and because I had trouble focusing. I told them a little about my past, about the contacts and the nail salon.

Eventually, they placed me in the major depressive disorder category. I recalled Dr. Hayes's diagnosis of me the previous year. He'd said I had "high-functioning" depression. It pained me to know that I had reached a point in my life where I was no longer "high-functioning." It was true. Though I'd struggled senior year of high school, I had enough strength and tenacity to push forward. Now I wasn't so sure. I no longer felt that ambitious pulse that once flowed through me. I'd exhausted all of my optimism, all of my faith, and any ounce of self-confidence I might have once had.

And I had never felt lonelier in my life.

The psychiatrist and therapists had me participate in group counseling sessions and occasionally art therapy. They told me they still hadn't heard from Dr. Hayes but would let me know as soon as they did.

At lunch one day, I noticed a pale, heavyset woman with thick-rimmed glasses sitting alone at a table in the corner of the room. She was in a wheelchair and seemed to struggle with eating. She stared straight ahead, unable to bring the fork to her mouth. Her movements were strange, slower than a snail's. I knew from my studies that this was a form of stuporous catatonia, characterized by immobility. Watching her was like watching a slow-motion video. Sometimes, she just stopped moving altogether, the fork halfway to her mouth, her mouth open, expecting the food but not getting it, a small line of drool sliding down her chin and onto her tray.

I worried about her. Mealtimes were strict, and by the time they ended, she had hardly been able to take a bite. But no one noticed. The cafeteria ladies served the food, then cleared the table in front of her when the meal was over. A nurse came in to wheel her back to her room. The same thing happened at dinnertime. I felt sorry for her and wondered how long it had been since she'd eaten anything, but didn't know what to do.

The next day, at breakfast, I summoned the courage to sit down across from her.

"Hi," I said. "I'm Ly."

She did not speak. But her eyes slowly centered on me.

"Um," I tried again, pointing at her food. "Do you need help with that?" Her eyes slowly looked downward at the food. The seconds crawled by, then her eyes slowly rolled back up toward me. No other response.

I tried to think. What could I do? How do I communicate with her? Maybe I could use her eye movements somehow, I thought. Maybe if I assigned looking right to mean "yes" and looking left to mean "no" we could get somewhere.

"I have an idea," I said. "If you could—"

But before I finished my sentence, she let out a groan. It wasn't much, just a small grunt of a groan accompanied by a very slight nod, but it was enough for me to understand. Yes, she needed help.

Okay. Now what? I still didn't know what to do. But it occurred to me that if I broke the food up into smaller portions and tried bringing the fork to her mouth, it might help. I waited. She did not open her mouth, but turned her head slowly and slightly to one side, then to the other side.

She was shaking her head no.

"I'm so sorry," I said, frustrated and disappointed. "I don't know how to help."

I was running out of ideas when I noticed that she was moving her index finger. Then I realized that she was trying to point at something. I followed her finger to the cup of applesauce on the far corner of the tray, and it dawned on me. Of course—the applesauce! I should have known. Applesauce would be much easier for her. She wouldn't have to chew.

So I tore open the cup and brought a forkful of applesauce to her mouth, which she finally opened and closed around the fork. Success! I was so thrilled, tears slid down my face. I waited for her to swallow and then brought another forkful to her mouth, until, by the end of breakfast, she managed to finish the whole cup. At lunch and dinner that day, I sat by her again. And continued to do so for the rest of my stay in the psych ward. I felt a special kinship with her. Though we could not communicate verbally, just being with her comforted me. Sometimes, I'd hold her hand in mine and we'd sit in silence at the end of the meal. I could feel her squeezing my hand. I felt like she somehow understood me.

I must have connected her catatonia to my own episodes in the bathroom, all the times I'd been unable to stop brushing my teeth until my gums bled, unable to turn the water on or off. I wanted to help her the way that I needed help.

After about a week or so, the psychiatrist in charge called me to his office. "We've finally gotten in touch with Dr. Hayes. He was on vacation, which is why we couldn't get ahold of him. But he says you're free to go."

His words pierced me like a bullet. On vacation? Dr. Hayes left me in a psych ward while he went off somewhere on vacation and never answered any of his messages? How could he have done that to me?

Later that day, as I was getting ready to go, several of the patients I'd befriended gathered in the communal space to bid me farewell.

"See you on the other side," a man I had played chess with said. A Korean woman rubbed my back. The catatonic woman gave me a slip of paper. She had managed to write on it in large shaky handwriting her phone number and email. "Look 4 me," the note said. "My name: Milagros." I could only imagine how long it took her to do that. I was and still am deeply grateful for that note. I gave each of them a hug and left with a heavy heart. I was going to miss them.

Now it was time for me to face the world again, and I was frightened. As much as I wanted to leave, I was returning to my life on the outside with no more understanding of what had been happening to me than I had when I was admitted. My time in the psych ward seemed only to delay the inevitable. It was just a matter of time before I stumbled and failed again.

Answered Prayers

DR. HAYES LOOKED AT me, waiting for me to begin. The seconds crawled by, but I had no idea where to start. I was back in his office, back to those four cream-colored walls, back to congested silence. But this time the silence was covering up a rage I didn't know I was feeling. After my release from the psych ward I'd made an appointment to see him.

"I thought it would be best to place you in the hospital while I was away," he finally said, once he realized that I was too blocked to speak. "That way, you could use the time away from school to get better. And we could have you medically excused."

"But why didn't you tell me you were going on vacation? Or that you would put me in the psych ward?" I asked, trying desperately to make sense of it all. "I tried to call you. And the doctors tried to call you."

"You're right. I'm sorry about that. I should have let you know that I would be on vacation. Do you feel like I abandoned you?"

I was silent. I didn't know how to put into words what I felt. After all this time, I was still lost at sea. I couldn't swim, the words I needed still locked away on that ship I could never reach.

"It's okay," he said. "You can be angry at me."

Somewhere deep inside, I felt immense pressure surging against the wall I'd constructed so carefully over the years. I felt that wall beginning to crack, emotion leaking out of me. Was I angry? Was that the word for what I felt? Did I even have enough confidence to allow myself to feel anger? I was reminded of the day I burst into Ms. Walsh's office to ask her why she'd called the ACS on my father without telling me beforehand. Was that anger as well?

How could he? I asked myself, as I had been asking every day since the day I heard those knocks on my dorm room door. How could he have put me in that place without warning and without being there to support me? Yes, of course I had felt abandoned, because I was—and I was shattered by that abandonment, so perhaps I *was* angry. But not only did I not have the words to express anger; I was afraid of what might happen if I did, afraid it would consume me.

I later learned that I was his first patient out of med school. Inexperience accounted for what a botch he had made of hospitalizing me. But the trauma I suffered because of his inexperience made me distrustful of Dr. Hayes for the rest of the time I remained within his care.

As planned, he wrote me a medical note attached to my discharge papers and sent it to Charlotte, my adviser. She and the director of the Honors College placed me on academic probation, the terms of which required me to maintain above a 3.5 GPA in the fall semester and have biweekly check-ins with her. If I met those terms, I could remain in the Honors College and keep my scholarship, dorm room, and laptop. For the rest of the spring semester, I was medically excused and granted official withdrawals from four of my six classes. The professors for the remaining two classes allowed me to take an incomplete, giving me two months to make up the work I missed.

Being placed on academic probation made me feel so ashamed of myself. *You had done so well the previous semester, but you just had to go and screw it all up, didn't you?* a familiar voice inside me asked. I had no choice but to accept the terms of probation and try to salvage whatever opportunity I had left to make things right again.

"We'll get there bit by bit," Charlotte told me in an email as spring semester was coming to an end. "Good luck this summer," she said. "I feel strongly that you will have a great fall semester."

I wanted badly to believe her. I was still having trouble waking up, still unable to focus. I had narrowly avoided disaster again, but how long could I keep this up? How long could I rely on the understanding and sympathy of others to pull me through?

"I think I'm depressed," I told Thinh and Phu in separate phone calls to them. Though Long had come back from Costa Rica the previous semester and was now living on the tenth floor of the Brookdale dorms, an elevator ride away, I didn't want to bother him. He was hyperfocused on his studies at the time, triple majoring and maintaining an almost perfect GPA. So I decided to reach out to the other two instead. It was the first time I'd spoken to either of them since I started college. We'd been so out of touch that I didn't even know Thinh had quit his job at Microsoft and was now working on several start-up ideas of his own. Nor did I know that Phu had moved to Washington after his one-year contract with Nike had expired, and was now living in Thinh's house, searching for jobs in the area. And, like my parents, they had no idea that I had been hospitalized.

"Nah, you're all right, Ly," Thinh said. "Depression is just a state of mind. You need to stop focusing on the past. You're in an awesome place now. Be grateful. What's there to be depressed about?" Thinh had bought contacts for me when he heard I was still having problems with my vision, but he'd originally thought that was a state of mind too—something I could overcome with determination. So I was skeptical about his casual dismissal of my problem.

"Just hang in there, Ly," Phu said. "You're gonna be fine. Look at me. I was struggling for a while too, but now things are looking up for me, and I've gotten a few job offers. Just be patient and take it easy."

It was all they could say. They didn't understand depression or mental illness. Or perhaps they'd found more effective ways of coping than I could. After all, we hadn't been brought up to deal with our emotions, only to repress and deny them. And since I never told them about my hospitalization for fear that they wouldn't understand or, worse, judge me for being weak, they couldn't have had any idea how serious my situation was.

When I moved back home at the end of the school year, since I couldn't stay in the dorm over the summer, it was back to Pitkin Nails. I couldn't help wondering if this was going to be my fate.

"How are you doing in your classes?" Charlotte asked me. It was during one of our biweekly meetings in her office, which was located on the main floor of the dorm. By then it was fall, and I was a couple of months into my second year at Hunter. Summer at home had gone by in a blur and my depression was worse than ever. I had finished off the two bottles of Lexapro and Dexedrine and stopped seeing Dr. Hayes. My mandated two years with him had come to an end.

"I'm doing well," I lied, too ashamed to admit that I was once again in trouble with my classes. I'd been showing up erratically. I attempted to complete my assignments but couldn't focus. There were days when I couldn't manage to wake up for more than a few hours at a time and couldn't get myself out of bed even when I was awake. And when I did get out of bed, I often just sat in my room, adrift in my thoughts, lost.

But I didn't want Charlotte to know what was happening. I didn't really know what *was* happening to me. I convinced myself that I'd snap out of it, so I lied to Charlotte during our sessions and even elaborated on how well I was doing to avoid her asking too many questions. I didn't know what else to do. I didn't want to disappoint anyone more than I already had.

"Great!" she said. "I knew you could do it."

After our meeting, I headed back up to my room and found more missed calls from my mother. She had been calling me for weeks, but I had stopped answering. I just wanted to shut out the world. This time, however, her missed call was accompanied by a long voicemail message.

"Lý." My mother's shaky voice filled my ears when I finally settled in to listen. "I was just attacked by a man in the store today. He had a big knife. Xuân, the new girl I just hired, was with me, but she ran into the bathroom and locked herself in. Can you believe it? She left me alone out there. Oh well, I guess I can't blame her. Anyway, I gave him everything I could, which wasn't much." She laughed. "It was another slow day so there were only three manicures and one full set."

I quickly did the math in my head. Six dollars a manicure and fifteen dollars a full set of acrylic tips. Free design.

"I'm okay, Kỳ Lý. I just wanted to let you know that I'm okay. Give me a call sometime, will you? Let your mother know how you're doing. You don't pick up anymore. Okay . . . well . . . I'm hanging up now." But she lingered a few seconds more before hanging up, the sound of that silence crushing me as I imagined her clutching the phone at the other end of the line, hoping I might answer after hearing about the terrifying experience she'd just had. Click.

I pressed play again and listened to the message so many times I lost count.

Lý . . . I was just attacked . . . big knife . . . can't blame . . .

Lý . . . I'm okay . . . Give me a call sometime, will you?

Lý . . . Can you believe it? She left me alone out there.

Lý . . . It was another slow day so there were only three manicures and one full set.

Lý . . . Okay . . . well . . . I'm hanging up now. . . .

I listened until I couldn't anymore, until, exhausted, I sank to the floor and wept.

I hated myself for not being there.

I hated myself for not being able to protect her, for never having been able to protect her all these years.

"I'm sorry, Mother," I whispered into the phone. "I'm so, so sorry."

Every day, I prayed to Quan Âm for something bad to happen to me. Did she even grant those kinds of wishes? I wondered. My depression didn't make sense to me. I had friends. I had contacts and could see now. I had a full scholarship to a prestigious college. I had my own dorm room. I had a part-time job with APICHA and was part of several school clubs and organizations. I needed something bad to happen to me to justify my inability to function.

Midway through the fall semester, something did.

It was a Tuesday evening, and I had just finished taking a chemistry exam that I was certain I'd failed. My head was spinning. All I wanted to do was get on the subway and go back to the dorm, back to the safety of my room, where nothing could hurt me. Exiting the subway at the Twenty-Third Street stop on Lexington, which was only about five blocks from Brookdale, I walked at a brisk pace, weaving through the masses returning home from work, trying to get back to my room as quickly as possible. I held my head down. A green traffic light. I stopped. A red light. I went. Green light again. Red light. Headlights. But I continued to walk since I had the right of way. But the sound of tires screeching rang in my ears. I looked up, but it was too late. I was suddenly airborne.

When I opened my eyes, a crowd of people had gathered around me. I was lying on my side in the middle of the intersection. The car that had hit me sped away without my ever having seen it.

"You'll be okay, honey. An ambulance is on its way." A black woman wearing pearl earrings, a white wool peacoat, and a red scarf knelt beside me. She was beautiful and had a warm sugary voice. She stroked my hair.

I sat up.

"No, no, sweetheart, don't move. Just wait until they get here," she said. But I barely heard her. All I could focus on was going back to my room to lie down.

"I'm okay," I said. And I was. Nothing seemed to hurt. Nothing was broken. I stood up, and the woman held on to the crook of my arm. "I'm okay," I said again. And she gave me a hug.

"Oh, sweetie," she said into my hair. "You're going to be okay."

Such compassion and warmth. I felt later that she must have been an angel passing by that night or an incarnation of Quan Thế Âm Bồ Tát, her kindness a temporary salve to my broken spirit. "Thank you," I said. And as the crowd of people slowly dispersed, I resumed my walk back to the dorm. Before I got very far a man on Rollerblades came up from behind me and stopped in front of me. He handed me a card.

"Call this number when you get home. This is a lawsuit. I'm your witness. That taxi-van ran a red light. I wrote down his license plates for you on the back of the card. Good luck." And he skated away. Another angel that night.

I made it back to my room, lay down on my bed, and drifted off to sleep.

The next morning, still in bed, I heard several knocks on my door and a familiar voice shouting my name. It was Pooja from next door.

"Come in," I called out, puzzled. Usually she just burst in without knocking.

"I can't," she said. "The door's locked." She tried jiggling the handle again. "That's so weird. Why is it locked? You never lock your door."

I scrambled out of bed and unlocked it. Pooja wanted to know where I'd been the last few days and whether I was ready to go to bio. She was one of the friends who was trying to get me to go to my classes and she knew my schedule as well as she knew her own, but I guessed she'd forgotten that I didn't have bio on Tuesdays.

"What are you talking about?" she said. "Today is *Wednesday*." She gave me a funny look. "You okay? You look terrible."

I nodded that I was okay and said I'd catch up with her later. After she left, I examined myself in the mirror. I had bags under my eyes and I was still wearing my clothes, even my coat, from the night before. Or was it two nights before? Was it Tuesday or Wednesday? Something didn't add up. Then I realized I was still in my sneakers. How could that be? What was going on? As I started to take off my soiled and rumpled clothes, that's when I saw the bruises in the mirror. The entire right side of my body was black-and-blue. And then it all came back to me, being hit by a car, walking back to the dorm afterward, passing out. It dawned on me that I'd slept for more than a day and a half.

I didn't tell any of my family members about the incident because I didn't want them to worry. And I decided not to contact the man on Rollerblades about pressing charges. It was probably my fault the car hit me, I thought, even though he'd told me the car had run a red light.

"You had a concussion," a doctor told me, months later, when I finally willed myself to get checked out. "You're fine now, but you're lucky. You should have gone to the hospital immediately. Who knows what could have happened?"

But something bad happening to me was exactly what I'd been hoping for. Punishment for my failures. Or at the very least, something I could use as an excuse for them, so that I could move on. But it didn't change anything. Instead, I just failed even more.

I went to my classes more infrequently than ever, instead spending most of my time in bed, sleeping long hours or just drifting. Every little noise bothered me, and sunlight hurt my eyes. I kept my room dim, blinds drawn during the day, and a small lamp lit at night so that it was never completely dark because the darkness terrified me. I started constructing my crystal domes again, but this time, they didn't work. They no longer made me feel safe. If I couldn't protect myself from the world, what hope was there that I could save anyone else?

Since I was spending so much time in bed, whenever I got hungry I would order takeout from a nearby Thai restaurant, the same shrimp *pad kee mao* dish every time. And whenever I could muster the energy, I would go to a nearby liquor store to buy beer and whiskey. I was only nineteen, but luckily for me (or unluckily), the store didn't check for ID.

I liked hearing the sound of my heart thumping loudly in my chest, the sensation of the blood rushing to my temples, the room spinning, the alcohol dulling my senses. I began to develop a high tolerance for liquor and often drank myself into a stupor. My fridge was stocked with alcohol and little else.

When I still cared, at least a little bit, I asked my friends to keep trying to get me to go to classes, and they did their best. One by one, they would come into my room and shake me awake for class. I'd pretend to gather my things and get ready for the day, but as soon as they left me alone, I'd go right back to sleep.

One friend, Noah, even asked one of my professors to give me extra time on an assignment in a class that we were in together. She explained the situation and the teacher reached out to me saying he understood and that he would grant me extra time. But I couldn't bring myself to do it. Everyone was rooting for me and everyone wanted to help, but I betrayed their kindness. I hated myself for that. A chorus of self-loathing voices swirled inside of me telling me that I was dumb and worthless.

So I drank and slept and ate and slept and stopped going to classes altogether. I felt completely hopeless.

"Dear Ly," an email from Charlotte began. "I noticed that you have a 2.77 GPA for Fall Semester. Before the Grade Review next Wed (Jan 14th), I will be meeting with all students whose GPAs are below the required GPA. Would it be possible for you to meet with me at some point between now and then . . . ?"

"Dear Charlotte," I wrote back. "I am sorry. I haven't been able to do anything I promised you I would do. I lied to you every time we reviewed grades, hoping that I could make up for it on the next exam—I never did."

The Macaulay Honors College was swift to dismiss me from their program, as I hadn't fulfilled the terms of the academic probation. But I wasn't being kicked out of school entirely. When a student is dismissed from the Honors College, they automatically matriculate to Hunter College—which Honors students refer to as "Regular Hunter." This meant I was still enrolled in school but would no longer be able to apply to classes meant specifically for Honors students, and no longer had the benefits of fellowship advising and network building. The scholarship money, dorm room, and laptop that had been provided as part of my Honors program package were also withdrawn.

It was late January when I received the official notice, first via an email forwarded to me by Charlotte, then a physical copy in the mail. I was sitting in my dorm room when I read and reread the letter, trying to absorb my new reality. It made sense. I couldn't even really complain. No matter what I did in life, it seemed, I couldn't escape myself.

I turned to look at the mirror hanging on my door. There she was again, that same face, that same ridiculous girl.

"Who the fuck are you?" I asked her. "Why can't you just leave me alone? This is all your goddamned fault."

Part V

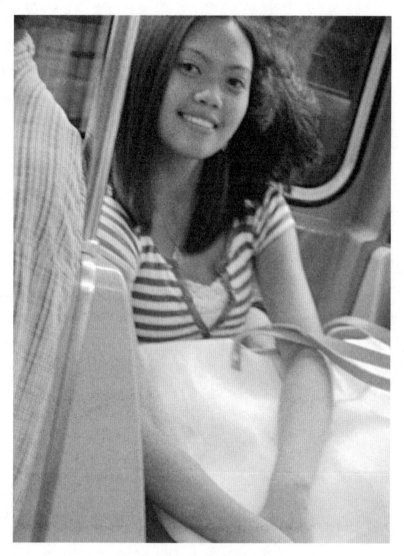

Summer 2007. Ly on the NYC subway.

Where Are You in Life?

I WAS ON MY way to visit Avery one February evening when I met him. It had been several years since I'd seen Avery. We were best friends during our middle school days, but a few months after high school began, she moved to Pennsylvania to live with an aunt. In the years that followed, we spoke on the phone for hours at a time and saw each other occasionally when she'd come back to New York for a day or two to visit, usually with whomever she was dating at the time.

I never knew who she'd be with, since she had no shortage of admirers, or even what she'd look like. She was always experimenting with her clothing and her hair, both cut and color. She had such a unique style that once, as we were ambling through the streets of SoHo, a young woman with a camera strapped around her neck approached us and asked if she could take a photo for her fashion blog. Avery stood there in the middle of the sunlit street and posed as though she had been modeling all her life. I loved her carefree and adventurous spirit, and secretly wished I could be as magnetic a personality as she was.

"What about you, Ly?" she asked me one day after she'd introduced me to her newest boyfriend. We were freshmen in high school, and she had come back for a brief visit. "Isn't there someone you like? Someone you have a crush on?"

I thought hard about her question. Someone I liked? I could no longer see the board in class and I was a disappointment to my family. I could barely hold myself together, tripping and stumbling blindly through life. How could I even think of having a crush on anyone? And for as long as I could remember, my parents, my mother especially, forbade me to think about boys and to focus on my studies. Besides, I thought, who would like me? I had no sense of style, and my hair was short and uneven because my father was still cutting it in order to save money.

"No, not really," I told her. "I don't really care about boys all that much."

But I could never bring myself to tell her the real reason. It wasn't that I didn't like boys. I had several male friends and enjoyed being with them. Having a boyfriend, however, was different. A lovely idea, maybe, but I didn't think something like that would ever happen to me, and I wasn't sure I wanted it to anyway.

Avery and I eventually lost touch. But one evening, shortly after the end of the disastrous first semester of my sophomore year in college, I found a voicemail on my phone and heard a familiar voice. It was Avery. She'd moved back to the city and had been living in Queens, staying with an aunt and uncle while pursuing a course in cosmetology at the Aveda Institute. But her aunt had passed away unexpectedly from lung cancer some months earlier, and a few days ago she'd found her uncle dead on his bedroom floor from a heart attack.

"I could really use a friend," she said through tears. "I miss you."

I called back immediately and made plans to visit her. It was early evening when I hopped onto the subway to head out to her aunt and uncle's house in Glendale, Queens, where she was staying until the title of the house was legally transferred to their heirs. She was all alone.

It was only a few weeks after I learned about my dismissal from the Honors College, so I was still raw from my attempts to process it. I'd already returned my laptop and I was supposed to leave the dorms too, but I asked if I could be allowed to stay at least a few more months while I sorted out my living situation. Charlotte informed me that I could keep my room, but I had to pay for the remaining months. How I would do that, I had no idea, but I told her I would. I couldn't bear facing the shame and embarrassment of moving out midsemester.

On the train ride, I mulled over how I would break the news of my dismissal to my parents. Beginning that summer, I would need to live at home for the next two years while I finished my degree at Hunter College. *Mày thấy không?* they would say. *What did we tell you? We were just trying to save you from this fate.*

After transferring from the 6 train to the L and getting off at the Myrtle-Wyckoff stop, I stood close to the edge of the platform waiting for the M train, blowing air into the collar of my coat to warm myself up. After some time, two bright lights appeared on the tracks. The M was arriving. I stared at the massive hunk of metal approaching the station, thought about how heavy it was, the impact it would make if it hit something. It would be so easy to just step right over this ledge, I thought to myself. Put an end to this misery. Just one foot in front of the other. Yes. One more step. *You're almost there.*

But instead I remained where I was and watched as the train pulled into the station, a rush of wind whipping my hair, the metal barely missing my nose. When the train opened its doors, commuters flowed in and out like schools of zebra fish, and I joined the crowd. As I continued my ruminations from the seat I found on an empty bench in the corner, I kept my eyes on the floor but was vaguely aware of a conversation between a man who was sitting on a neighboring bench and another who was across the aisle.

I leaned my head against the wall behind me and closed my eyes. I wondered what Avery would look like this time. Would her hair be short or long? What color? And I thought about what to say to make her feel better. I'd never experienced the death of anyone close to me so I worried about whether I would say the right thing. As my mind ran through various snippets of possible dialogue—maybe I could just ask her how she was feeling and let her lead the conversation—I had a funny feeling that I was being watched. I opened my eyes and noticed the man across the aisle looking at me. He grinned.

I wasn't sure how to react. I thought he might have been grinning at something he read on the poster behind me. More than once I'd been guilty of staring at an ad, not realizing that this could be mistaken for staring at the passenger in front of it. I smiled a half smile at him, then quickly averted my gaze. He returned to his conversation and I settled back into my reverie.

Finally, the train slowly pulled into the Metropolitan Avenue station. Last stop. I walked over to the doors, waiting for them to open, when the man who had grinned at me appeared by my side. I hadn't really noticed his appearance until then. He was a large man, with a mustache and goatee, a black beanie pulled over his head, and an orange turtleneck sweater visible beneath a leather jacket. He looked at me and smiled again. This time there was no mistaking it. He was smiling at me, and he was so close that I felt a sense of panic. I did not smile back, and as soon as the doors opened, I walked briskly out of the train station.

I stepped into the cold night but didn't get very far before I realized I had no idea where I was going. I'd forgotten to bring the directions Avery had given me. I was about to turn back, but suddenly I had the feeling I was being followed. Not wanting to appear lost, I walked on, pulling out my phone to call Avery. She didn't pick up.

The further I walked from the train station, the darker it became. My pulse quickened. I called Avery again. No answer. I heard footsteps behind me. I was right. I was being followed and I just knew it was the man from the train station. *Oh no . . . not this again*, I thought. I had no idea what to do. I was sure I couldn't outrun him and I couldn't fight him either. Walking back to the train station was best, I decided, because there was a bus stop in front of it where people were waiting and the station at least was well lit.

But it was too late. He'd already caught up to me. I heard a low voice behind me say, "Excuse me, miss?"

I turned around to see the man from the train looking straight at me, this time with a more uncertain smile.

"Y-yeah?" I managed, trying to appear calm and collected.

"Hi," he said with a small wave. "Uh, I'm really sorry to bother you, I, uh, I saw you earlier on the train and, well, I, well, I was just wondering if there might be a chance I could get your number?" He smiled sheepishly, then added, "Sorry, I have no game whatsoever."

I blinked. That's what this was about? Taking a good look at him, I decided he didn't seem so scary. In fact, there was a sweet charm about him as he stood there waiting for my reply. But still, I had to be cautious. If I responded negatively, he might lash out. But if I said yes, it might give him the wrong idea. Maybe I could say yes and give him a fake number, I reasoned.

"Uh . . . sure," I said.

"Oh, wow, really? I can't believe that worked!" He laughed, and I saw kindness beneath a seemingly rough exterior. His eyes were bright and playful and he had one dimple on the left side of his face.

"Um, I'm Joseph, by the way." He extended his hand. I shook it.

"Ly."

"That's quite a handshake," he said, grinning. "Anyway, since you have your phone out, give me your number, and I'll give you a call so you'll have my number too."

Dammit. My plan had backfired. I'd forgotten I had my phone out. But there was no turning back now. I had to give him the real number. I reluctantly typed the digits into his phone, and he tried it out.

"Awesome. Thanks," he said when the call went through. "Well, it was really nice to meet you, Ly. I'll give you a call one of these days. Have a good night." And with that he walked away.

I clutched my phone to my chest and let out a sigh of relief. That wasn't so bad, I thought, and continued in the direction I had been walking. Then my phone rang again. It was Avery. I told her where I was and that I'd forgotten the directions she gave me to her house.

"Oh, it's easy," she said. "Just wait for the Q54. That's the bus right in front of the station. Take it to Cooper Avenue, and I'm just a block and a half away."

I headed back to the train station, and then I saw Joseph coming toward me again.

"Hi again." He waved. He pointed to the sign for the Q54. "You're not waiting for this bus, are you?"

I nodded, unsure how to feel about this second encounter.

"Oh, shit. I am too," he said. "I was hoping to get your number and remove myself from the situation before I fucked anything up. I'm telling you, I seriously have no game."

I laughed. It had been a while since I'd heard the sound of my own laugh. I was grateful to him for it. I relaxed a bit. After a brief awkward silence, I decided to break the ice.

"Where are you in life?" I asked. It was the first question that popped into my mind. I guess it was the question I had been asking myself all this time.

"Whoa," he said, laughing. "What the fuck kind of question is that? I mean, do you *really* wanna know?"

I understood his point and tried again. "Okay, what's your educational background?"

Later, friends would tell me these were the two worst questions I could possibly have asked.

"Oh yeah, like this one's better," he said, grinning. "But okay, I'll answer it. I went to Princeton, Yale, and Penn State."

"Wow, really?" I said, impressed. "What did you major in?"

"Nah, I'm just kidding," he said. "I went to prison, jail, and the state pen."

I stared at him and chuckled nervously. It was a clever enough joke. If that's what it was.

"Yeah . . . I wish the whole thing were a joke," he said. "But only the first half is. The rest is unfortunately true."

"Oh," I said, trying to process what he'd just told me. I'd never known anyone who went to prison, besides my father, and being a political prisoner didn't count.

"I'm not proud of it," he said with downcast eyes. "It was a different life. A different me. But yeah, I'll understand if you don't want me to call you after knowing this. I'll respect that." I observed him closely and cautiously. There was no malice in his voice, only earnestness. I looked at his eyes and slumped shoulders, felt the pain he was in, and wanted, in that moment, to give him a hug.

"What happened?" I ventured.

"It's . . . a long story." He winced. "I did a lot of fucked-up shit with my friends when I was a teenager."

"Like what?"

"Like . . . oh, I don't know . . . multiple armed robberies?" He looked at me, waiting for judgment. I was too stunned to say anything, so he supplied the judgment himself. "Yeah, it's shitty. We were reckless and young and just plain stupid. And some of us eventually got caught and paid the price. We deserved it. I still regret what I did. Man, do I regret it. But . . . but you know what? Prison, as strange as it sounds, turned out to be a positive and transformative experience for me. I reflected on all the mistakes I'd made, and I read a lot. Like, a lot. I read more in prison than I ever did in school. I mean, there was nothing else to do, really. We had access to a library and I enrolled in a few literacy classes they offered to the inmates. I read Shakespeare and Dostoyevsky and Sartre. I really got into philosophy. I had a lot of time on my hands, as you can imagine."

I appreciated his honesty. The way he spoke about his experience made me see him as a person who had made mistakes in life, not some dangerous ex-convict. It might have been naive of me to be so trusting, but there was just something in his eyes, in the way he carried himself, that resonated with me, that told me I didn't need to be afraid of him.

"Go on," I said.

"Damn, you were being serious when you asked me where I was in life, weren't you?" His smile returned. "Anyway, that's pretty much it, I guess. My friends and I grew up during an age when gangsta rap in hip-hop was on the rise, and since most of us, including me, didn't have fathers in our lives, we took our lessons about how to be a man from the lyrics in all those songs. For us, those crimes were like a rite of passage. We took to the streets to define our manhood."

He continued, telling me what it was like growing up in New York during the eighties and early nineties. Suddenly he stopped and looked at me with suspicion. "Wait a minute," he said. "How old are you, by the way?"

"Guess," I told him, feeling playful. I couldn't remember the last time I'd felt playful—half an hour before I'd been thinking about killing myself, and now I was being almost flirtatious—but something about Joseph seemed to bring out another me.

"Uh, I don't know. . . . Twenty-five . . . ? Twenty-six, maybe?"

I laughed. "I'm nineteen," I said. Many of my clients in the salon often guessed that I was older, so it didn't surprise me that Joseph would as well. However, the gap between our ages did surprise him.

"Whoa! What the fuck? You're only nineteen?" He took a step back, his eyes wide with shock. "I just turned thirty-one last week. Holy shit, you're young." He thought about it for a few seconds, weighing possibilities, then quickly composed himself and shrugged his shoulders. "I mean, it's okay with me if it's okay with you."

I giggled, amused by his reaction. "We can still get to know each other," I said. "We can be friends." He was twelve years older than me, but somehow *I* was the one reassuring *him*. I liked it that he seemed almost more vulnerable than I was.

"All right, all right, cool. I like the sound of that," Joseph said, flashing his dimpled smile. "Oh, and one more thing." He sucked in his breath. "Since we're being honest here, I might as well tell you everything in one go." He paused, bracing for my rejection. "So, uh, I have a son . . ."

With that, he beckoned to someone standing in the shadows a few yards away from us. It was the guy he'd been talking to on the train. I'd been so focused on my conversation with Joseph that I hadn't noticed anyone there, and also hadn't noticed the man had a small child with him.

"Ly, this is my brother, Beto." Beto and I shook hands. "And this is my little munchkin, Ethan. Ethan, say hello to Ly." Ethan was playing on a Game Boy, puffs of Afro peeking out from under a hood. He looked up with bright eyes and long curly lashes. He quickly mumbled a hello and returned to his game. "He's a little shy," Joseph said. "He's six."

"Oh, he's adorable," I said. I was enchanted.

The Q54 arrived and we all climbed on. Joseph and I spent the rest of the ride until my stop talking about our families, what we liked to do for fun, what kind of music we liked. I didn't go into any details about my troubled family life and just told him the basics, like the fact that I was mostly Chinese, but born in Vietnam, and had been raised in Ridgewood, along with three older brothers. He had been born in the Bronx but sent to live with his grandmother in the Dominican Republic when he was only two. He didn't come back to the States until he was eleven. He was half Dominican on his mother's side and half Puerto Rican on his father's. And Ethan was half Jamaican.

The more we talked, the handsomer Joseph looked and the more I began to feel self-conscious. Did he maybe think I was "cute"? Did he truly want to get to know me?

But I couldn't let him find out the real me. When he asked me where *I* was in life, I told him that I was studying neuroscience on a premedical track at the Honors College at Hunter, conveniently leaving out the fact that I'd just been kicked out of the program. I wanted to reinvent myself in his eyes as the person I'd been just a few months before—sailing through her courses, feeling on top of the world. Sure enough, Joseph was impressed.

"I'll call you one of these days," he said when we arrived at my stop and gave me a quick hug.

"I look forward to it," I told him. And I meant it. He waved at me through the window as the bus rolled forward, and I waved back, thrilled at the prospect of meeting him again. For the moment I'd forgotten all about my troubles. I half walked, half skipped the block and a half to Avery's house, then composed myself when I remembered what I was there for and rang the bell.

"Hey, girl!" she said when she opened the door. Her eyes were puffy and her cheeks flushed, but she still looked as radiant as ever. I threw my arms around her and we hugged for a long time.

"I'm so sorry about everything you've been going through," I told her. "I wish I'd known earlier." I didn't know what else to say, where to start, or how to comfort her. "How are you holding up?" I attempted. "Is there . . . Is there anything you want to talk about?" I winced. What a stupid thing to ask, I thought.

"Not really," she said. "I mean, you heard everything on that voicemail. That's pretty much the gist of it. I've been crying too much these past few weeks, as you can probably notice. I'm so-o-o done with that. It's been rough, but I'm getting better. And now I just want to catch up with my old best friend."

"Okay," I said. It was clear she didn't want to dwell on recent events, and I didn't want to push it.

"Come on into the living room," she told me as she headed down a long hallway. "You hungry? I've got some rice crackers, ice cream, and half a bottle of Grey Goose."

I laughed. "How 'bout all of the above?"

We sat down at a small table and she poured a shot glass of vodka for each of us.

"So what's up, girl?" she asked. "How have you been? I haven't seen you in ages. I know you're busy being a rock star at Hunter and all, but you could reach out sometimes, you know."

"I know, I know," I said. "I'm sorry. I've been bad at that." Again, I decided not to mention my dismissal. I sipped the vodka instead, feeling the familiar trickle of liquor down my throat, warming my insides.

She dished mint-chocolate-chip ice cream into two bowls, then giggled.

"Come on!" she said. "I haven't seen you in centuries! What's new? I wanna hear some juicy details."

I looked at her piercing blue eyes, still so full of delight and wonder despite everything she'd been through. And she looked back at me, fully expecting juicy details.

"Well," I began. "I met this guy . . ."

The Lost Days

MY EXCITEMENT WAS SHORT-LIVED. I had to return to the mess of a life that I'd created for myself. I forgot all about Joseph. The next day, I began to gather my things to bring them home, thinking I'd be moving out of Brookdale within a month or two and should probably get started. As I packed, I reflected on everything I had been through up to that point, and I began to feel an intense rage build up within me. Why? I thought. Why, no matter how hard I tried, could I never make things work? Something kept holding me back, but what the hell was it? Poverty? Circumstance? Post-generational trauma from the war passed down through my father? A lack of love and care? Shitty luck? Why didn't my parents just let me get glasses, dammit? Why didn't they love me enough to see how much I needed help, how badly I wanted to succeed in this life? Was I so undeserving?

I'd felt this rage before, but this time, I'd had enough. I was sick of once again being lulled into a false sense of success only to have it pulled out from under me. By the time I arrived home that evening, with bags of clothing and boxes of school-related paraphernalia, I'd worked myself into a state. My parents looked at each other quizzically.

"What are you doing here? What's going on?" they asked.

"Oh, don't even pretend you don't know what's going on," I said. "Go ahead. Tell me what you've wanted to tell me all these years. Tell me I'm worthless."

"*Hỗn láo!*" my mother said. "How dare you talk to us that way, you insolent girl."

But I didn't care anymore. In that moment, I blamed them for everything. I blamed my father for his paranoid delusions and my mother for being powerless to stop him. I blamed them for failing me.

"You wanna see something funny?" I asked them. I reached into one eye and popped out a contact, then popped out the other.

Both my mother and my father were speechless, mouths open to berate me, but not knowing what words they could possibly say to their disobedient, defiant daughter.

"Lý, what have you done?" my mother whispered.

I could see the madness creep onto my father's face, his eyes bulging out of their sockets, the capillaries in his cheeks reddening. He clutched his chest. He grabbed at his hair. "*Trời ơi,*" he muttered. "My God."

"You were right all along," I said quietly. "I was never meant to amount to anything."

I braced myself for the violence I knew would erupt, the violence I'd been frightened of all my life. I didn't care anymore. I wanted him to beat me. I wanted to be punished for being a bad daughter and for failing to save my parents, from their poverty, from their pasts, from the monsters in the dark.

Later, when I tried to describe this scene, not just to others but to myself, I remembered it as dramatic. I remembered it as a moment when my father completely came apart, unstrung by rage. In the telling of it, ceramic bowls were flung against the wall, broken glass littered the floor. It was so much easier to believe it happened that way, as it had so many times before. Otherwise, how could I justify the depths of my anger at him in that moment—anger that, once I finally felt it, would last for a long time.

But all these years later, after my anger has dissipated, I remember it differently. I remember the truth of how it happened:

A single smack across the face, just like the day I came home in the third grade with a note from my teacher saying I needed to see an eye doctor. That's all. No dishes were broken, no rage unleashed.

When he hit me that day, I saw the familiar look in his eyes, the look that used to send me cowering in a corner. But this time, I recognized that look as *fear*.

What I didn't understand then is that it wasn't fear of the government being after me. Nor was it fear that the government was after him, which was what he'd felt when the caseworkers from ACS came knocking on our door. No. This was a fear greater than that. It was the fear that he had failed, failed to protect me, failed to be a good father. And failed to recognize that his daughter truly did need glasses.

It would be a long time before I could arrive at that understanding. And when I finally did, it would be with his help.

"Shit, Ly. That fucking sucks," Long said when he found out about my dismissal some days later. He'd come home from the dorms to have dinner with our parents that night. "What are you gonna do?"

"I don't know," I said. "I guess I'll just finish my degree at Hunter. And I can stay in the dorm for a little while longer, but now I have to pay for it."

"Yeah," he said. "You'll be fine. It's not the end of the world."

"Just move back now and get it over and done with," my parents said. "You can't afford to pay for the dorm." Which was true. Even though I still had my Pell and TAP grants, there would be a lot of new expenses now that I was no longer on full scholarship.

"I'll pay for it," Long told them. "Don't make her move out midsemester. Don't you guys know how embarrassing that is?" He had saved money from the various scholarships and fellowships he'd racked up over the years, so he wrote me a check for the full balance of the dorm room for the spring semester, which was about to begin. And I was too miserable to utter even a simple thank-you.

I signed up for a full course load and returned to live in the dorm, but this time without any motivation to try to do well. What would be the use? I thought. I'd probably fail anyway. Being able to see hadn't done me any good after all. One night shortly after the spring semester started, lying still in my dorm room and praying to Quan Âm for the strength to move past this phase of my life, I heard my phone buzzing. It was Joseph.

"Any chance we could get together one of these days?" he asked.

I couldn't believe he had called. I was flattered and excited but also hesitant to say yes. Should I really be going out? I asked myself. Did I *deserve* to go out? I thought about all the things I had to do, all the responsibilities that weighed on me, but they didn't seem to matter anymore. Even though classes had just begun, I was already feeling overwhelmed and hopeless. Everything was falling apart, no matter how desperately I tried to put back the pieces.

Joseph's voice was full of warmth and I was taken back to the evening we met, back to the delight and ease I had felt in our connection. I wanted to feel that again.

"Sure," I told him. "I'd love that."

First Date

"SO YOU'VE REALLY NEVER had a boyfriend before?"

Joseph and I were walking around Fresh Pond Road in Ridgewood, one stop away from where we met.

"No," I told him.

He looked carefully at me and shook his head. "No way. I don't believe it. How are you nineteen and you've never had a boyfriend?"

"Is that bad?" I asked, a little embarrassed.

"No, no. It's not bad at all. It's just . . . unusual. I mean, I kissed a girl when I was five, and I had my first girlfriend when I was eleven. I've never met someone who's made it this far without having a relationship."

"Oh," I said.

"Don't get me wrong," he said, sensing my insecurity. "I'm not trying to make you feel bad. I'm just a little shocked, that's all. Maybe we just come from different worlds. I mean, clearly we do, but holy shit, this puts a lot of pressure on me. And I don't really have much to offer, to be honest."

"What do you mean?"

"Well, what I mean is that I have to make this experience as memorable for you as possible."

I laughed. "It's already memorable," I said, breathing a small sigh of relief. So he was nervous too, I thought.

He jutted out an elbow, inviting me to take his arm. I slid my arm through his, and we continued walking through the street this way. It felt surprisingly natural. He took me to a little fried chicken spot on the corner of Fresh Pond and Sixty-Eighth Avenue, where he ordered food to go.

"We're not eating it here?" I asked.

"No, I figured we'd go back to my place and watch a movie there. What do you think?"

I wasn't sure what to think. It hadn't occurred to me to question where we were going. I had just agreed to meet him in Ridgewood since that was where we first met. "Where exactly do you live?"

"Just one block down. Fresh Pond and Sixty-Seventh."

"No way," I said. "I didn't know you lived in this neighborhood. I live just two stops away, on the Seneca Avenue stop. I mean, I live in the Brookdale dorms during the school year, but my family's home is on Bleecker and Seneca."

"Wow," he said. "So we must have walked past each other a bunch of times all these years without knowing it. Looks like it was meant to be." He winked at me, and I could feel my cheeks getting warm.

After we got our food we walked back to his place, which was on the second floor above a bank and a pizzeria. As we climbed the dark stairs, a part of me wondered what sort of girl would go to a man's apartment on the first date. And another part of me wondered if he could be trusted. Who knew what I could be walking into? My mother's voice crept into my head. *Foolish girl. Why would you follow a stranger into a building? Why would you let someone take advantage of you like that?* But he hadn't yet given me any indication that he was dangerous, and I decided, once again, to go with my gut. Still, I was nervous.

"Ta-da," he said when he opened the door.

His apartment, which seemed to consist of just one room, was dimly lit by a single light bulb dangling from the ceiling. The wooden floor was worn and splintered, his bed frame the sawed-off upper half of a metal bunk bed. Rectangles of spackle were splattered on dark red walls, a repair job left unfinished. Bags of laundry filled a corner of the room. Tools and machinery filled another corner. Drills, table saws, routers, cords. Certainly not what I had been expecting. I walked in tentatively, planning my exit route if he gave even the slightest hint that he might be a danger to me.

He set the food down on a little blue plastic table and pulled up two small folding chairs.

"Sorry for the way things look," he said, eyeing me, trying to gauge my reaction. "After I separated from my son's mother, I had to move here to get my life back in order. I do construction, as you can probably tell, so I'm gonna eventually tear down these walls, the ceiling, and the floor, and just redo the whole room, especially these walls. I hate this ugly-ass red color and all these cracks everywhere. I started spackling it, but I was like, fuck it. I'm gonna tear this whole shit down and make it look so much better. I like working with my hands. I wasn't very good in school, I think because I could never see the point. But with construction, you can see the before and after, and it's such a rewarding feeling. Like, yo, I actually made that."

He told me all about his plans for redesigning the room. His eyes lit up as he talked, and I found his enthusiasm infectious, felt myself being drawn to him.

"But anyway," he said, "I'm rambling. Sorry the place is such a wreck."

"It's okay," I said, wanting to relieve his embarrassment. "My apartment looks pretty bad too," I reassured him. "We've got holes in the walls and some of the light fixtures haven't worked since we moved in more than fifteen years ago. The ceiling leaks when it rains. . . ."

"Damn, really? That's worse than mine," he said. "So you must be glad to be out of there and living in the dorms." He took off his sweater, his T-shirt underneath revealing muscular arms, one with a tattoo of a Japanese symbol engulfed in flames.

"Oh, yeah," I said quickly. I didn't want to mention that I'd be moving back to my parents' place soon. Not yet. I just wanted to forget my bleak situation for a bit. And besides, I didn't want him to know what a failure I was.

Changing the subject, I asked about his tattoo.

"Oh, this thing? I got it when I was seventeen with my boys. We smoked several blunts while we were waiting to get tatted up and decided we should all get Japanese characters. My boy Angel got the character for 'love' in Japanese, Luis got 'family,' and I forget what the others got, it's been so long now, but I decided on a 'demon.'" He laughed. "Damn. Now that I think about it, it sounds really bad compared to the others, but I guess what I wanted it to represent at the time was for me to conquer my demons."

I thought of my own demons.

"How 'bout you?" he asked. "Any tats?"

I shook my head. I was suddenly very insecure about the way I looked. Was I "cute" tonight? Was there something in my teeth? Was I dressed okay? I'd worn one of the outfits that Guille had picked out for me, a pair of dark blue skinny jeans with a gray polka-dot top, but I was unsure if I could pull it off.

After we finished eating, Joseph turned on a television mounted on the wall facing his bed. "All right, so what do you say we watch a movie?" he asked. He walked over to a dresser next to his bed that had a large selection of DVDs piled on top. "Any movies you've been wanting to see lately?"

"Anything is fine," I said. "I don't know much about movies."

"Wow, really? I love movies. Can you tell?" He laughed, gesturing to his collection. "Anyway, if you really don't care, how about *Slumdog Millionaire*? It just came out and I've heard good things about it."

"Sure," I said.

"Yay, awesome," he said with a goofy grin. "So why don't you get comfortable and we can sit on my bed to watch it. I really gotta do something about the chair and table situation in this room. Obviously, this is Ethan's table, and these folding chairs are not the most comfortable."

Where was Ethan anyhow? I wondered, but felt it might be rude to ask. I took off my shoes and cautiously sat down on his bed. I was getting nervous. The date wasn't what I expected. But then again, I didn't know anything about dates. Joseph slid the disc into his DVD player and turned off the lights. Then he sat down next to me and put his arm around me. I flinched and immediately balled my hands into fists. Thoughts of the man in the nail salon resurfaced in my mind. I had forgotten all about him. Why was he appearing in my thoughts now? I pushed him out of my mind. *No*, I thought. *This is different. I am in control now. I can leave if I want to. This man will not hurt me.*

"Relax," Joseph said. "Let's scooch backward a little so we can lean our backs on the wall."

I was so nervous, I could barely manage an "Okay."

"You all right?" he asked.

"Oh, yeah, I-I'm okay," I lied.

He still had his arm around me and gave my shoulder a squeeze. "Just relax and enjoy the movie. I hear it's great. And let me know if you're uncomfortable in any way."

I tried to focus on the movie, but I was hyperaware of every movement, every breath, every heartbeat. His and mine. I'd never been so close to anyone before. I steadied my breathing and tried to focus on the movie. *Just calm down*, I told myself.

Luckily, one of the opening scenes was hilarious. We both laughed, which took the edge off and put me more at ease. Then the movie quickly took a dark turn. Rioters ravaged a village and brutally slaughtered a child's mother right before his eyes. I thought of my own mother and became flushed with emotion, turning inward. Joseph gave me another squeeze.

"Damn, that was pretty fucked-up," he whispered. Then he gave me a kiss on the forehead. It was a small gesture, but one that had an enormous impact on me. Maybe it was all of the emotions that I was feeling at once, but I suddenly felt as though a door that had always remained closed was opening up, and I was now free to go someplace I'd never been before. I took a deep breath and settled into the crook of his arm, taking in his smell and sensing his strength. He also shifted his weight, pulling me closer, my body folded up neatly into his. It seemed to me we somehow fit perfectly.

The movie was intense, and when it ended, we looked at each other, neither of us knowing what to say.

"Well, that was not what I expected," he finally said. "Especially not for a first date."

I laughed. "I liked it," I said. "I thought the actors were brilliant."

"Yeah? You didn't think it was too heavy?"

"Well, I mean, it was, but I didn't mind."

He looked at me and smiled. "Good," he said, turning to face me. "I'm glad you liked it."

I could tell he was nervous too, searching for the next words to say. It made me feel better that we were both struggling, that even though he was much older and more experienced he was as uncertain as I was about what would happen next.

"Okay, so I have to ask again," he said. "You've really never been with anyone before?"

I laughed. "Really," I said.

Then he leaned in closer and took my hand in his. "May I kiss you?" he asked softly. I nodded, surprised that I wanted to be kissed. His hands were much larger than mine, warm against my cold fingers. He pulled me in.

The credits were still rolling, a faint light coming from the screen. He wrapped one arm around my waist. I flinched, nervous, excited, and scared. In the dark, I could hardly make out his lovely almond-shaped eyes as he gently pressed his lips against mine.

Letting Go

"YOU EVER HEARD OF 'Bachata Rosa'?" Joseph asked me. It was the next evening, and we were back in his room.

"No," I said. "What's that?"

"Oh man, I gotta show you. It's this song by Juan Luis Guerra. And I mean, so beautiful. The lyrics are something else, man. He's like . . . He's like this modern-day Shakespeare, the way he uses language. But in Spanish 'cause he's Dominican. You mind if I show it to you real quick? It's a little difficult to translate but I'll give it my best shot."

He turned on his television.

"I think you're gonna love this, watch," he said, his voice full of excitement as he slid a DVD into its slot. The song opened with sweet melodic vocals, the sound of maracas and bongos, and a guitar.

Te regalo una rosa, a man sings.

"I give you a rose . . . ," Joseph translated.

La encontré en el camino

"I found it on the path . . ."

Joseph sat with his chin resting on the palms of his hands, brow furrowed as he concentrated on giving me the best translation he could muster. The track titles were in white against a bright blue background, like the blue of a polyethylene tarp, the blue of my first memory, and it illuminated his silhouette in the otherwise dimly lit room.

"*Ay, ay ay ay, amor,*" he sang along in a soft voice, switching to Spanish. "*Eres la rosa que me da calor . . .*"

I heard his voice crack as he sang, and when I looked over at him I could see tears filling his eyes.

"Sorry," he said, chuckling, rubbing his eyes. "I don't know what it is. It's just . . . the way he describes things, man. I wish I could speak Spanish like that. Or any language, for that matter. I mean, listen to this part. He's saying, 'I am the satellite, and you're my sun, a universe of mineral water, a space of light, that only you fill, my love.' What do you think? Beautiful, right?"

But I couldn't answer him. It was in that moment, in the dim lighting of his cluttered, halfway-spackled room, that I found myself feeling something I'd never felt before. Was this what people meant when they talked about falling in love? The beauty of the moment overwhelmed me. I couldn't speak. I could only act. I took his face in my hands and gave him a long, deep kiss. *Ay, ay ay ay, amor. Eres la rosa que me da calor.*

"What was that for?" Joseph asked.

"Just 'cause," I whispered.

"There are a lot of assholes out there," he said later that night. "At least in the world where I come from. I'm glad for your sake that you didn't meet some asshole in the street instead of me. I mean, I'm not saying I'm perfect. I've got my fair share of baggage, as you know, but I think we can make this work. So how about it?"

It took me a moment to figure out that he was asking me to be his girl-friend. It wasn't the most romantic invitation, but I didn't hesitate to say yes. I trusted him. He was exactly who he claimed to be, never trying to be anyone else. He was the same person who'd found me on the street on a cold winter night. His kindness and authenticity came at a time when I felt so much of it was lacking in my own life, when I felt a stranger to myself, lost. Who was I supposed to be? Was I supposed to remain the obedient daughter of Vietnamese immigrants, bound for a life in the nail salon, or was I supposed to do what other immigrant children and children of immigrants were doing all around me—finding ways to live out their American dreams, to move beyond the constricted lives of their parents? Now I'd found Joseph, and I felt like I was moving on too.

By the end of our second date, Joseph and I had become lovers. He called me beautiful. It was the first time anyone had ever called me beautiful other than the man in the nail salon. And this time, there were no strings attached, no price to pay. This time, I welcomed his touch and blossomed under it. In his arms, I felt the stirrings of a new freedom, a sense that life might take me somewhere exciting after all. At night, when I looked at myself in the mirror, it was through his eyes that I would look at myself. It was temporary and yet another illusion with which I shielded myself. But it saved me from my own condemning gaze.

During the next few months, I got to know Joseph better. He worked at a hardware store in Queens from Monday to Thursday, which left his Fridays free. That's when I would visit him in Ridgewood, or he would visit me at my dorm.

I liked it that he felt protective—that he always wanted to be sure I was comfortable with his behavior toward me, that he worried about whether he was good enough for me. Around him, I didn't need to be anyone other than myself, and for the first time, I felt safe—though not safe enough to tell him the truth about my status at school. It wasn't so much that I feared his judgment as that he was my escape from reality, so I was much more eager to hear about his life than to talk about my own.

Besides, I really loved getting to know who he was. He inspired me. After returning to the States when he was eleven, he'd lived with his mother in Queens (his father had left shortly after he was born). He struggled in school and eventually dropped out, turning to the streets and ending up in prison for a time, as he'd told me the first night we'd met. Seeing the man he became gave me hope. His past did not define him.

"I'm concerned about Ly. She needs to get her act together," I heard a friend say one day after I had brought Joseph to the dorms to introduce him to a few of my friends. "It's like she doesn't care anymore; she's practically stopped going to her classes, and all she does is hang out with this guy. Who is he anyway?"

I was insulted, but I lacked the energy to defend either myself or Joseph. And it wasn't a simple matter of caring or not caring. If getting my life together were that easy, didn't they think I would have done it by now? All those years of guilt and grief, of fighting so hard to have things that came to others so easily—if only they knew what that felt like, if only they could see the world through my eyes and walk the streets in my shoes. But there was no use trying to explain. They'd never understand. So I withdrew even further and began to distance myself from my friends. I thought it was better that way.

Though I loved spending time with Joseph, as the weeks went by, I began to withdraw from him as well. Sensing my distance, he would call me and ask me if everything was all right, but I couldn't bear to tell him. I couldn't bear for his image of me to be shattered. Even though it was just an illusion, it was the only thing I had left.

Very late one night in mid-March, I suddenly found myself walking on the East River Greenway, a pedestrian pathway along the FDR Drive, looking over the East River. I didn't know how I got there. It was only a short walk from the Brookdale dorms through Waterside Plaza, but there seemed to be a strange gap in the events of the day. What had I been doing before this? When had I left my room? I seemed to be either waking up from a dream or entering one. I was exhausted and cold. I looked at my phone and saw several missed calls from Joseph.

"Where are you? I've been calling," he said when I finally picked up.

"I'm just walking along the FDR Drive." I could hear cars whizzing by on the other side of the plaza to my left.

"This late?"

"It's just a short walk. I'll go back soon."

"Why don't you start heading back?" he asked, his voice tinged with worry. "Do you want me to come get you?"

"No, no, I'm fine. It's just a short walk. Really. It's nothing."

"Sweetheart, you're alone, it's two o'clock in the morning, and you're walking on the FDR Drive. That's not safe. Look, I'm gonna come get you. I'm worried about you."

"Joseph, I'm fine," I insisted. "Look, I'm walking back right now. Are you happy?"

"You're such a pain in the ass," he said, laughing. "But yes, I'm happy. Text me when you get home, please?" I could tell he was still worried so I reassured him once again that I would call in a few minutes, as soon as I got in the door.

We hung up. I continued walking along the drive, staring out at the dark river, at the short fence that I could easily climb. After all this time, I thought, I was still afraid of swimming.

Maybe that's just because you're scared. Maybe, just maybe, if you jump, you'll discover that you've known all along how to swim. But you have to go for it. You'll never know if you don't go for it.

I stopped walking. I had a sudden urge to sit on top of the fence. I gripped the metal bar, hoisting myself up, surprised at my own strength. I swung one leg over the railing, feeling the blood pumping in my veins as I balanced myself. A blast of icy winter wind threatened to carry me off as I swung the other leg over and I held on as tightly as I could. I was freezing, but the wind felt refreshing somehow, purifying. I stared down at the black water, lost in a trance as the waves beckoned to me. Slowly, I loosened my grip on the railing and relaxed.

It would be so much easier this way, wouldn't it? a part of me thought.

But what about your parents? Your brothers? Joseph? Everyone who loves you.

What about them? This way, they wouldn't have to ever worry about me again. I won't be a burden anymore.

I stayed there for a long time, unable to move, unable to decide. *What if I'm the light?* I'd once asked my mother. If that had ever been true, that light seemed to have been snuffed out long ago. There was only darkness now.

Then my phone buzzed again, breaking me out of my reverie. It was Joseph. I let it buzz as I stared at the soft glow of the screen in the dark, the wind whipping wisps of hair against my face.

No, a voice within me said. *No, it's not over yet.*

I took one last look at the river, got down from the railing, and hurried back to the dorm.

———

I never told Joseph, or anyone else, about that night, about what I'd con-templated as I stared into the river. I didn't want anyone to worry or make a big deal out of it. But I eventually had to tell him about my situation at Hunter when I asked him for help moving out of the dorms at the end of the semester and he wanted to know why I was leaving. I confessed that I had been dismissed from the Honors College and had lost my scholarship and all the perks that came with it, including my laptop and dorm room.

"Wait, what?" he said. "Why permanently? I thought you had this room for the next two years."

I sat him down and told him the truth of what had led to my dis-missal. Or part of it, anyway. Not the part about my hospitalization and how depressed I'd been. Just that I'd been skipping classes and failed my courses.

"Why didn't you tell me?" he asked. "This isn't good, sweetheart. You need to go back to class. You need to finish your degree. Don't make the same mistake I did." He gave me a good hard look. "Am I the reason you're neglecting your schoolwork?"

He threatened to break up with me if that was the case, but I assured him it wasn't. I explained that I couldn't bring myself to go to classes anymore, that I was too ashamed to show my face around the halls of Hunter. I didn't want to see my friends from the Honors College. I didn't want to see their pitying glances.

"Please, Joseph," I pleaded. "I just need time to sort out my life. I can't do this right now."

"I know, babe. But you need to. You need to get through this because you have so much to offer. It would be a damn shame to let it go to waste," he said. "Next year will be better."

But I didn't believe him. It wasn't the first time someone had told me this, and every year seemed worse than the last.

Still, he showed up to help me pack. Then we ordered in and he stayed the night. The next morning, we awoke to a loud knock on my door.

"Yo, Ly, you don't answer your fucking phone. I've been calling you all morning. Mom and Dad are outside waiting in the car." It was Long. I'd totally forgotten that my parents had offered to pick up Long and me and drive us home. I panicked. No one in my family had met Joseph or even knew about him, and I sure wasn't ready for them to meet.

"Sorry," I yelled through the door. "I'll be down in twenty minutes. Just tell them to wait."

Joseph and I got ready as quickly as possible, and I asked him to leave through the back door of the dorm. I felt terrible that he had to sneak out, but he understood.

"I'll be ready to meet them when you're ready. No rush," he said.

"Thanks so much for helping me pack last night," I said. "I really needed that."

"Of course. Anytime, babe," he said, giving me a kiss on my forehead. "And hey, listen, no more secrets, okay? I wanna know what's going on in your life and if you need help. I worry about you, and it's really not cool being lied to."

Okay, I promised him, no more secrets. No more lies. And I told myself that one day soon I'd be completely honest with him. About my depression, about what I'd been through that led to that depression, and about where I was headed. Just not yet . . .

Returning to Pitkin

THAT SUMMER, I RETURNED to Pitkin Nails to reclaim what I feared, more and more, was going to be my future. My parents were happy to see me around the salon again.

"It is good karma to be helping your parents," my mother told me. "Don't worry about school. You made it past middle school. That's more than I did. You went all the way to college. You should be proud of yourself."

I nodded my head in quiet defeat and settled back into the rhythm of the salon. Old customers greeted me with hugs.

"Where you been, girl? I missed you like crazy. Ain't nobody design my nails like Ms. Ly do," one woman said, to which I responded with a smile, grateful to hear those words. At least I wasn't a complete failure in this department.

That June, news of Michael Jackson's death spread like wildfire through the salon.

"The king is dead." Clients came in one after another telling me the news.

"Did you hear?"

"The world done lost a great man."

"Ain't that a shame."

"Not Michael. No no no, not Michael."

"I never believed that shit they said about him being a baby molester. That's probably what got him in the end. Those assholes ruined a legend and a great human being."

My father arrived a little later in the day, after coming home from his job at the Michael C. Fina factory.

"Did you hear?" I asked him.

"Hear what?"

"Michael Jackson died today."

"And? Why should I care?"

"I thought you liked his music."

But he made no response. He sat down at a manicure station and was already beckoning a customer in. He hadn't even taken off his cap.

The customer sat down. "Michael Jackson died today," she told him.

"Yah, I know," he said. "My dawduh, she jus toe me."

She shook her head in mourning, joining a choreography of heads shaking all throughout the salon.

"Mm mm mm," they said. Some even shed tears. They spread their hands out in front of us with pleading eyes as if asking us to bring him back somehow. "Can you paint me something in memory of Michael, honey?" they asked.

So I painted his initials on their nails with a crown on top. On longer nails, I painted the outline of a square-jawed face, a few curls peeking out from underneath a fedora. Grief was quickly replaced with excitement.

"Damn, can you do that to all my nails? I'll pay extra, 'cause that shit is dope," a client squealed. I adorned their nails with music notes, the letters "RIP MJ" spelled out across the tips of their fingers. They wanted to wear their mourning on their hands.

I looked at my own hands, imagined myself with long nails, and wondered what scene might be painted across them that could express my own grief, my fears about what the future would hold.

"Your aunt called me this morning," my mother began. She was referring to her older sister. We were having a lunch break during a brief lull between clients. Although it was hard facing up to the possibility that the nail salon might be the only future I could hope for, I did enjoy having time to spend with my mother. It eased my guilt and made me remember the closeness I'd felt to her when I was younger.

"How is Big Auntie?" I asked, slurping the hot-and-sour soup I'd picked up from our local Chinese takeout restaurant.

"Oh, you know. They're traveling again. Your uncle likes to travel."

"Do Amanda and David stay behind to look after the shop?" My aunt and uncle own a fish-and-chips in Brisbane, Australia, and they have two adult children.

"No. The whole family goes. They don't have a care in the world. Isn't that great?"

"Maybe we should follow in their footsteps," I said. "Maybe we can save up some money and do the same."

"No, no," she said quickly. "I don't want to go anywhere anymore. I just want to work and take care of my children and be a devout Buddhist, and maybe in my next life, I'll get to travel too."

"Oh goodness." I rolled my eyes. "Here we go again with this."

She smiled to herself. "It's true," she said softly. Sometimes it seemed to me that she actively embraced martyrdom, with her absolute refusal to protest the injustices of her life.

She chose another conversation topic instead. "There's this girl in Vietnam I used to know. One day, she just looked up instructions on how to make little desserts and pastries. She got pretty good at it and started to sell whatever she made right from the front yard of her hut. After a time, she became very popular and everyone in the village started going to her. She made so much she was able to open up her own dessert shop and became very wealthy."

"That's so nice that she was able to find her 'passion.'" I said the word in English, since I didn't quite know how to translate the word into Vietnamese. "Do you know what 'passion' means?" I asked.

"You mean like the latest clothing styles?"

"No, that's 'fashion.' This is 'passion,' p-a-s-s-i-o-n," I spelled aloud. "It's when you find a job you really love doing, so it's not so much a chore as it is something you enjoy. You would do it even if it wasn't your job."

"Oh."

"Do you have a passion, Mom?"

"Doing nails, I guess," she replied.

"No, doing nails is just your job. But it isn't a job you *like* doing, do you?" I could sense her struggling to understand. "Like, if you could do anything in the world, if you had all the options available to you, and all the talents and skills and intelligence to do anything, what would that be?"

"Wait. I'm thinking," she said. And it dawned on me that this might be the first time anyone had ever asked her this question.

"I guess I would like a big house that has space for a shop in front and I would sell clothing and little knickknacks and maybe drinks on the side, and then whenever I was tired and business was slow, I could just go lie down. That's my 'passion.'" She struggled to say the word in English.

I thought of all the things I wanted to say to her, all the conversations we could have had if only our tongues obeyed the same laws. The bells above the door jingled as a woman walked into the salon, and the conversation was cut short.

"Hi, how may I help you?" my mother and I said in unison. We looked at each other and giggled.

"Just looking," the woman said.

"Okay, if you have any questions, let us know," I said.

But after a few moments, she left. I was glad. I was not yet ready to have this moment with my mother end. As we continued eating, she suddenly moved to another topic. This time, she was in a nostalgic mood.

"Back in Vietnam, your father and I used to carry this huge wheelbarrow full of clothing from the shop to our home every night at around one or two a.m. Sometimes, we would drop clothing and not even realize because we were too tired. Your father would pull the wheelbarrow from the front, and I would push from the back. It was really heavy."

She opened a thin bottle of polish with a narrow brush typically used for nail art and she began to practice a new design she'd come up with on a piece of paper towel: three tiny pink flowers with wisps of golden polish weaving between them.

"Thinh used to come out and help us close up shop. He was so sweet. And it was so far, almost half a mile out, which is a long distance to walk for a child.

"I was at home when my water broke with you inside me. Your father was in the shop. So Thinh immediately set out with a lantern to tell your father to come home. He was only six, and he walked all the way to the shop in the darkness. It isn't like America where people keep their porch light on and there are streetlamps. There wasn't any electricity back then. After eight or nine o'clock at night, people went to sleep and blew out all the candles. I can't believe how brave he was. Even I was scared and I was a grown woman!" She laughed.

"How old did you say he was?"

"However much older he is than you," she said. "Six? Seven? One time, and this was during the day, he was walking back home from the shop and I had given him a little bit of money to buy ice cream on the way. A neighbor came to me and said, 'Auntie Five, your son just fell down into a ditch! Come quick!'" I rushed out of there so fast, but

319

when I arrived, he had already managed to climb back out of the ditch, his face and body covered in dirt and ice cream all mixed together. I remember how pale he looked."

"Was he hurt at all?" I asked.

"I don't think anything more than a bruise," she said. "No, he was pale because he thought I would beat him."

"And did you?"

"No, of course not," my mother said. "I'm not your father. And besides, I felt so sorry for him. His face so small and dirty. My brave son."

As I finished my lunch, I pictured Thinh walking on a dirt path along the Mekong, bathing in the rays of the afternoon sun and licking his ice cream cone, immersed in sugary delight. I imagined the ground suddenly giving way beneath him, plunging him into darkness, ice cream splattered everywhere, and I imagined the pain from the fall and the rising fear that he would be punished for it. I was so lost in thought that I cried out in sympathy, forgetting where I was.

"Huh? What's the matter with you?" my mother asked as the bells above the door jingled again. "Hurry up and finish your food. We have customers."

Self-Preservation

FOR THE NEXT YEAR of my life, beginning in the fall of 2009, when I became a junior, I bobbed along lifelessly, frozen between a state of existence and nonexistence. I don't even remember much of what happened during this time. That first semester of my junior year I signed up for a full course load at Hunter, just as I had done before, and then, just as I had done before, I attended my classes erratically—or not at all. I wasted my Pell and TAP grant money. I believed, at some point, that I could somehow pull myself out and suddenly get better. But I didn't.

Eventually, midway through the spring semester of 2010, I dropped out altogether, giving up on the idea of ever returning. It was a matter of self-preservation. I had the feeling that if I continued to push myself, it wouldn't end well for me. I felt I was on the brink of a terrible breakdown from which I might not recover. There was something else too . . . a small voice within me that begged to be heard and grew louder and louder as time went on. I was tired of blaming my parents for my failures. I was tired of blaming the past. And I was tired of just being swept along in the current of chance and circumstance. I wanted to regain control over my life. If I was going to fail, it would be on my own terms. It would be my own decision, a choice I'd made to turn my back on this chapter of my life and move on to something else, even though I had no idea what that would be.

So I took one last look at Hunter College, roamed its crowded halls one last time, and even visited the Honors College lounge before I left, never to return.

Next was figuring out how to deceive my parents. I couldn't tell them what I'd decided. I couldn't face their disappointment again, as I could barely face myself. I came up with a plan to leave the house every day at the same time. This would create the illusion of going to school. Then I would take the subway to random stops in the city and wander around until Joseph got off from work, when I would meet him at his apartment. It was a foolproof plan. My parents would never find out. And neither would Joseph, I thought. Who would suspect it?

I started spending all my evenings with Joseph. Being with him made me feel alive again in a way that nothing else did at that time. I had never been touched in the way that he touched me. I hadn't realized that of all my senses, touch was the one of which I had been most deprived. My mother had hugged and kissed me when I was a child, but I couldn't remember the last time she did so. From my father, I seemed to remember only the beatings, the fear of his wrath. And my brothers and I rarely expressed affection for each other, either physically or in any other way. Touching just wasn't done in our household.

When I gave myself to Joseph for the first time and every time after, I did so with complete abandon. In the days that followed I wanted to hold his hand at every opportunity, kiss his lips and cheeks, embrace him. And Joseph welcomed it all. For someone who, at first glance, might have seemed rough and hardened by life's circumstances, Joseph was even more affectionate than I was.

He was also gentle and generous, and we delighted in each other's company. We never ran out of things to talk about. However, we still weren't talking about what was happening with me.

"Uh, weren't you supposed to have class today?" he asked one afternoon. He had the day off, so I had come over early. But he was suspicious. He was beginning to catch on, and I remembered my promise to him. No secrets.

"I just don't feel like going anymore." I sighed.

"Again?" he asked. "Come on, babe . . . Don't you think this is getting out of hand?"

"Well, actually," I finally admitted, "I've dropped out." He looked at me as though I'd committed the most egregious act and insisted that I return to school. But I had made up my mind. The more he pushed me, the more I pushed back.

"Look, I know what I'm doing," I told him.

"Oh yeah? And what's that? Dropping out? Throwing your future away?"

"My future isn't at Hunter," I said. "I just know it isn't. I can't tell you why or how I know. I just feel it in my gut. If you don't like that I'm here, I'll leave or we'll just break up. But no matter what you say, or anyone else, I am not going back to that place."

He looked at me in defeat. He didn't know what to do. He knew he couldn't stop me. And even I was surprised by the strength of my own conviction.

"All right, babe. I trust you," he said. "I don't agree with what you're doing, but I dropped out myself, so I really don't have a right to tell you anything. I honestly think you're doing yourself a disservice, but hey, who knows what the future will bring? You might find something better. That's the way life has worked out for me, so I guess we'll just have to be patient. But what are you going to do in the meantime?"

"I don't know," I said. "I'll figure it out."

While I was in limbo, I committed to spending more and more time with Joseph. He worked as a contractor on the side to make ends meet and he started bringing me to his job sites, teaching me how to put down wood flooring, repair ceilings, put in a kitchen backsplash, spackle, and paint. He was an excellent teacher. He knew how to explain things in a way that made it very easy for me to understand. He'd set me up to complete a task, then trust me to accomplish it. Occasionally, he would check a few things here and there, but he never micromanaged.

Learning something new gave me a sense of purpose and allowed me an escape from my fear that my life was going nowhere—because despite my saying that I knew what I was doing, I had no idea what my next steps would be. I just knew that I needed to get out of Hunter. The work I did with Joseph was proof to me that I still had curiosity about the world, that I still had an interest in learning and doing, and I knew that as long as I could keep that fire burning within me, I would find a way to get back on my feet again.

My growing attachment to Joseph's son, now seven years old, also gave me a sense that my life was in some way meaningful. Ethan lived in Upstate New York with his mother but would join us every other weekend. He was quiet and shy, but a very kind and thoughtful child. He had bright eyes, a little afro, and a habit of rubbing his shirt collar against his lower lip whenever he was sleepy.

One day, Joseph received a letter in the mail notifying him that Ethan was at risk of being left back in school.

"What?" I asked. "How can that be?"

Joseph sat down and rubbed his eyes until they were red. He sighed heavily and explained to me that because Jamie, Ethan's mother, was in the army, she had to move around often.

"Just in the past two years, he's had to move schools three times. He's had no stability, and I don't know how to help him," he said.

"Well, why doesn't he just live with you?" I asked.

"Because Jamie is his mother. The courts would never allow him to live with me."

I could tell he loved Ethan dearly but, having grown up without a father himself, he didn't know how to help his son. I foresaw the trajectory of Ethan's future. Without a support system, he would fall through the cracks just as Joseph did, and the cycle would repeat itself. It wasn't a matter of intelligence. It was a matter of circumstance. Though I was only nineteen, a strong maternal instinct kicked in.

"Look," I told Joseph. "If you really care about him, you have to fight this. He needs to live with you. He needs stability. If there's anything he needs help with in school, I can help him."

"I don't know . . . ," he said. "You sure about that, babe? I mean, I'd appreciate any help you can offer. School was never a strong point of mine, as you know. But that's a lot to ask of you."

"You're not asking," I said. "I'm offering. But first things first, he needs to live with you. If you want to be the father you never had, you have to figure out a way to support Ethan and be there for him. These are some of his most formative years academically. This is the time for him to build good study habits and develop a strong foundation. If we don't do something now, it may never be possible to get these years back."

My persistence surprised me. I don't know why I felt so protective toward Ethan. I saw myself in him somehow, a child who was struggling and had no way of controlling his circumstances, a child who needed someone to intervene at an early age. I didn't want him to get to a point in his life where he would be facing the struggles that I was now facing. And the struggles that his father faced too, from not having the proper support growing up. I didn't want him to feel that he never had a choice, never had a chance. I was so adamant, Joseph eventually gave in.

Through many conversations and arguments, he eventually worked out a plan with Jamie to have Ethan live with him during the week. We enrolled him in an elementary school nearby, P.S. 88. He was severely behind in his class, but I started tutoring him, reaching out to his teachers when he wasn't doing well. I scheduled meetings with his principal, went to his parent-teacher conferences, remembering that no one had gone to mine when I was younger. I figured if I wasn't going to make it, I might as well give this child a chance.

Little by little, his grades improved, and I began to feel that if I could help this child succeed in life, then my own life might be worth living.

Sibling Reunion

"COME ON OUT TO Seattle and visit us for a few weeks," Phu had suggested to me the previous year. "You should take a break from your studies. It'll be like a mini-vacation. Thinh and I will buy your tickets for you."

Now seemed the right time to take him up on that offer. Though I'd found some sense of purpose with Joseph and Ethan, I'd just dropped out of school and was reminded, everywhere I went, of my failures and the fact that I was still directionless. Going to Seattle would at least be a temporary distraction.

It was midafternoon on a Saturday in April 2010 when I finally reunited with my brothers.

I found myself in a BMW with all three of them, racing along the Lacey V. Murrow Memorial Bridge under an overcast Seattle sky. It was only the second time I had visited Thinh and Phu since 2005. Thinh was now working as lead website designer for a high-end marketing company. Phu had gotten a job at Pokémon as a marketing program manager and was renting a room in Thinh's house. Long was also with us. A former Teach For America instructor, he was now teaching high school math to gifted middle school students in a South Side, Chicago, charter school and was on spring break. We had just dropped our luggage off at the house Thinh had bought in Kirkland and were now on our way to Seattle to have lunch in the city.

I stared out the window at the wide expanse of Lake Washington beneath. The bridge we were on, measuring 6,620 feet, is the second-longest floating bridge in the world. "Floating" is an apt descriptor. Suspended. Adrift. On my left, dark waves crashed against one another, sending white foamy peaks into the air. On my right, the water was light blue, smooth as glass.

"Nice," I said under my breath.

"Yeah? You like it?" Thinh asked, letting go of the wheel momentarily and spreading his palms outward as though he had built the bridge with his own two hands.

"Yeah, I forgot how gorgeous the view is. It's been what, four years now, since I visited?"

"Sounds about right," he said. "The bridge is okay. I'm used to it."

Long sat in the back seat next to me. Phu sat in the front passenger seat next to Thinh.

The drive was quiet. We were not expressive people—at least, not raised to be expressive, so even basic questions like "How have you been?" and "What have you been up to?" were awkward for us to ask each other. Still, I had questions that needed to be answered.

"Why'd you move?" I asked no one in particular. A light rain had begun to fall, droplets of water hitting the windows and obscuring my view. The rain made me pensive, and I felt the sting of abandonment acutely. I'd missed my brothers. We'd been so close, sitting on the living room floor, making those ties and cummerbunds all those years ago. Who were we to each other now?

Phu looked out of his window. Long was silent. Only Thinh answered, telling me that there had been nothing there for him in Queens. "Now *this, this* is the life."

"You don't ever call," I said to Thinh. "You've spoken to Mom three times this year, and Father even fewer times." The accusation wasn't only on behalf of my parents. It was for me as well. He seldom called me, rarely reached out to see how I was doing at a time when I needed him most.

"Uh-oh. Here we go," Thinh said. He'd no doubt heard the same from our parents. Having his little sister admonish him too was probably not something he'd bargained for. Trying to change the subject, he told me he was hungry and couldn't wait to "grab some grub," some idiomatic expression he must have picked up because he thought it was cool, made him sound more American. And he really was becoming more American. I examined his face in the mirror. He looked straight ahead, his jawline taut and speckled with stubble. It was the first time I'd ever seen him with facial hair. How different he looked after all this time.

Sitting in my brother's car then, trying to make sense of the rift that had grown between us, I suddenly remembered something Monet had said: "When you go out to paint, try to forget what objects you have before you, a tree, a house, a field or whatever. Merely think here is a little square of blue, here an oblong of pink, here a streak of yellow, and paint it just as it looks to you, the exact color and shape, until it gives you your own naive impression of the scene before you." That's how I felt about my brothers in that moment, like I was seeing only an impression of them.

But then they came into focus again, and I saw how differently they had grown into their American identities. Thinh's hair was still spiked, though a little more to the right this time, not straight up like in his high school days. And it was blown out, not gelled. He wore a fitted white Armani button-down with expensive dark jeans. Unlike the rest of us, he'd always had a great sense of fashion, always cared a lot about the way he looked and presented himself to the world. In contrast to Thinh, Phu was wearing a tracksuit. He always dressed as though he might be called upon to play in some volleyball or handball tournament at a moment's notice. Long, the thriftiest and least materialistic of us all, always just wore whatever Thinh and Phu could no longer fit into, but I don't remember what it was that day.

The rain was falling harder now, in sheets. I opened my window and squinted through the drops hitting my face, the wind whipping my long hair all around. I looked toward the river and watched the violent waves. Triangles of white on blue water. No, on blue parallelograms.

"Hey, what are you doing?" Thinh cried out. "Are you crazy? Those are premium leather seats. Close your window!"

In the restaurant, which was one of those sushi restaurants where the dishes ride around on a conveyor belt and the customers serve themselves by taking whatever looks good, we made small talk like casual acquaintances. I had the disquieting sensation that I no longer knew my brothers. And it occurred to me that they barely knew who I was either. They knew almost nothing about what I had gone through in college. We were each on separate paths, each of us trying both to make sense of our past and to escape it. They didn't have time to hold my hand.

It had been years since the four of us had shared a meal, and we'd been together for only a couple of hours, yet already we couldn't find anything to talk about other than the novelty of conveyor belt sushi. When that subject was exhausted we sat silently, plucking the occasional dish from the conveyor belt and focusing, apparently, on our food. Outside, the rain had become a torrential downpour. By the time we got back to the car, we were drenched, our dripping bodies soaking the leather seats. I tried my best to wipe them down.

Back at Thinh's house, I wrung the water out of my hair with a towel. He lived in a quaint residential neighborhood on a hillside in Kirkland looking out at Mount Rainier. There were three floors, five bedrooms, and two and a half bathrooms. Tenants occupied two of the five bedrooms. Phu's and Thinh's rooms were on the second floor. Long was to sleep on the couch in the living room, and I would sleep in the spare bedroom.

We congregated in the kitchen area, where a sliding door gave onto the backyard terrace. I sat at the dining table with the towel around my neck, watching as my brothers horsed around, comparing bicep sizes. A tenant came out at some point to get something from the fridge.

"Oh, Kent," Phu said. "You haven't met our little brother and sister yet. This is David and Lisa."

I flinched. No one had called me by that name since the fifth grade, when I'd gotten my citizenship. We all had an a.k.a. attached to our names on the citizenship certificates, the names we'd come up with years ago. Tony, Peter, David, and Lisa. Thinh and Phu still used their American names, whereas Long and I held on to our birth names.

"It's Ly," I said to Kent. "Lisa is my American name."

Kent shook my and Long's hands. We chatted briefly about our plans for the next few days before he disappeared back into his room.

"Yeah, don't worry about Mom and Dad, Ly," Thinh suddenly said, as though it were something he had been mulling over all this time. He assured me that when he launched his business plan, things would change. He was going to get our parents out of Ridgewood and out of that nail salon in Brownsville. It was the same promise he had been making for years now. In the meantime, though, I would have to be the one to hold the fort.

"That's why you gotta graduate and get yourself a good job. We're all depending on you, Ly."

I stared out the terrace door. I know now that it was his way of encouraging me to move forward, to finish what I had started and get to a better place in life. At the time, however, it didn't seem fair to me. I had three older brothers who had made it or were on the verge of making it. Why did I always have to carry the burden of helping our parents? I didn't realize then that my brothers too were struggling under the weight of our shared past, trying to defy the poverty that had defined us for so long. Thinh's house was a symbol of his defiance, his car an affirmation to himself that he was in the fast lane toward the Dream. But the reality, as I later discovered, was that he was up to his ears in debt: student loans from RIT, house loans, and car loans—he was struggling more than he let on. In a way, I suppose that *was* the American dream, buying more than one could afford and dealing with the repercussions later.

Phu had tried to emulate Thinh and even moved in with him, but at that time had yet to find his footing. And Long. Well, Long just happened to have chosen a profession that didn't pay very much. At least, not in the beginning.

We're all depending on you, Ly.

"How was it?" My mother and father questioned me when I returned two weeks later. "What'd they say?"

"Nothing," I replied. "It was nice. They have a big house, white, three floors. They drive stick shifts. Thinh has a BMW. It's black. Phu has a white Civic Si. Sports edition. We ate in restaurants. There was a floating bridge."

What else could I say? My parents smiled, wrinkles deepening on their lined faces. "Good," they said. "As long as they are happy." I looked around at our small apartment. Roaches like raisins scurried along our walls, dark brown ovals on a plane of eggshell white.

A Glimmer of Hope

ONE FRIDAY THAT SPRING, I decided to make an appointment at the Mount Sinai Adolescent Health Center to get a physical. I'm not sure what prompted me, but it had been years since I'd had a checkup and I was feeling run-down. Besides, other than tutoring Ethan, I'd been doing nothing useful with my life. I was still just roaming the streets, aimless and hopeless, with no aspirations and not a single clue as to what my future would look like.

As I was filling out paperwork in the reception area, I ran into Pamela, the legal advocate Dr. Hayes had introduced me to the summer after my senior year of high school. I aimed a tentative wave in her direction, thinking she might have forgotten me, but she came over right away and gave me a hug.

"Oh my goodness! Ly! How are you? What a surprise to see you here!"

She asked me how school was going, and when I let on that things hadn't quite gone according to plan since last I'd seen her, she ushered me into her office, where we could have some privacy.

We talked for hours. Pam had a way of wresting information out of a person. She asked question after question and listened sympathetically to my story. I hadn't really planned on divulging everything to her, but she was so sincere and so nonjudgmental that it all came pouring out. The pressure of keeping the truth locked up within me had become too great. And Pam was the perfect person to tell it to. By the time I finished my story, she'd filled out several pages of notes on her notepad.

"Okay," she said, setting her notepad to the side as soon as she felt she had all the information she needed. "This is what I think. You need to go back to school. There's no other option. You're too bright not to."

"But my grades are terrible," I told her. "I failed all my classes. What college would accept me?"

"Well, that's why we need a plan. When you apply, schools will need to know the reasons behind your grades at Hunter, but they'll also need to see that that won't happen again, that you've changed since then and are ready to move forward. So first things first: we're gonna need to get you a job. That will let colleges know you're serious about getting back on your feet." She was calm but focused, speaking with such conviction that I almost believed it was possible. I was in awe that she could come up with a plan so quickly and decisively.

She could also tell that I wasn't in any state of mind to do the work necessary to move forward. So she took it upon herself the next few days to research jobs and internships for me. She heard from a colleague about City Year New York, a subdivision of AmeriCorps that offered internships to students taking a gap year between high school and college or college and graduate school. The internship was to work with struggling elementary and junior high school students through tutoring and mentorship. She invited me back to her office to discuss it.

"Ly, this sounds like it's right up your alley," Pam said. "You have a lot to contribute here, especially with your background and experience with academic struggles."

I was hesitant. Although I was tutoring Ethan, I wasn't sure if I was cut out for the job of tutoring other students. But Pam left no room for doubt. She had someone from City Year on speakerphone before I could even decide how to respond. She told them that they should look out for an incoming application from a bright young lady who would be perfect for the work. She wrote me a two-page recommendation letter, and reached out to Dr. Hayes for another letter of recommendation. He sent one immediately.

"Putting you in the psych ward and going on vacation might not have been the best move on his part, but he clearly cares a lot about you," Pam said.

After completing a screening and selection interview for City Year, I received an email a few weeks later. I'd been accepted into the program and would begin mid-August. I was ecstatic. After a string of rejections and failures, it was invigorating to finally be on some kind of track. Toward what, I didn't know. But at least it was something. There would be no more wandering about.

"These kids are gonna be so lucky to have you," Joseph said. "Ethan's grades are already improving because of you and I know you're gonna do the same for them."

I was terrified, but Joseph's and Pam's support gave me the confidence I needed and the strength to fight through my depression. Though thoughts of guilt and worthlessness still haunted me, I tried to summon the optimism I once had as a child and the faith that things would work out. For the first time in a long time, I prayed to the goddess of compassion, asking for just one more chance. I confided in Pam about my depression, and she coordinated with the psychologist at her clinic to have me see an extern there by the name of Jodie. I wasn't sure if I wanted to go back to therapy after what had happened the previous year, but Pam was once again persistent.

"Sometimes, it's just a matter of finding the right therapist for you," she told me. "But it's worth it when you do."

Again, I trusted her and agreed to see Jodie, who turned out to be incredibly kind and understanding. She was young, and I was one of her first patients, but I felt so at ease speaking to her, as though I were speaking to a friend. I saw her every week for forty-five minutes, and since her office was in the clinic, I'd check in with Pam after I was done. She'd take me out to lunch at Nick's, an Italian restaurant near her office, or order takeout for me, always making sure I was well-fed, and she would tell me stories about her husband, her sons, and her pets.

I was beginning to feel better about myself. The depression was still there, still lurking in the background, but knowing that I had support, and knowing that I was finally headed toward something, diminished its power over me.

Later that summer I arrived at the City Year New York orientation event, to a room full of people from all over the country ready to give a year of their time to a good cause. I could feel my insecurities rising to the surface as I looked out at unfamiliar faces. Every single one of my endeavors thus far had been a failure. Would this just be more of the same? Only time would tell. But one thing was certain: I couldn't stay where I was, stuck in an endless loop going nowhere. And I couldn't let Pam down.

I was assigned to a team of ten people, all from different parts of the country. We would be working together that school year at J.H.S. 13, a middle school on Madison Avenue and 106th in East Harlem. We were given uniforms to wear, black shoes, beige cargo pants, white tees, and a red winter coat and blazer with the City Year logo emblazoned across the back.

Back home, my parents were proud of my City Year uniform. Because I now had a job in addition to what they still believed were my school obligations, they accepted that I would no longer be working with them in the nail salon.

I worked for City Year New York from 7:00 a.m. to 6:00 p.m. five days a week, and sometimes on weekends. The hours were grueling, and the pay was nothing more than a $221 stipend every week. Still, it was about as much money as my mother made working in the nail salon, and because I was helping students who had fallen between the cracks of an over-burdened school system, I felt I was doing something meaningful.

Many of these students had major gaps in their learning. Eighth graders were still at a third-grade reading level. Seventh graders didn't know their multiplication tables. They didn't get enough sleep and were often late to school or didn't show up at all. Many came from single-parent homes.

My team and I developed after-school programs for them and were in constant contact with their guardians. I drew on my own experiences and knew what a difference having the right kind of support could make. In fact, I was in the middle of experiencing it myself. I was even able to secure therapy for several of my students with Pam's help.

Several days a week, Joseph would pick me up from the school and I'd get to his place just in time to spend a few hours helping Ethan with his homework. He was making a lot of progress in school and had even been awarded a certificate for Most Improvement in his class. My work at City Year helped me become an even better tutor for Ethan, and he helped me become a better mentor for the students at J.H.S. 13.

During these months, Pam urged me to work on college applications. It was difficult because I was still fighting my depression and my symptoms were now psychosomatic—headaches, stomach pains, and nausea. It was hard to get myself to wake up each day and go to work. But Pam wouldn't allow me to use my depression as an excuse. She was my advocate in the truest sense of the word, a combination of under-standing and firm.

"Is there anyone else you can think of who would be helpful?" she asked me. "Anyone who can speak about your potential? Former teachers?"

The only person I could think of was Ms. Liu, my English teacher at Bronx Science in my freshman and sophomore years. I'd done fairly well in her class those years because, unlike my other courses, it didn't require my being able to see the board to take extensive notes and my love of books and reading motivated me to try my best.

Introducing herself as my legal advocate and explaining my situation, Pam immediately reached out to Ms. Liu and asked for her support. Ms. Liu was living in London at the time, but she responded right away. She was now working as a college counselor and knew how to navigate the system, which colleges would be a reach for me, which would be safeties. I now had two strong, capable, and caring women on my team, fighting for me. And neither one of them was going to let me give up. I began to work on filling out the common application for the schools they recommended: Drexel, Wesleyan, NYU, Smith, Barnard, Bryn Mawr, and Mount Holyoke.

One evening Pam invited me to her apartment on the nineteenth floor of a building on the Upper East Side near Gracie Mansion to help me work on my application. The apartment had large windows that looked out onto the East River, and two garden terraces, one connected to each bedroom. It was beautiful—the most elegant apartment I'd ever seen, but also a very homey, comfortable one.

She introduced me to her husband, Steve, a real estate lawyer for Columbia; her two sons, Brian and Jeremy, who attended Yale and Wesleyan, respectively; her two Sheltie dogs, Anja and Tucker; and a Burmese cat named Little Oh. Brian and Jeremy were in the living room playing video games when I arrived.

"Boys," she called out to them. "Come say hello to Ly. She's the young woman I've been telling you about."

She ordered Japanese takeout and we all sat down at her long wooden table to eat. Her sons were sweet and welcoming, and really sharp. It was difficult for me to keep up with their witty banter at the dinner table, but I very much enjoyed listening to them. It was a completely different scene from my own family life, the six of us around a rickety dinner table, eating my mother's *bún bò Huế*. It made me miss my family. When would be the next time we would sit down together, my brothers, parents, and I, at a dinner table?

"So, Ly," Pam started. "I told the boys a bit about your story, but I figured maybe you might want to share a little more with them about your background. No pressure, of course. I just think it's an incredible story. I also think it's good for you to be able to articulate it since you'll have to be writing a lot of personal essays for these applications, and colleges will want to know the story as well."

I didn't know where to start, so I started from the very beginning, from Vietnam. As I spoke, I thought it all sounded ridiculous and unbelievable. A sense of shame and embarrassment swept over me. But they were kind and encouraging in their remarks.

"I think you should apply to Columbia," Pam said to me when I finished.

"Are you kidding?" I asked, thrown off guard. "An Ivy League? With my grades?"

"Yeah, but I heard that Columbia has this program, the School of General Studies, that considers their applicants' personal history and extenuating circumstances. It's a program specifically for nontraditional students, students who dropped out for whatever reason, or students who decided they weren't ready for college and took a gap year instead. I'm not sure, but I think you fit this bill, Ly."

"I don't know," I said. The whole thing seemed so far-fetched. How could someone like me even think of applying to such a prestigious school as Columbia?

"Just apply. What's the worst that can happen? Boys, don't you think she should apply?"

"Of course you should," they echoed. "She's right. What's the worst that can happen?"

"Just tell them your story," Brian said. "Tell it the way you've told it to us."

I was pessimistic but I couldn't really argue with them. I was already skeptical about my chances of making it into the other colleges where Pam and Ms. Liu wanted me to apply. Adding one more wouldn't make much of a difference to me. Besides, it was hard to say no to Pam.

After dinner, she and I retreated to the living room, where there was a row of computers, one for each member of the family. She looked up the application process for the School of General Studies and reviewed it with me.

"This is due in two months," she said. "That's right around the corner. You better start working, kiddo."

She sent me home with a list of tasks to do, deadlines to accomplish them by, and a bag of leftovers. At home, I set to work on my application half-heartedly. When it came time to write the personal statement, I froze. I had to explain in detail all the reasons I considered myself a "nontraditional student," which meant diving into the nontraditional life I had led and all the trials and traumas that went along with it. When I really thought about it, my story was incredible even to me, so much so that I doubted anyone would believe me if I told them.

Just apply, I heard Pam's voice say in my head. *What's the worst that can happen?*

So I pushed through my resistance and ended up writing a nine-thousand-word essay about my life as a Vietnamese immigrant. I went through many drafts before I felt ready to let go of it. Though my understanding of myself and the events that had molded me was still very limited, writing the essay allowed me to understand just a bit more of my past, of all the events that helped shape me into the person I was then, and how they would continue to shape me for years to come. Writing allowed me to connect the dots and made me feel more grounded within myself. It was as though all the words I could never say suddenly tumbled out of me and onto the page.

The application to Columbia went out with all the others in December. I was relieved to be done with them but so burned-out from the stress of applying, the exhaustion of working my City Year job, and my fear of failing yet again that I couldn't muster any optimism about the results.

Winter was especially cold and dark that year, and it seemed endless, as did the limbo I was in. Friends of mine from school would be graduating that year, while my chances of getting a degree seemed nil. What a mockery I'd made of my parents' sacrifices and the opportunities I'd been given.

But eventually, just as it did every year, spring arrived—and this time it came with an invitation to an interview at Columbia. Though I knew I didn't have a chance, the buds and blossoms appearing on the trees were enough to propel me forward. I took the 1 train to 116th Street in Morningside Heights. Nervous, I walked up the steps to Lewisohn Hall, barely taking in the beautiful campus around me. I was directed to a room where I met Yvonne Rojas, my interviewer. She had my transcript from Hunter in hand.

"I read your essay," she said when I stepped into her office. "It was very moving."

"Thank you."

"But I'd like you to elaborate a little more on your grades at Hunter," she said, indicating the transcript. "I see here that you started off very well. What happened?"

I struggled to come up with the words to explain my three semesters of Fs. I knew "I was depressed" wouldn't quite cut it. She looked at me dubiously.

"This is a difficult case," she said. "I am sympathetic, but while Columbia does look holistically at a student's background, I'm afraid these grades will work against you."

"I understand," I said. I was calm. I'd had years of letdowns and setbacks to prepare me for more, and the latest round of rejections—first from Barnard, then Wesleyan, Smith, Drexel, and NYU—had already begun rolling in, just as I expected. Another rejection couldn't break me further. I had already reached rock bottom. But even as I contemplated getting in nowhere, I felt my heart still beating. This time would be different. I was prepared to move forward regardless of the outcome. I was alive and, somehow, still fighting.

It was around that time that I decided I had to tell my parents about Pam. I didn't tell them that I had dropped out of Hunter and I didn't tell them that I was reapplying to other colleges. But I felt guilty about hiding Pam's existence from them, so I explained that she was the one who found the City Year job for me and described how nurturing she was, all the meals and MetroCards she'd given me, all the support. I worried about what they might think of the relationship, but their reaction was not at all what I expected.

"She's your angel," my mother said.

"Please tell her and her husband I said thank you," my father said. "Thank you for helping our daughter when we could not."

Their response shocked me. I thought they'd be disappointed or even jealous that I had found someone who was akin to a surrogate mother. Instead they embraced her and thanked the Buddhas for her presence in my life.

I began to look at them in a new light and finally understood that they had always wanted what was best for me, had always wished for my success, but lacked the tools and knowledge to help me. They did what they could, escaping poverty and persecution to bring my brothers and me to what they saw as this promised land. They could not have anticipated all the hardships we would face here. Faith was all they had. They saw Pam as proof that their faith had been rewarded, their prayers answered. Once again, an angel had appeared when she was needed.

Another conversation, another day—this time about my contact lenses. After the scene when I'd flaunted my contacts in a fit of rage, my father had taken to asking me the occasional question about them.

"Do those really help you see?" he asked one night over dinner.

I nodded yes, and he asked how much they cost.

"Not too expensive," I lied, not wanting him to worry about the price.

"Do you have to wear them all the time?" he asked.

"Yes," I said, explaining to him once again that without them everything was a blur. He looked at me with sad eyes and shook his head, finding it hard to accept that I was, in a sense, handicapped and that there wasn't any amount of wishful thinking or denial that could erase that reality.

In May 2011, I was in the middle of a class at J.H.S. 13 when I received a phone call. I asked to be excused for a minute and stepped out into the hallway.

"Hello, Ly," a familiar voice on the line said.

It was Yvonne, my interviewer at Columbia.

"I just wanted to say congratulations to you for your acceptance into the School of General Studies at Columbia University. It was such a pleasure meeting you a few weeks ago and to hear your story. Your essay was incredibly strong. We hope that you will accept this offer."

I couldn't believe what I was hearing. I could barely speak as tears filled my eyes. Of all the schools I'd applied to, how was it possible that the one I had the least hope of getting into would accept me? I looked down the long hallway, toward the midday light streaming in through the windows and bouncing off the waxed floors. It was as though my path forward was being illuminated for me.

"Hello?" Yvonne asked.

"Yes," I managed to whisper. "Yes, I accept the offer."

"Holy shit, Ly! Congratu-fucking-lations!" Long texted me from Chicago.

"Well done," Thinh said when I called to tell him and Phu the news.

"Nice job, Ly. Now come visit us in Seattle again. We'll go out to celebrate," Phu said.

Since my parents were still under the impression that I'd be graduating from Hunter that year, their reaction was a mix of shock and fear. "How much longer will you be in school? And how are you going to pay for it?" they wanted to know.

"I'll find a way," I told them. "I know I'll find a way."

I had to. How, I didn't know. I had only one semester left of my Pell and TAP grant money, which, in any case, would barely cover even one course at Columbia. And as a transfer student, my eligibility for financial aid was limited. The rest of my tuition would have to come from institutional and private loans.

Then there was housing. Pam insisted that I had to live in university housing, where I would be within walking distance of campus, independent of my parents, and in an environment where I could develop a community of friends. She wanted me to have a true college experience. Using her own money, she paid my admission fee of one thousand dollars and five thousand dollars for the first semester of housing. She also went with me to meetings with the director of financial aid at the School of General Studies, telling him my story and asking that they give me as much assistance as possible—which they did. But even with grants, scholarships, Perkins Loans, Stafford Loans, and institutional loans, it was not enough.

So Ms. Liu had an idea. She decided to write a letter, which she later forwarded to me.

"Dear Friends and Colleagues," the letter began.

I hope that this message finds you well . . . I am writing to you because today is my birthday. Chances are you know that I am not a "birthday" person. I don't really enjoy birthday parties, though I am always touched by the effort. I have never felt entirely comfortable receiving gifts. Perhaps this is my Asian upbringing. Every birthday, though, I make a wish. I always, always make a wish. It's my favorite part of my birthday.

This year I am hoping you can help me with my wish. Because this year, I am wishing that Ly Tran, a former student of mine, will be granted the opportunity to finish college. I am hoping you and I can help her. But first, let me share her story with you.

Ly was my student at the Bronx HS of Science eight years ago. I was her English teacher during her 9th and 10th grade years, and she was one of my best students. She didn't earn the highest grades, but she had a genuine passion for literature and a great talent with language. What I remember best about her is that she was the one kid in class who was able to see the humanity in any character, even those characters that are often considered bad, mean, or just plain reprehensible. She was THAT kid. . . .

There were things though, about Ly, that were confusing. First, she asked to sit near the board. I mistakenly thought she was asking for some kind of privilege. Years later, I learned that she was severely nearsighted and had gone to school for ten years without corrective lenses.

Second, Ly consistently turned her work in late and this baffled me because students of her caliber usually turn homework in on time. Years later, I learned that from the age of 12, Ly had worked every week at her parents' nail salon. She turned her homework in late because she had no time to do it outside of school.

In fact, there were many things that I—that we, her teachers—did not know about Ly. We did not know that she lived below the poverty line in a small apartment in Brooklyn, with three brothers and her parents. That her family was relocated here under the

U.S. government program "Humanitarian Operation." That her father served nearly 10 years in a prison camp in the Vietnam War and suffered from extreme Post Traumatic Stress Disorder. That she lived in a household where she was discouraged from going to college. That, in fact, Ly almost didn't make it to Bronx Science, because her father told her not to bother taking the specialized high school test, since her three older brothers hadn't gotten in.

In my lifetime, I have never seen, in any student, such a desire for education, combined with steel will and courageous tenacity . . . If Ly is admitted [to Columbia] for fall 2011, she anticipates she will have to work full-time. This is a girl who has worked since she was the age of 12. Although she has worked 13–14 hour days at AmeriCorps, her net income was $4,000.

As the daughter of immigrants, I have to say that Ly's story really resonates with me, especially the cultural barriers she has faced. But I was lucky. My parents went to college and they supported my efforts to go to college. I was privileged enough to have—through none of my own doing—the means, the support, and the access to attend university. Ly has none of these things. . . .

If I were in NY, or in London, I might throw a birthday dinner. You might bring a bottle of wine or maybe even a gift. But this year I am asking that you take whatever money you would have spent and instead donate it to Ly Tran. Whatever we raise together will make a huge difference to her—even if we were to raise $800, this would already constitute 20% of her current income. And this money, for Ly, would mean freedom—freedom to work fewer hours next year, or freedom from some of her loans, something.

All of this is a very long way of saying: my birthday wish this year is that you consider donating to Ly Tran . . .

A check for nearly three thousand dollars arrived for me that summer along with the names of dozens of people who had donated to my cause and a package from Ms. Liu. Inside was a beautiful blue-and-brown maxi dress and a card with a fifty-dollar bill in it.

Dear Ly,

You can do this. I believe in you. We all do.

Love,
Ms. Liu

P.S. If the dress doesn't fit, use the $50 and take it to the tailor. I hope you like it.

I didn't know how to feel. What did I do to deserve such kindness? And what could I do to ever repay these incredible women?

There was only one thing to do. I had been accepted to Columbia University with their support, guidance, and unending faith in me. I was going to prove to everyone who believed in me that their faith was not in vain. I vowed never again to let my circumstances decide my fate. I would take the helm of my ship, and this time, I wasn't going to let anything get in my way.

Standing outside the iron gates of Columbia on my first day was surreal. Thoughts of whether I belonged at such a prestigious institution flooded my mind, but I pushed them away. The workload that first semester was much greater than what I'd had at Hunter, but I didn't let it deter me this time. I attended all my classes, kept impeccable notes, and showed up to TA sessions when I had trouble understanding a topic. I stayed in my room and kept mostly to myself, rarely hanging out with classmates, unless there was a study group. I was afraid of overwhelming myself as I had done when I was in the Honors College.

There was only one thing I felt I had to keep doing, and that was tutoring Ethan several times a week and helping him with his homework. I wanted him to have a sense of structure and stability, and I hoped he'd see me as a good student who also had to work really hard, and that that would inspire him. The semester flew by and ended before I knew it. I had made the Dean's List, which meant my scholarship would increase the following semester. I was going to make it.

On the way home from temple every Sunday, my parents would drive to the corner of 121st and Amsterdam, where I shared an apartment with three housemates, to drop off food for me. They rarely came upstairs, always in a rush to get home, so I'd stand outside their car and chat for a while. I'd ask them about the nail salon.

"Oh, it's fine," my mother would say. "Same as always. Don't worry about us. You just keep working on your studies. Your brothers have been telling us what a big deal Columbia is. They said it means you're very smart."

"Really?" I asked. It was the first time I'd ever received praise from my brothers. It was almost strange to hear it.

"Really," my mother said. "Just make sure you're taking care of yourself."

"And what about your eyes?" my father asked one day.

"What about them?" I asked defensively.

"Are you going to do something about them?"

"Like what? I can see now, remember? I wear contacts."

"Oh, right." He nodded solemnly. I could see that he still couldn't accept the reality of my myopia.

On another Sunday, he brought up the subject again.

"Are you sure it's okay putting those things in your eyes all the time? Are you sure they're not going to get stuck in there?"

"*Đừng có lo, Ba,*" I told him. "Don't worry. They're not going to get stuck."

"What . . . what about LASIK surgery?" he asked in a measured tone, cautiously, as though trying out the sound of those words for the first time.

I was shocked. How on earth did he know about LASIK surgery? And why would I ever have considered it? It cost a lot of money, money I certainly didn't have. Besides, wasn't wearing contacts and hiding it from my parents for years sinful enough?

"I heard about it on the news," my father said. "Everyone's doing it now. The technology is developed, and it—it looks safe. So maybe . . . maybe you can too." As he spoke, I could see all his anxiety about me surfacing, and there was a tenderness in his voice that I hadn't heard since the early days of my childhood.

I didn't know what to say to that. I had thought he would never forgive me for my betrayals—the contacts, the visit from ACS, my flunking out of college. And perhaps, on a level deeper than I understood at the time, I wasn't sure if I could ever forgive him. But the man before me seemed different somehow, at once familiar and unrecognizable.

"Think about it," he told me. "Your mother and I, we have a small amount of money saved from the sweatshop labor. We can help with the costs."

"Do you know how much it costs?" I asked him.

He looked down, his eyes heavy with pain.

"Yes," he said quietly. "I know how much it costs."

Outside the Prison Gates

"ALL RIGHT, CLASS, SO what did we think of Ly's piece?" Adam asked.

Sitting in a fiction workshop of about twenty students the spring of my first year at Columbia, I was sweating. It was my turn to be work-shopped. I wasn't allowed to speak. I could only listen and take notes on my classmates' critiques of the piece I'd written. Although the piece was fiction, it was loosely based on my life and that of my parents, and I had made no attempt to conceal that fact.

The man in the story was a Vietnamese soldier in the South Viet-namese army. He was captured after the war ended and sent to the reeducation camps of Vietnam. The narrative was framed by two time-lines, that of the man's time in camp and that of the man working at a nail salon decades later, old and frail, memories of bloodshed and plot-ting coordinates for bombs running through his mind as he scrubbed the corns off clients' feet.

The class had mostly positive reactions to the piece. Sure, the writ-ing was amateurish and needed work but there was a lot of heart there, they said.

It was my first attempt at being a writer. The experience was complicated, extraordinarily difficult, yet at the same time exhilarating and liberating. Writing for myself was one thing, writing for others something else entirely. But I found that the voice I'd been unable to access all my life came through, in little spurts here and there, on the page. It was as though I'd conquered my inability to say what I felt, to speak up for myself. It was just as scary as I'd always thought speaking up would be, maybe even more so because there's a permanence to the written word that isn't present in speech. But I felt somehow that I was made for the written word. Could I really do this? I wondered. Could I major in writing? Become a writer?

I ended my first year at Columbia with high scores. It wasn't easy. I had to pull a lot of all-nighters to hand in assignments on time or cram for exams, and I didn't make straight As as I had at Hunter. But I held my own.

I did, however, struggle financially. Even with loans, money was so short that I sometimes went hungry. I needed to graduate as soon as possible, so as not to rack up any more debt, but I also needed to make some money. During my second year at Columbia, I took a part-time job as a medical receptionist. It was the only way I could pay for my dorm room that semester and afford to eat and buy essentials. But in the end, having to work and go to school at the same time was so exhausting that I got severely ill with bronchitis and my grades began to slip.

No, I said to myself firmly. Not again. Not this time. I told Pam about my situation.

"You need to quit your job," she told me. "Don't worry about money. We'll figure that out later. But right now, you need to stay in school and focus on your work."

As difficult as that decision was for me, Pam was right. If I didn't want the past to repeat itself, I had to quit. I couldn't let this situation hold me back the way I'd let poverty, ignorance, and fear hold me back my whole life. I had to stay strong, I had to have faith that it would work out in the end, and above all else, I had to do well in school. It was my only ticket out of the life I had been living.

To have gotten this far and fail was not an option.

HD Eyes

A MALE NURSE WALKS me into the operating room. I'm the first patient of the day. I pass by other patients as they prepare for their turn, putting on the same light blue surgical cap that is on my own head, like a shower cap. In the room, a surgeon sitting down at a computer stands up to greet me. "All ready for us, Miss Tran?"

I give a quick, nervous nod. My vision is blurrier than usual from the medication I'd been instructed to administer the night before. The nurse guides me to the operating table and I lie down. Using his thumb and forefinger to open my lids wide, he squeezes numbing medication into each eye.

"Would you like a stress ball or bunny?" he asks me, holding in one hand a yellow-and-blue stress ball, and in the other a gray stuffed bunny.

I choose the bunny. Not very soft, I think to myself as I pass my hand over its coarse gray fur. I wish I had my stuffed turtle with me instead.

"Okay!" The doctor claps his hands together and speaks with a slight Russian accent. "So, vat you're going to feel in few moments is lot of pressure in eyes, one at a time, about thirty seconds for each eye. During zis time, I'll use blade to cut tiny thin flap in cornea, so zat I have access to stroma. I'll pull flap back, and zis is where I make changes to cornea. Remember, any changes to cornea cannot be undone after zis surgery."

The surgeon moves a large contraption into place over my left eye, its edges sinking deep into the outer bases of my eyelids, causing them to peel back. I begin to tear up. I see a red dot that seems to be hovering right above me in a circle of black.

"I vant you to stare at dot no matter vat happens," the surgeon says, "and continue staring until I remove machine. Zis is very important to procedure, and complications vill occur if you blink or look away. Okay, ready? One."

I am scared. What if I have to blink? I already feel like blinking. What if I accidentally look away? What if my eye moves involuntarily? What if something goes wrong and I become blind forever?

"Two."

I think about clarity. I think about sight and healthy eyes. I think about crisp, sharp lines. I think about my father.

"Three."

An overwhelmingly painful amount of pressure bursts into my left eye.

"Focus on red dot," I hear the surgeon's voice say.

I'm pinching myself, hoping that the pain from the pinch will overwhelm the pain from the pressure of the machine. I smell burning flesh. I hear a high-pitched whirring sound.

"Okay, we are detecting some movement," the surgeon says. "Remember, focus on ze red dot."

I will myself to stare at the red dot. I don't want to go blind from this, I think. *I don't want to be blind anymore.*

The sound from the machine stops suddenly and the pressure eases. The doctor has cut open the flap in my eye and slowly folds it back on its hinge. As the flap crosses over my pupil, I watch as the red dot becomes hazy and out of focus. Then, without warning, more pressure. Even more than the first round.

"Cutting cornea now," the surgeon tells me, almost as an afterthought.

But his voice barely reaches me. The smell of burning flesh is pervasive, the pressure unbearable. I begin to slip out of consciousness.

"Focus, focus! That's right, you've got this," he says as I feel my eyelid drooping. I just want to sleep. My mind wanders. A red blur dances before me. I want to stop this. Can we stop this? I don't want to do this anymore. I've changed my mind.

"Three, two, one. Okay! Done. Next eye. You're doing great." Then the whirring stops. The pressure stops. He removes the machine from my left eye and works on attaching it to my right.

I breathe. I haven't been breathing. I'm doing great?

"Thirty seconds, see? No biggie," a voice says somewhere in the distance.

No biggie.

"Okay, same thing here, got it? Red dot. Focus."

Because I know what to expect, this one goes by somewhat faster. Pressure, burning flesh, high-pitched whirring sound. I endure it once more.

"Okay! You're all done. Why don't you go ahead and open your eyes. Look at zat clock! See zose numbers! Amazing, yes?" The nurse and doctor clap in the background.

I try to open my eyes, but they are so heavy. Everything hurts. They open a crack to reveal numbers on a clock hanging on the wall in front of the operating table. When was the last time I saw the numbers on a clock with my own eyes, without the use of contacts? But a sharp pain shoots into my right eye. Something is wrong.

"I-I feel something in my eye," I stammer, holding one hand out, unable to open my eyes again, clutching the bunny tight in my other hand.

I feel two fingers pull open the eyelids to my left eye. I see two hazel eyes peer into mine. The surgeon shines a light into my eye, the brightness temporarily blinding me and sending arrows of excruciating pain through my head.

"Okay, zis eye is good. No complications here. Now let's try other one."

When he tries to pull open the other pair of eyelids, my eyes refuse to open and tears start to stream down my face. I feel my face contorting at the pain.

"No no no," he gently admonishes. "Just relax. Pain is normal."

He forces my eyelids open. A bright light. This time he is silent for a few moments, shining the light around my eye.

"Daniel," he calls back to the nurse. "Forceps, please. And ze Zymaxid. Thank you." He turns back to me. "Ah, I see problem now. Don't vorry. Flap somehow moved in ze process of blinking. Zis happens occasionally when eyes dry out from operation. I vill move flap back into place now."

Daniel hands him the forceps and moves another microscope-like contraption over me, into which the surgeon peers. He reaches in with his forceps. They are sharp, causing my eyes to immediately blink. The surgeon clicks his tongue against the roof of his mouth in rapid succession.

"Ah ah ah," he says. "Hold still or flap vill not go back into position."

I will my eyes open, tears running down the side of my face and into the cotton pads over my ears. My legs shake and I am certain I am bleeding where my nails have dug into my skin above my thigh.

"Okay." The surgeon exhales sharply. "Daniel, please put more of ze Zymaxid drops in her eyes to avoid infection." Daniel squirts the small bottle into my right eye, then opens my left and does the same. "All done. Feel a little better? Vy don't you try to open your eyes now?"

I try. It still hurts, but the sensation of having something in my eye is no longer there.

"Yes, better," I reply weakly.

The nurse and surgeon open the doors to the operating room and lead me out to the waiting area, where I will find my mother and father. I open my eyes a crack. They are already standing up from their seats, eager to take my hand. My mother rushes over to me, a knot of anxiety between her eyebrows.

"How was it?" she asks. "Are you okay?"

My father moves excitedly from side to side, like a child, and tells me he saw the whole thing on a television in the waiting room. He tells me how cool it was.

"Lý, we saw it. We saw the whole thing. Technology nowadays, huh? The things they can do, huh? Did you know there's a big screen out here where you can see everything? Your mother and I watched the whole operation in real time. It was incredible!" He grins widely. My mother holds on to my hand, squeezing it.

"Oh, my daughter," she says, feeling my forehead and cheeks as though I might have a fever. "How do you feel? Are you in pain? I was so worried."

I close my eyes to minimize the pain and nod weakly at my parents. I am tired. I want to sleep. The doctor hands my father a pair of sunglasses to put on my face, and I feel the arms of the glasses sliding over my ears.

"You can't open your eyes for the next six hours," the doctor says. "Take a nap if you can."

"Thank you so much, Doctor," I hear my father's voice say. "Thank you, thank you, thank you." I think of that time I saw him at the donut shop years ago thanking the owner for giving him free donuts. I imagine him bowing to the doctor now as he thanked him. *Thank you, thank you, thank you.*

My mother leads me to the elevator, and we descend to the ground floor. My father hails a cab.

"Let me help her into the cab," my father tells my mother.

"No, a mother's touch is better," she argues. But it is an argument just for show. She knows how special this moment is for my father. She gives me a squeeze and I feel her small hands replaced by my father's large and rough ones.

It is a strange sensation. When was the last time I held my father's hand? I wonder. Though his hands are rough, his touch is gentle, and he moves me slowly from the curb to the cab. I hit my head on the hood of the car.

"Be careful!" my mother yells.

"It was an accident," he says, rubbing the spot on my head where I had bumped it. "I'm sorry." His apology echoes across the years of my life, soothing like salve on a wound.

The ride home is unbearable. My eyes throb painfully.

"It hurts so much," I whine, and start to cry.

"Shh," my father coaxes. "It's all over now. Don't cry. It might ruin the results. You don't want that, do you? Your eyes are beautiful now." I hear his voice crack. "They're beautiful."

I try to hold it in.

The cab stops. My mother and father open the door of the car and they both lead me up the steps to our apartment, my father still holding on to my hands and walking backward up the stairs, my mother with her hands at the back of my waist, telling me when to step. We enter the apartment, and they lay me down gently on the bed. My mother tenderly brushes my hair.

The familiar smell of incense wafts through the apartment and I hear the sound of a switch as my father turns on the lights of our altar. I hear him recite a prayer to Quan Thế Âm Bồ Tát. My mother joins him. I too whisper it, imagining the gentle touch of one of Quan Âm's thousand hands on my shoulder. More tears slide out, both because I am in pain and because I am healing.

"So how long is recovery going to take?" my mother asks. "What did the doctor say?"

"It's not going to take any time at all," my father says. "She probably just needs to rest."

"Just like that, huh? Wow, technology these days. We never would have been able to do this in Vietnam."

"Definitely not. At least not for another few decades . . ."

They talk excitedly to me. I nod, but I don't hear anything they say. I fall into a deep sleep and dream of bright colors, sharp lines, the world in HD.

Almost There

I WAS STANDING ON the edge of a wooden bridge jutting out and into a touristy lagoon in the Dominican Republic, Joseph coaxing me into the water.

"Go ahead, babe. I got you."

"No, no. I can't. I'm scared."

"Don't worry, I'm right here, right by your side," he said. "I won't let anything happen to you."

I stared into the turquoise waters, at the fish swimming by, the detritus shrimp nibbling on the dead skin around the cuticles of my toenails, and the small red-eared slider turtles languorously poking their heads above the surface, suspended in the water and bored by my indecision. Across the lagoon, tourists and locals alike took turns sitting and posing for cameras on a low-hanging tree branch that dipped into the water. It made for a very scenic photograph.

I closed my eyes and held my breath. *You can do this*, I thought.

I had been studying abroad in the Dominican Republic that summer, analyzing the ecosystems of Punta Cana. It was the end of my second year at Columbia and this was a summer elective, a chance for me to earn enough credits to graduate the following year. I'd been doing well in school, better than I expected, having made the Dean's List every semester. It was enough to increase my scholarship, and my brothers were pitching in to help with any costs that I couldn't cover.

I'd gotten my eye surgery just a few months before, and studying abroad on the breathtaking island of DR could not have come at a better time. During those days, I would wake up at the crack of dawn and walk a two-mile stretch of beach, ankle-deep in the water, watching the sun slowly rise red-orange over the horizon. *Aguaceros* connected ocean and sky in the distance, and white herons soared above the clear blue water. I couldn't believe that I was seeing all of it with my own two eyes.

When the five-week, six-credit summer course came to an end, and our reports on sunscreen and its effects on the bio-regeneration of algae in the Ojos Indígenas lagoons were handed in and graded, Joseph flew in to join me. I was in his country now, and I wanted a grand tour, so I'd extended my stay by a week.

We booked a few bed-and-breakfasts around the island, rented a car, and explored to our hearts' content. He showed me La Romana and Santo Domingo, the places where he spent much of his childhood, and, since I wanted to show him my research, we eventually circled back to Punta Cana, and I took him to the beautiful lagoons of the Indigenous Eyes Ecological Park and Reserve, where I had spent the previous five weeks.

"Come on, babe," he coaxed. "The longer you think about it, the harder it's gonna be. You've got the snorkel on. I'll be swimming right beside you. Nothing's gonna happen." Reluctantly, I took Joseph's outstretched hand and sat down on the platform, my feet dangling into the water.

"There we go," he said, crouching down beside me. "Now, just hop in."

He demonstrated, letting go of my hand and slipping smoothly into the water. He swam out several feet, then returned, raising an expectant eyebrow at me. I lingered there, feet immersed and swaying. The water was warmer than expected for freshwater lagoons, which were usually colder than ocean water.

Kids barely five years old were plunging in from a ten-foot wooden diving board a few meters away. Surely, if they could do it, I could too. I looked around. It was the weekend and entire families with their *tías* and *abuelos* and *nietos* and *suegras* were all gathered right there in the water.

I thought about my own extended family, my parents, my brothers, my aunts and uncles and grandmother in Vietnam, and legions of unknown cousins and distant relatives dispersed over oceans and across four continents: Asia, North America, Europe, and Australia. I thought about the prayers we whispered into our pillows late at night that we would make it somehow. I thought of the incense that burned daily on the altar, the wisps of smoke carrying our hopes and dreams high into the heavens.

Somewhere I heard a father call out to his little boy, *"Mira, m'ijo, con tus manos! Como así!"* The little boy looked to be not yet four and was just learning to swim, his torso in the hole of a donut floater. The father cupped his hands, pointed them downward, and pushed backward in the air to demonstrate dog-paddling.

"Aww, look at that. Just look at that," Joseph crooned while treading water. "He's adorable."

The father shouted more instructions I couldn't understand. He paced back and forth on the wooden bridge leading into the water, and his voice became higher pitched, more aggressive, as his words began to take on familiar tonal qualities.

"Kỳ Lý, mày đang làm cái gì vậy?" I heard him say. *"Mày phải dùng hai cái chân của mày đá lên đá xuống mới lội được!"*

"I know, I know," I muttered. "I'm trying."

"I'm waiting," Joseph sang. "Any day now."

I swung my feet in the water, staring into my rippled reflection. A smile escaped me as I was, for the first time in my life, not surprised by the girl staring back at me, her eyes bright and full of gratitude. *You can do this*, she seemed to say.

I took a deep breath, despite having my snorkel on, and jumped into the cool water. My heartbeat spiked. I saw a flash of chlorine-blue pool water, as I was taken back to that moment so many years ago when I fell into the Astoria public pool. *Calm down*, I told myself. *Calm down. Just do like he said.* I cupped my hands and moved them backward, feeling myself propelled through the water. I straightened my legs and kicked them up and down. It was working. I opened my eyes, and could see the section of branch where it dipped ever so slightly into the water.

"*Gần tới rồi, Lý! Con gần tới rồi,*" I heard the man's voice say. And I moved diligently toward the branch, listening to my father's muffled encouragement reaching my ears below the water.

Almost there, Ly.

You're almost there.

Acknowledgments

ALL THE LIFETIMES IN the world would not be enough to express my gratitude to everyone who has made this book possible, who has made this life possible, but I'll try as best I can to fit it all on these pages.

Saïd Sayrafiezadeh, I'm forever indebted to you for taking the time to read *Twenty Thousand Cummerbunds*, for believing in my story, and jump-starting this journey for me. Sarah Levitt, my incredible agent, I can't thank you enough for your careful guidance throughout it all, for never letting me give up, and for always being in my corner. My sincerest gratitude to Liese Mayer, for pushing this boat out into the sea and to Beth Rashbaum for being the wind that has carried me to shore.

To my extraordinary editors, Valerie Steiker and Sally Howe, thank you so much for your divine insight and patience in taking this book to the next level. And many thanks to the entire team at Scribner: Nan Graham, Colin Harrison, Roz Lippel, Brianna Yamashita, Mia O'Neill, Michelle Chung, Jaya Miceli, Kathleen Rizzo, and Stephanie Evans, as well as Cordia Leung and Sabrina Pyun for their thoughtful early reads.

In order of appearance in my life, to Michelle Puleio née Weisenthal,

Nate Dechongkit, Joan Liu, Dena Ford (I miss you more than words can express), Pamela van der Meulen, Sylvia Richards, and Rorianne Schrade, I will carry the enormous impact you've had on me for the rest of my life.

Special thanks to the staff at MacDowell, Art Omi, and Yaddo for the space and freedom to create to my heart's content. And to the Whiting Foundation for their generous grants, without which I could not have accepted these residencies.

To the friends and extended family members, teachers and professors, acquaintances and strangers, to anyone who has ever lifted my spirits with a caring word or gesture, your kindness is deeply embedded in my soul and shall never be forgotten.

Trần Tỷ và Hứa Diệp: Làm thế nào con có thể cảm ơn Ba và Ý vì đã hy sinh tất cả vì con? Sẽ không bao giờ có đủ trang sách để bày tỏ lòng biết ơn bất tận của con, nhưng con hy vọng đây là một sự khởi đầu. Con thương Ba Ý rất nhiều.

Hia Thịnh, Hia Phú, Hia Long, my dear brothers. This book is as much for you as it is for our parents. For all of us. Look at how far we've come. Remember that story Mom used to tell us? How she'd gone to see a monk after we were all born to inquire of our fates, and the monk said to her, *"How did these four walk through the same door?"* As though he'd recognized us somehow. I don't know what that means any more than you do, but I, for one, am glad we did walk into this life together. Thank you for putting up with your annoying little sister, for all the love and support throughout the years, the fights, the laughter. For the chimp video.

Finally, to the one and only Joseph Vidal, thank you for your wisdom, for never letting go of my hand, and for joining me in all the silly dances and uncontrollable wiggles over the years. I love you.

About the Author

LY TRAN graduated from Columbia University with a degree in creative writing and linguistics in 2014. She has received fellowships from MacDowell, Art Omi, and Yaddo. This is her first book.